Contents

Foreword

Sigrid Gareis, artistic director of Tanzquartier Wien,
on behalf of the Tanzquartier Wien Team

The recent development of dance and performance into artistic disciplines from the turn of the 20th century up to the present of the beginning 21st century is clearly marked stronger by eruptions and breaks rather than continuities: The sudden end of *Ausdruckstanz* brought about by National Socialism, the "new beginning" of contemporary dance development since the 1960s, the body investigations of the 1960s and again of the 1990s, the first dance boom in the 1980s, and another in the 1990s can be mentioned here as headlines.

It is remarkable that analyses of the development of the discipline often fail to consider two great "breaks": the political division of Europe after the Second World War, and the fall of the "Iron Curtain" – followed by the political restructuring of Europe. If European dance and performance studies up to today quite often write "parallel histories", in practice a dynamic field of artistic body work has established itself which implements and connects protagonists from Western and Eastern Europe alike. They share an interest in conceptual art formats as well as scepticism concerning established institutions and structures.

At the beginning of March 2005, more than forty speakers from theory and practice – key figures of this dynamic field – were invited to take part in the congress *Inventur: Tanz und Performance* to reflect and present their work. The congress – curated by Martina Hochmuth / Tanzquartier Wien and Georg Schöllhammer / springerin – became an "all-European manifestation" of contemporary advanced dance and performance creation.

Superficially, one may wonder that the aim and ductus of the discussions during this congress strongly pointed in the direction of an establishment of mutuality, confirmation of artistic diversity and an effort toward better consolidation and conscious definition. And it doesn't seem to be coincidence that this discussion is accompanied by a growing acceptance not only throughout Europe but world-wide, as well as – and more decisive at that – successively increasing artistic relevance of the fields of dance and performance. Could it be that now, in a new Europe there begins a new chapter of a continuously developing dance and performance history? The future will show … But one thing already became clear in Vienna: We are far from a dichotomy in the development of Western and Eastern European dance and performance. And there's more: Reading this congress publication may convince you that an attribution of Western and / or Eastern European with regard to the status quo of dance and performance development in Europe eventually has become obsolete.

Tanzquartier Wien would like to thank all speakers and moderators of the congress, as well as the authors of this publication. Furthermore, we would like to thank the City of Vienna, Department for Cultural Affairs, Erste Bank and Boris Marte, Head of Corporate Sponsoring, KulturKontakt Austria and Annemarie Türk, the network THEOREM (association supported by the Culture 2000 programme of the European Union) and the State Secretary for the Arts and Media, Federal Chancellery of Austria, without whose support neither the congress would have taken place, nor this publication realised. And our special thanks go to the co-curator of the congress, Georg Schöllhammer, and the magazine *springerin – Hefte für Gegenwartskunst*.

Preface

Krassimira Kruschkova / Georg Schöllhammer / Martina Hochmuth

In his commentary on *Who Can Sing a Song to Unfrighten Me* Tim Etchells lists the scenic "Inventory" of this wonderfully poetic 24-hour marathon performance by *Forced Entertainment* as follows: "Dogs, alphabets, panda bears, casualties, fairy tales, gothic stories, dances and jokes".[1] This rhizomatic list corresponds with Jorge Luis Borges' famous (in any case, since Michel Foucault's *Les mots et les choses*) "Chinese encyclopedia"[2], with the paratactical subversion of every taxonomy. It notates – thinking the impossible – a shaking, a tremor of word levels, a collapse of the orderly surfaces, a failing taxonomy of the scenic, an inventory which mainly marks gaps, absence, which calls to mind not only what is missing, but missing itself as a mark of representation, as a presence of absence[3].

As a marking of significant empty spaces, as archive, revision, investigation of the traces and vacancies which since the 1990s have influenced contemporary dance and performance this publication also reads the singularity of the congress *Inventory: Dance and Performance*, which – curated by Martina Hochmuth and Georg Schöllhammer – took place from March 3 to 5, 2005 in Tanzquartier Wien: As an inventory in the mode of its impossibility, knowing about its interminability, a potential inventory, an inventory of the potential; as an event of what can not take place or as one of the "impossible possibility of talking about the event"[4], as an inventory "in vain" ever deconstructing itself, a list voiding instructions and inscriptions. Or, to put it differently: as a "weak" list destabilising itself in the sense of "teatro debole"[5], which commits the sense to the spectator, or as a kind of "weak dance strong questions"[6] – especially in a time of strong questioning of dance and performance in the new politico-cultural and artistic context since 1989.

It takes place when it doesn't. On dance and performance since 1989 follows the congress of Tanzquartier Wien to which we had invited participants from all over Europe to talk about new geographies and artistic workforms and workspaces in the fields of dance and performance, about the widely interweaved and cross-referencing, often indistinguishable and multiply coded cultural figures of production, reception and reflection. The focus was a form of exchange beyond the well-proven cultural positions of artist and spectator, beyond the borders of disciplines and beyond the classical play of presentation and interpretation. Also, it was about showing spaces of action that lie outside the hermetic and taxonomic models of representation of a medial and academic discourse mostly reproducing areas of terminology or dichotomies like Western / Non-Western, which by now have become canonical. The meeting, on the other hand, should enable a moment of open discussion. Instead of endeavouring to stake on lexical and indexical coherence, and thus on categorical closures, the congress played with the dangers of those closures and with the possibilities of invent(or)ing. Against representative conventions and categories which always are liable to petrify, strategies should be stressed which subvert and destabilise the borders of classification. The intention was to create transdisciplinary and translocal constellations and fade-overs.

Of course, any temporary fixation of an open constellation such as the fields of dance and performance at the moment present, includes a dynamic of presences and absences, as well as empty spaces caused, e.g., by tour plans and agendas that could not be correlated. During the editorial work, however, we did not retrospectively try to reduce the openness and methodological as well as formal multifariousness to a single format. The ductus of colloquial formulations was left colloquial, ambivalences – with the exception of a few thematic excursions only understandable from the internal context of the event – were not revised away and homogenised *post festum*. *It takes place when it doesn't* doesn't follow the chronology of the event which often was determined by the calendar. However, the publication on the whole retains its groupings which were co-determined and co-invited by the interests and fields of reference of those integrated in them.

Since 1989 in the subtitle stands for the overcoming of a division, and marks a geographic figure which it presents as restrictive, excluding, transgressable and transgressed simultaneously. Playfully, it should work against the canons of still active cartographies of the local, and instead reveal a complex network of conceptual and practical relations. According to this, the chapters of the tome can be taken as an aid to navigation. Like in the congress itself, as the result of a dialogue between inviters and guests, it groups the texts around certain areas, follows thematic traces to fields of practice, takes up their vocabularies, refers to mentalities and positions within a field which in a double sense is in constant motion, unconcludable by interpretation.

The gesture of an inventory in the double sense of stock-taking and invention (from the Latin *invenire*) – thus the double meaning of the congress title – is, one could say, the gesture of an off-setting setting, an abysmally affirmative discourse performance, an "afformance". Werner Hamacher calls "afformative" the "making possible which in no form can find its fulfilment, as enabling and disabling, as action and non-action at the same time: as the afformative of language"[7]. The afformative is "not *aformative*, not the negation of the formative"[8]. In this sense, the gesture of the inventory can be thought as a stock-taking of its own impossibility, as affirmation of a not-taking-place taking place, a pure event, a nothing-but-event that makes impossible what it enables, excludes what it expects. One could say that the inventory opens a scene which immediately deplaces, deconstructs, off-sets every discursive setting. The oscillating inventory / invention brings into motion a kind of affirmation, assurance, asseveration, confirmation, corroboration, an affirmation albeit without an affirmed subject.

If the Latin *affor* means addressing, talking to, then "afformance" approximates prosopopeia, the artistic device of apostrophe which simultaneously enables addressing and omitting, which "gives mask and face to something missing"[9]. Academic discourse can only shake its head at that – though "afformatively". Every assumption that the intentions and inscriptions of inventories take part in a conclusion, a finiteness, is simply mistaken: The invention of the inventory takes place on condition of its interminability[10]: it takes place when it doesn't, it takes place as a mistake, as productive failure, as constructive absence, as potentiality, as promise.

....

Krassimira Kruschkova / Georg Schöllhammer / Martina Hochmuth

In the sense of retracing more toward the future; in the sense of Roland Barthes' text *La mort de l'auteur,* which means the birth of the reader; in the sense of apostrophe, which simultaneously marks addressing and omitting, we decided to begin this publication with the topic *The spectator's act:* An inventory as apostrophe addressing the inventive reader – aware of all the omissions in whose mode it happens.

[1] Tim Etchells: "Forced Entertainment. Einige Anmerkungen zu den Arbeiten 'Dirty Work' und 'Who Can Sing a Song to Unfrighten Me?' und deren Entstehungsprozeß", in: Programme folder for *Dirty Work* and *Who Can Sing a Song to Unfrighten Me,* Wiener Festwochen 2000.

[2] Michel Foucault calls to mind the "Chinese encyclopedia" quoted by Jorge Luis Borges, in which it is written that "animals are divided into: a) belonging to the Emperor, b) embalmed, c) tame, d) sucking pigs, e) sirens, f) fabulous, g) stray dogs, h) included in the present classification, i) frenzied, j) innumerable, k) drawn with a very fine camelhair brush, l) et cetera, m) having just broken the water pitcher, n) that from a long way off look like flies". (Michel Foucault: *The order of things. An Archeology of the Human Sciences.* New York 1970, p.xv).

[3] See also the publication of the lecture series of Tanzquartier Wien of the season 2003/4 (Krassimira Kruschkova (ed.): *Ob?scene. Zur Präsenz der Absenz im zeitgenössischen Tanz, Theater und Film.* Wien: Böhlau 2005).

[4] cf. Jacques Derrida: „Une certaine possibilité impossible de dire l'événement". In: Nouss, Alexis (ed.): *Dire l'événement, est-ce possible? Séminaire autour de J. Derrida* (avec J. Derrida et G. Soussana), L'Harmattan, coll. „Esthétiques", Paris 2001, pp.79-112.

[5] See also the contribution by Emil Hrvatin in this book.

[6] Thus, e.g., the title of the performance created in 2001 by Jonathan Burrows and Jan Ritsema.

[7] Werner Hamacher: „Die Geste im Namen. Benjamin und Kafka". *Entferntes Verstehen. Studien zu Philosophie und Literatur von Kant bis Celan.* Frankfurt a.M.: Suhrkamp, 1998, S. 323.

[8] Werner Hamacher: „Afformativ, Streik." *Was heißt „Darstellen"?* Hg. Christiaan L. Hart Nibbrig. Frankfurt a. M.: Suhrkamp, 1994, S. 346/360. Also cf. – referring to theatre – Hans-Thies Lehmann: *Postdramatisches Theater,* Frankfurt a. M.: Verlag der Autoren 1999, S. 459-461.

[9] Paul de Man: *Autobiography as De-facement.* In: the Rhetoric of Romanticism, New York: Columbia University Press 1984.

[10] See also the contribution by Gabriele Brandstetter in this book.

Acknowledgements

The editors would like to thank

13

All contributors of the congress and the authors of the present publication:
Ric Allsopp, Daniel Aschwanden, Maja Bajević, Jérôme Bel, Cezary Bodzianowski, Andrea
B. Braidt, Claudia Bosse, Iara Boubnova, Gabriele Brandstetter, Roger M. Buergel, Bojana
Cvejić, Maja Delak, Alex Demirovic, Nataša Govedić, Marina Gržinić, Philipp Haupt,
Christian Höller, Emil Hrvatin, Stefan Kaegi, Veronica Kaup-Hasler, Lois Keidan, Klaus
Kieser, Mala Kline, Július Koller, Bojana Kunst, Brigitta Kuster, Xavier Le Roy, Isabell Lorey,
Hubert Machnik, Boyan Manchev, Ralo Mayer, Tomislav Medak, Gil Mendo, Louise Neri,
Christine Peters, Goran Sergej Pristaš, Jan Ritsema, Gerald Siegmund, Mårten Spångberg,
Christine Standfest, Robert Steijn, SUPERAMAS, Emese Süvecz, Ritsaert ten Cate,
Attila Tordai-S., Ana Vujanović, Yosi Wanunu, Christophe Wavelet, Isa Wortelkamp,
Katherina Zakravsky, Dragan Živadinov

For financial support of the congress:
The City of Vienna, Department of Cultural Affairs
Boris Marte, Head of Corporate Sponsoring, Erste Bank
Annemarie Türk and KulturKontakt Austria
The State Secretary for the Arts and Media, Federal Chancellery of Austria

For copy-editing:
David Ender, Jill Winder

For project management:
theater & kunst: das Schaufenster

Sigrid Gareis and everyone of the Tanzquartier Wien Team

The spectator's act

The terminal spectactor

Emil Hrvatin

Let us begin with the articulation of the dwelling spaces of the future as presented by the Italian architect Franco Purini in his vision of the ideal, hundred-million-people city and houses that form it:

> Life will become increasingly solitary – but not necessarily less happy, and will be lived out in large detached houses. These will consist of a vast environment, a bare loft in which all life's functions will be played out like on theatre stage, with no need to isolate oneself or find private space. Electronic equipment, which extends the senses, will be integral part of the house. Its simple space will have no relationship with the exterior, since this would only offer the image of the outside, because all houses will tend to be the same. Each house will be the terminal of the energy and IT networks, but also a transmitter station, a place for telecommuters and an interactive centre for communication with the entire planet. People will no longer be buried in cemeteries. Instead, the house will be the tomb of those living in it. (Franco Purini, *A thousand times one hundred thousand houses*, project for the Venice Biennale of Architecture, 2000).

Purini's project is on the one hand attractive due to its precise definition and operability of the old modernist utopia, and terrifying on the other – considering the terminality of the subject's position within the house of the future, or rather, within the terminal space.

It is the terminal space that constitutes the subject in a double, Althusserian sense of the word: as *sujet*, active and dependent at the same time. Terminal space is the dwelling of Virilio's terminal citizen, who employs various telecommunicational prostheses to connect to the outside world from his elementary cell. It is a place that enhances the image of the isolated nucleus of the individual's freedom to the subject, organising the city as a de-centred conglomerate of micro-centres. To a terminal citizen, the external reality is an abstract construct that can be arbitrarily appropriated. It is a reality of total individual irresponsibility.

Theatre topos: from the extremely public to the extremely private

In Purini's architecture of the terminal individual, the latter occurs as a performer. We are witnessing a shift from the *teatrum mundi* concept to the concept of the panoptic intimate theatre where the terminal individual is at the same time performer and spectator. His living environment is a scene (scene in the double sense of the setting and the realisation of the act), upon / within which he acts for himself and the world, and the world acts for him.

At first it seems that we are dealing with a panoptic situation: my intimacy is made completely visible while the external reality is an archive of multiple images / environments that I can virtually project into my intimate panopticon. In the economy of social organisation, individuals sacrifice their privacy, gaining the illusion of the teleportational democracy instead: "at any given moment I can participate in any given sphere of social life – from buying shares to voting pro or contra capital punishment". But the totalitarian image of the panoptic intimate theatre also has another, postmodernist, side. The Orwellian Big Brother whom I can never escape and who I desperately want to hide from is now joined by a younger – Dutch or by now trans-European (but not American (!), although the father of the idea is no other than Andy Warhol, with his "five minutes of fame") – brother that makes me reveal my entire privacy. To the new Big Brother, I am willing to sacrifice the last fragment of my privacy just to receive his attention and gaze. That is why I am turning my living room into a theatre and myself into an actor desperately fighting for an audience.

This perverse "big-brotherly" shift from the subject trying to escape Big Brother's gaze to the subject that would sacrifice privacy to receive his attention, signals the decline of the private and consequently the decline of the public, since the modern age concept of "public" is nothing but a field of fighting for the untouchability of one's integrity (privacy, rights, property …). Privacy made spectacle, intimacy as the means of pleasing the TV auditorium, obscene interpretation of the human right to publicly express and perform … are the consequences of the narrowing public space and the narrowing space of the public. In the nineties, the channelled, controlled and ritualised expression of the public resulted in a radical depolitisation of the voters (abstinence, emergence of antipolitical parties …). If participation in political life is reserved for the members of political elites exclusively, I will find alternative means to establish myself as the subject of the public. The only means of achieving that is to sell my privacy. The media radically exploit this notion, turning their programmes into gladiators' games of revealed privacies. The Italian public was shocked by the explicit sexual act in their version of *Big Brother* (*Il Grande fratello*). During a Jerry Springer show, a thirteen-year-old girl admits – in front of her mother, the studio audience and the cameras – that she prostituted herself. A girl tells her boyfriend, who has just confided how much he loves her and how idyllic their relationship is, that she has been cheating on him for the last six months with the boy who at that precise moment appears in the studio and in front of the TV cameras. The two boys start fighting and the members of the TV crew are trying to stop them. The audience is simultaneously disgusted and pleased.

The solitary position of the terminal citizen / spectator eradicates close-range communication and develops long-distance communication. The local is subordinated to the global, the concrete to the abstract and the material to the virtual. Social practices become tele-practices. It is easier to confess to the TV cameras than to one's own mother, boyfriend, friend. The society is structured as a huge therapeutic device.

But in between the two Big Brothers there is a third, transitory area best illustrated in Peter Weir's movie *The Truman Show* (1998). The main protagonist Truman Burbank, whose life is created in a huge TV studio and whose every move is followed by cameras under the watchful eyes of the obsessed director and his creator Christoph, is basically a postmodern Kaspar Hauser. Truman's environment is basically your everyday American reality in which all the subjects know that they act for him and for the public (and are thus a kind of primitive terminal spectactors – see the following pages). Truman is the only one experiencing that reality as genuine; he is not even bothered by eventual bizarrely performed *product placements*.

....

Emil Hrvatin

The terminal state of Truman's position is revealed at the moment he becomes the child from Andersen's fairy tale *The Emperor's New Clothes*, telling everyone that the emperor is naked, that genuine reality and cosiness around him actually are a 24-hour reality show where all the people are performers, all the individuals characters in a gigantic show.

What is supposed to be the individual's authentic reality is actually virtual reality. For Žižek this is the embodiment of the paranoid fantasy of an American "who suddenly starts suspecting that the world he lives in is a sham, a spectacle created to convince him that he lives in the real world. (…) Hollywood is not the only one producing images of real life with no weight and material inertia – in the former capitalist consumer society the 'real social life' itself somehow assumes the features of a performed sham in which our 'real' life neighbours behave as actors and walk-on's".

What is scary is not the revelation that the environment I live in is a lie but the fact that this lie is actually all my truth, that even though I recognise it as simulation I will not moralistically reject it, I will continue living it. The subtlest feature of Weir's movie is the fact that the revelation of the spectacularity of Truman's every day does not really change anything. Truman's drama did not primarily take place in Truman himself but in the eyes of the viewers, who were – unlike Truman who had lost his reality – losing their fiction. The symbolic universum in which every single one of them had a role came crashing down, providing the economy of belonging and high rates in return. As Truman's moment of truth takes place, when he "murders his father" (at that moment, his name should be *Trauman* or *Traumaman*), the viewers suddenly take his side, supporting his decision to leave the show. This, however, has nothing to do with affection for Truman – who, by the way, leaves the show with the same sentence he had started it with every morning ("Good morning, good day and, in case we don't see each other, good evening") but out of sheer relief, since Truman's return to the show would entirely destroy the existing relations and, putting it politically/pathetically, "nothing would ever be the same as before" (Truman's collision with the dome of the studio). Truman's exit from the studio after it had become clear that the symbolic universum of the show was destroyed released the audience of responsibility, they left the studio together with Truman and continued to live his new life. The masses are convertible just like money is, the only question remains which economy of the subject is behind it all.

Reality shows, including *Big Brother*, emerge from an obsession with unmediated reality: the media world has been perfected to the point where its credibility can only be preserved by live reports, documentary style and real personalities. What does *Big Brother* do? It creates a theatrical situation within which characters playing themselves are placed. The theatrical situation is completely isolated, which basically makes it theatre – there are no connections with outside reality whatsoever[1]. Furthermore, all known reality is to be left at the studio entrance to enter the new one. The last thing the authors of BB want is the mediation of the performance: the participants – which is probably the best description of what they are – have certain guidelines how to behave that can hardly be considered scripts. What they are in the outside, open reality is present also in the closed one, although the very punctum of BB is creation of a new reality. The participants play themselves because the eye of the no longer hidden camera forces them to; just like Truman they can pose for it at any given moment. So what is real about the reality shows? The place, time, situation etc. are constructed artificially. Perhaps the identity of the participants?

Let us examine Belgian BB hero Betty who became a media star although she had not won. After leaving the BB containers and facing the fan euphoria, she suddenly started referring to herself in the show in the third person: "Betty did that, Betty was like that …", in short, she talked about herself as a character. At first we can laugh at the infantility of her fascination (when we are children we refer to ourselves in the third person singular) but her words confirm that the whole thing is acted out.

What can be considered real in the BB context, however, is the participation of the viewers. This is, of course, primarily a gladiator situation in which we are practising media Darwinism. "I have the power to eliminate the one I do not like." In the nineties, this pattern of thought has massively invaded the political sphere. We are talking about a phenomenon we could call *the electorate of revengism*, evident not only in states in transition, where the voters massively support nationalists and right-wing parties but also in the so-called developed democracies, where some traditional parties have disappeared and a number of new ones with marginal or even apolitical programs appeared instead. In the societies of the post-utopian (but not post-ideological), it is much easier to motivate the electorate to vote against than to vote for.

But motivation against is always decidedly more aggressive and destructive than motivation for, as Christoph Schlingensief has demonstrated with his project Bitte liebt Österreich, placing containers with Austrian immigrants along the streets of Vienna. On www.auslaenderraus.at spectators could vote, eliminating the ones they did not like. The results were as racist as expected, enhanced by anonymous participation. Schlingensief has shown that anonymous participation dismisses discomfort and places the viewer into a directed situation in which the viewer – precisely because of anonymity – does exactly what the direction demands.

Anonymous participation is the common trait of both the big brothers: Orwell's Big Brother provides citizens with the institution of the "two minutes of hate" and the Big Brother of today offers the institution of elimination. In both cases we are dealing with organised racism, in the public sphere most commonly encountered in readers' letters or radio talk shows. In the eighties, the Slovene political theoretician Tomaž Mastnak called the phenomenon "totalitarianism-from-below", referring to the outbursts of racist and chauvinist opposition to gay gatherings. Anonymous participants' totalitarianism-from-below does the dirty work for the governing elite. In the media sense, participation raises tension in BB. The turning points in the lives of the participants are brought about by impulses from the outside, the only permitted one being elimination.

....

Emil Hrvatin

Participatory, voyeuristic and terminal spectactor

Purini's vision takes us back to the two classical statuses of the spectator in a theatre event, the participatory and the voyeuristic. As it is well known, the participatory status of the spectator is typical for the theatre that aims at generating a certain community and for whom the theatre is the event. The ultimate participatory spectator is, according to Rousseau, a spectator who not only participates in the event but also becomes the protagonist / actor / performer of the event; who becomes – to use Althusser's terminology – the subject of the event. The voyeuristic status of the spectator is typical for the theatre that addresses the anonymous individual as part of an unidentified crowd.

On the ideological-political level we are talking about two different concepts of the individual and his / her place in the public structure. To speculate with Tönnies' terminology a bit, we could say that the participatory spectator stems from the understanding of society as (undifferentiated) community, while the voyeuristic spectator is a product of regarding society as (differentiated) society. In contemporary societies, democratically developed, transitional and undeveloped alike, the voyeuristic status of the spectator prevails, although it is constantly challenged by projects of experimental performance. In his article / manifesto *Ten points for the actors*, Einar Schleef indirectly states that it is the bilateral economy of pleasure that keeps the voyeuristic spectator and his complementary exhibitionistic actor together: "The spectator has paid for and is here precisely because of that exhibitionism, which is why he sits in the dark".

The voyeuristic status of the spectator is constantly challenged by projects of the experimental theatre. The ever-present paradox of the contemporary participatory spectator lies in the fact that theatre rarely produces a non-manipulative situation or a situation inducing no discomfort in the participatory spectator (Richard Schechner and Herbert Blau wrote a lot about this; at this point we are leaving aside those participatory spectator theatre practices which deliberately produce situations spectators are not comfortable with). The position of the performer in the above cases is just as uncomfortable.[2]

Purini's terminal spectator presupposes a different performance. Interactive, we could still call it today, although the performative power of interaction is still rudimentary. As long as someone merely observes interactive activities, we cannot talk about true interaction – interaction is not observed but performed, participated, created. Today, we generally connect interactivity with technology but it basically means a larger selection of possibilities granted in advance, with chance optionally in-calculated within them (with an emphasis on the word in-calculated); technology, however, never reacts unpredictably (unless, of course, due to an accident or a higher power). We will be able to talk about interactivity only when the machine will be able to produce a paradox, when it will be possible to program an unpredictable reaction, unpredictable for the programme itself.

In the theatre of the terminal spectator (who is at the same time the actor, therefore terminal spectator / actor will be called terminal spectactor), the physical reality is the hypersensory reality. The body of the spectator is in constant link with the surrounding physical reality functioning as the mediator for long-distance connections. The spectactor navigates in space, adapting it to his needs. Each movement of the body creates a new information for the computer that becomes a sensitive instrument for the detection of the terminal spectator's moods. The computer literally becomes "my fellow man", the emphatic alter ego comprehending (even) user's caprice.

We are talking the sensorial theatre beyond senses. No smell, no taste, no touch. The body of the terminal spectator is not in virtual reality – but which reality is the reality of his body? Because virtual reality is no longer a space. The term used for entering virtual reality is immersion, which, of course, still anticipates the existence of certain physical laws analogue to the spatial ones.

Theatre in Weightlessness

Developing Purini's idea of the terminal spectator by searching for a corresponding physical reality, we would ultimately discover reality in which space coordinates no longer define the body's up-down-left-right-in front-behind. What does the dwelling space of the terminal spectator actually presuppose? Surroundings formed by screens capable of producing the effect of teleportation at any given time. I am not moving yet I am everywhere – which is Virilio's definition of the terminal citizen.

Let us examine a unique event in the history of performance and art in general, the *Biomechanics Noordung* performance by the Slovene director Dragan Živadinov. The event took place in December 1999 aboard of the Ilyushin 76 military aircraft, otherwise used for parabolic test-flights for future cosmonauts in the course of their training. During the flight, the aeroplane performed 11 parabolas, each providing 25 seconds of gravity 0 or the state of weightlessness.[3]

Transitions from one gravitational state to the other are transitions from one physical reality to the next, an experience absolutely incomparable to any other bodily experience. Despite the seeming brevity of the intervals, the half-minute "dramas", the intensity of the transitions and the novelty of the situation forced the body to concentrate upon its every move. Fixed to our seats, we, the spectators observed the mise-en-scene unfolding in real time – the rehearsals for the event took place in normal gravity (the creators of the performance were only granted one test-flight four months before the show). Thus, we were literally attending the transposition of the body through different physical realities. The noises formed in these communications were predominantly the noises of our bodies, since we shared the same physical realities as the performers. After three parabolas, the tables preventing us from floating were removed. Performers, spectators, technicians and instructors hovered in a unified reality of gravity 0. The libertine idea of the theatre of participation (Rousseau) with no boundaries between the performer and the spectator was here realised. The standard semiotic wall structuring the theatre event was demol-ished, and at the same time, the matrices of new interpellations of the theatre medium were open. The performers, the spectators and the rest of the crew shared multiple physical realities in which the intensity of the preoccupation with self prevailed over everything

....

Emil Hrvatin

else that was going on, either structured or improvised. No more discomfort as arises in the manipulative situation of theatre projects based on cooperation with the audience.

At first we feel as if our bodies were alienated from us and we desperately want to control them (in psychoanalytical terms, what we experience is the process opposite to the mirror stage that is crucial for the identification and construction of a subject – in our case, the image of the body is alienated from the subject). We must become reacquainted with the body, which has literally lost its footing but can find a new one on the ceiling, the sides or on any other fixed object in the area. The true "drama" is the drama of the subjects' fight for control over their bodies. But then again, the drama is caused merely by the deep rooting of normal gravity in the body's memory.

The body quickly absorbs the rules of weightlessness, it reconstructs and starts functioning within new physical realities. It learns to navigate in conditions where no weight is pulling it downwards or anywhere else. As astrophysicist Herman Potočnik Noordung wrote: "The bodies move only according to the law of inertia (persistence) – unless an obstruction appears in their arbitrary and rectilinear direction – and they are subject only to their own forces (molecular, electric, magnetic, mass attraction and others) working among or within them".

Is the first terminal space, then, a space station, and its first terminal citizen a cosmonaut? The cosmonaut is placed / shrunk into a space from which he communicates with the supra-terminal on Earth by means of prosthetic media. At the same time, his body is placed into an environment of zero gravity, into a physical reality where the space co-ordinates pertaining to conditions of Earth weight or gravity 1 are relativised.

<u>End of private = end of public</u>

The theatre that the terminal spectator creates is his own life that on the formal level functions as an amalgam of fascinating visuality, the two-dimensionality of computer games and the media ghetto Big Brother trivia. What in this regard seems much more important than Baudrillard's catastrophicality is the point of the terminal spectator's identity constitution through the relation between the private and the public.

In the theatre, the positions of the public and the private are transparently defined. On the side of the public we have the performer who delivers a certain artistic gesture to public consumption. On the side of the private there is the spectator who consumes the offered artistic gesture through an organised public event that grants him / her privacy (the spectator's respect for the order of the event is awarded with the freedom of own opinion – the situation of Kant's *Sapere aude!* Enlightenment). With the terminal spectator we are witnessing a narcissistic situation, in which the performer is his / her own public and vice versa, and where the difference between the public and the private is blurred. But with the blurring of both, the question is: where, in which field, can we locate the subjectivity of the terminal spectator? If the public can access all areas, if nothing is private anymore, then the notion of the public is abolished as well.

. . . .

At first sight we could say that Živadinov's project places the individual into a certain totalitarian situation, in which he / she is totally manipulated, following the precise dramaturgy of transitions through the three gravitational conditions. But the situation is totalitarian only if the reality itself is totalitarian. Živadinov, namely, accepts the ever-avoided yet time and again dreamt about basic risk of the theatre: what if the performance (presented material, articulated event) slips out of control, itself becoming a reality in which the spectator no longer deals with the dramaturgy of fiction? The moment of the spectator's hovering in the air and the following moment of getting the body back to the floor, *re-corporating* it, are the moments in which we are the performance to ourselves. There are no more spectators, there is no more material to be observed. The brilliance of Živadinov's dramaturgy of the spectator lies in the fact that he did not invent the third spectator (the observer, as he called him in *The Praying Machine Noordung*, 1992) given the status of the "objective" witness of the event (even the cameras were floating freely). The performance is not observed, it is physically experienced – a concept established by the Italian visionary Giulio Camillo in the Renaissance already and further developed by many post-Freudian theoreticians, let us just mention Merleau-Ponty and his concept of synaesthetic perception.

Il teatro debole – theatre with no demands (of me)
This is the point of physical experience in theatre, upon which a number of contemporary dance and theatre projects rely. If Martha Graham hypostasised truth in the body ("the body does not lie") and if Wim Vandekeybus searched for something that would not be a sediment of Marcel Mauss's body techniques in the body (*What the Body does not Remember*), then the dance and theatre projects of the nineties' generation (from BAK Truppen and Jérôme Bel to Showcase Beat LeMot, Tom Plischke, Jonathan Burrows & Jan Ritsema and many others) reveal a certain fetishisation of the pre-theatrical quotidian. The search for a dance / theatre language that would differ from the one postulated by the Flemish dance and theatre scene of the eighties, employed powerful visual and choreographic authorial modes of expression and managed to achieve an excellent standard of performance as well as define the performer as a responsible subject. But their search was fundamentally a methodology of de-theatricalisation of both the performer's and the dramaturge's narrative, a decomposition of the musical, and de-authorisation of the director / choreographer. By analogy with the Italian philosophical school *il pensiero debole*[4], such theatre could be called *il teatro debole*, the weak theatre, the theatre with no demands (of me), the theatre that plays with and through the theatre, the theatre in which authors / performers could not care less whether someone considers them the performers of a certain event or just a group of people who found themselves in front of an audience merely to organise an event in which the others will participate. De-theatricalisation of the performer is, of course, one of the strategies of establishing new theatricality, most radically carried out by Elizabeth LeCompte and the Wooster Group. However, in com-

parison to the youngest generation of the weak theatre (*il teatro debole*), an important distinction is observed:

namely, the hypostatisation of the quotidian, urban subcultures, youthful unencumbrance, pop culture. *Il teatro debole* is the theatre of distance, but not permeated with the *Gestus* in a Brechtian or the Wooster-Group sense, in which the form of acting subverts ideological presuppositions of a given theatrical mainstream. What is important is that the weak theatre does not want to be a theatre in the first place, or, in case it wants to be, searches for a new form of authentic theatricality within the quotidian. Their stance when encountering the public is that of the spectators' participation; it is up to the spectators to find the meaning and place within the event. Radicalised execution of the concept (not within the *teatro debole scope*, however) would result in articulation of the participatory impulse as terminal.[5]

Ethics of the performance: to make an audience without the performance
Let us conclude with a couple of thoroughly banal questions. Why do actors in the theatre as a rule behave as if the spectators were not there, thus actually making fools of themselves? And: has the spectator ever felt like participating in the theatre? *Il teatro debole* addresses participation by lowering the level of theatricality. Taking the reality of the activity on stage to the level of the spectator's reality means counting on deconstruction of the theatre's representational frame. But the problem is not only the fact that the spectator is the first to theatricalise the event, that it is his presence in a theatre event as theatre event, which constitutes theatre as theatre, but also the fact that theatricality is already inscribed within each and every gesture intended for public performance. If we wanted to, we could do a performance even without any public. The key question of the theatre is exactly the opposite: can a public be made without the performance? The answer was, for example, offered by the futurists, but most consistently conceived by Samuel Beckett and John Cage, making clear that participation is only possible when there is nothing to participate in, when the public becomes a theatre event and perceives itself as such. *Biomechanics Noordung* further developed the concept, uncompromisingly producing the situation in which at the moment of participation the spectator splits into the subject and the object of observation, making clear that there is nothing to see except one's action in gravity 0. Thus the participation becomes terminal, meaning that if we insist on the terminal spectator, we have to renounce the performance.

[1] The producers' rigidity in preserving isolation of the "heroes" can be illustrated by recent events: the participants in American *Big Brother* were not told about the attacks on WTC and the Pentagon, despite the fact that family members of one of the participants were among the victims.

[2] I recently attended Felix Ruckert's performance at the Berlin Dock 11, where I was laid down on a comfortable bed and then caressed by a female dancer. I gave in to her rather cold and unfocused touching which I found extremely pleasurable after a hard day. But as I started to return the touches, as I, evidently, accepted the play and became her partner, I felt an insurmountable distance from the other side. In the conversation after the performance, the performers told me that they themselves did not have precise instructions on how to react to certain reactions by the spectators.

[3] Short resume of my article "Živadinov's Biomechanics in Weightlessness", Janus, no. 6/2000, pp. 38-42.

[4] The Italian philosophical school places weak thought between "the powerful mind of the one who tells the truth and helplessness similar to that reflected in the mirror of the one who observes his own nothing" (Pier Aldo Rovatti). Gianni Vattimo upgrades the metaphysical and metaphysical-historical (Hegelian) approach to the problem of the starting point with the "empiricist formula" of the weak thought: "Experience that can serve as a starting point and to which we can remain true is primarily the experience of the mundane, which is also and always determined historically but full in the cultural sense" (both quotes from the collection of essays *Il Pensiero debole*, Milan, 1983). Elsewhere, Vattimo explains that everyday media reality is neither the Hegelian absolute spirit nor a perversion. It contains cognitive possibilities and experiences, which probably predict what is yet to come (in *La fine della modernitá*, 1985).

[5] A number of web projects play through different theatricalities that ultimately constitute a terminal spectactor. Interesting examples of that are projects by the Slovene net artist Igor Štromajer (www.intima.org), the Russian net artist Olga Lialina (will.teleportacija.org), the Italian net artists calling themselves 0100101110101101.org (www. 0100101110101101.org), etc..

Translated by Mojca Krevel

Emil Hrvatin

Their job is not to dance,
but to watch other people dancing – if they dance

Jérôme Bel / Jan Ritsema

Jérôme Bel: Hello everybody, my name is Jérôme Bel and this is Jan Ritsema. And of course there are two microphones to interfere if you want – because I have to tell you that I am a little bit shocked to see the house full, because in the last days there were many people talking, very interesting, more articulated than me for sure, and it was not so full.

Jan Ritsema: Shall we start?

Bel: Yes.

Ritsema: All the time we were talking with each other about what is really important for the performances we make, it boiled down to that we like performances that problematise something, research something, that want to know something in comparison to performances that want to impress, want to have our admiration or that kind of things. This wanting to know can be different, can be expressed in two ways. When you make a performance, you can search for something, you can want to know something – so you research something, and then you find a solution, which ends up in a certain form, and that form is the performance. This is what you want to share with an audience. You can also make a performance that still wants to know something while it is actually taking place, so that the audience is needed to fulfil the performance. The performer fulfils 50%, and the audience is needed to fulfil the other 50%. Jérôme's performance of *Nom donné par l'auteur* which was here yesterday is a good example of a performance where the audience is needed to fulfil the thing. You have to think. And it is made for you to think. There are propositions all the time to share secretly with what is offered to you. Why I like this especially is because I adore (and I never wanted to be an audience that admires) the way this performance looks at me as a member of the audience. I am treated as a mature person. I am not treated like a child that is manipulated in all kinds of directions, mostly with clichés and stereotypes of performance making. I am treated as someone of whom the performance does not ask anything, does not want anything. There is no economy, no cash to be made, it is not about being good or not being good. I can stay entireely in my own sovereignty and dignity. And Jérôme provides this not only with *Nom donné par l'auteur* but also with many other performances. He looks at me in a dignified, in a non-repressive way. And repressiveness is the natural state of performance makers. It is only repressiveness that people in the audience want to be treated with.

Bel: Yes. To make a performance is to take power over the audience, and people are expecting this. If you refer to *Nom donné par l'auteur* the goal was to give a lot of space to the audience to resolve the enigmas we put on stage, and many people couldn't stand it, some fell asleep because of course the piece is boring, I know it. I have to admit it but this was the only possibility for me to force, excuse me if I use the word, the dignity of the audience. I did not want the performers on stage to dominate the audience. And then people did not like it at all. They felt free so they came on stage. So, if you don't dominate the audience they try to kill you. Right?

Ritsema: Yes, Yes ... Don't laugh about it. That is a horrible situation – what people do to each other. Every time you go to a performance you are getting educated, treated to be repressed, and you are educated to accept this repression. There are hardly any performances which do not suppress you. And in my opinion we have to get rid of this. As an audience we have to get emancipated. That means that you can control what is represented to you. That there are no illusions, no mystifications, no manipulations wanting to get you into a good mood or a bad mood or smiling.

Bel: The performers do no more than the audience.

Ritsema: Exactly.

Bel: That's why I, for example, in *Nom donné par l`auteur* use a vacuum cleaner, a carpet, a salt cellar, things that everybody knows. I am not talking about Romania in the 15th century. Because I want to have the same subjects as the audience. For *The show must go on,* it is also the music that everybody knows. I try to find equality between audience and stage. But every time, somebody has to take the power.

Ritsema: I think this is clear. You want to ask something?

Ana Vujanović: I'd like to say that there is no innocent relation between the audience or spectatorship and performance, because you forget that you make the context of understanding and relating to your performances at all. For example, there are so many people here who make context in which we as audience are able to relate with your performances. So there is no enigma that could be resolved innocently in direct relation with the spectatorship.

Ritsema: But that is not what we said, that it presents something innocently.

Vujanović: I'd like to say that we are all prepared to understand the performance in a certain way because of the context that is prepared before we enter the performance.

Ritsema: I don't think so. That presupposes that people are informed about how they have to look at a performance by Jérôme. When these performances started, they had a lot of problems with the audience which was not prepared for this, because they wanted to be entertained and they did not get the entertainment. That's why Jérôme called it boring.

Vujanović: Yes, but that's because there are many contexts of reading one single piece, not because the piece is boring.

Ritsema: But this is a context where you are not treated like a child, he does not want to direct you. You are free to go with his propositions or not.

Vujanović: I cannot remember my childhood, so I cannot remember when I was free. So I am speaking about the present.

Ritsema: So you mean that you cannot distinguish between performances where you might recognise repression and others which do it a little bit less?

Ana Vujanović: Of course I do.

Jan Ritsema: I think I like performances (and it is necessary that there be more such performances), which try to not be repressive, or at least try to be more transparent. That means that the whole audience can verify what is happening to them by the transparency of the means used by the makers.

Goran Sergej Pristaš: Do you expect for the audience to feel any joy while watching performances?

....

Jérôme Bel / Jan Ritsema

Ritsema, Bel: Yes.

Pristaš to Bel: How do you deal with the situation of joy? You just said you don't want to make entertainment.

Bel: I did not say this – entertainment is okay.

Pristaš: Sorry, can you then repeat what you said? The performance of *The show must go on* in Zagreb was kind of a celebration of your work, people admired you. People were singing with you, putting lighters up, people really celebrated with you. What do you say to this?

Ritsema: It is exactly the problem that people are so accustomed to repressive behaviour that they start to behave repressive too at a performance that offers something else. They go on stage thinking that they feel free, but it is just the repressiveness that they put on themselves. It is not what *The show must go on* itself proposes. It is dangerous that they treat themselves like this. It is horrible what people do to each other. You have to stop them from doing this.

Bel: I don't want them to clap hands during the performance. I want them to shut up and to watch the performance. And especially in the National Theatre of Zagreb. I don't perform in a kindergarden.

Gerald Siegmund: Jan, can you just clarify what you mean by repressive performance?

Ritsema: All of them, 99%.

Siegmund: What would be the repressive element in them that prevents the freedom you have when watching Jérôme's performances? I would be very interested in this point.

Ritsema: I feel repressed when there is an oversized ego wanting to sell itself to me. I don't want to be put under pressure by somebody who thinks he is superior because he has the microphone and can stand on stage. The stage wants to do a lot with me (the audience) but when I cannot control it, when it is not transparent but illusionistic or mystifying, when the realm is certain emotional aesthetics (aesthetics always represent an ideology, mine too), I refuse. Like you said earlier, a crucial thing for you is when you feel that a piece has a soul. I don't know what you see when you say you see the soul, but I don't want to see a soul. I want to see a transparent way of acting / moving, meaning that I want to recognise the structure, the scaffolding, want to recognise how the piece is organised, that the makers want to share this with me instead of wanting to impress me, to manipulate me, to treat the audience as a whole rather than individual spectators, that they respect the audience. I mostly feel disrespected. Like Godard said: it is of less importance that you like the performance than that the performance likes you. I don't want to be sucked into the stage and certainly not with cheap emotional aesthetic clichés. That stupefies the audience. Represses them, makes them dependent of the stage. As Rancière, the French philosopher reasoned: First, no theatre without a spectator. Second, looking is the opposite of knowing. Looking makes the spectator passive, the opposite of active. Spectatorship is a bad thing because it forbids knowledge and action. So far Rancière. Spectators are too often treated, are expected to put their brains on zero. To undergo. So-called experience. I want to experience by thinking, to which a performance like *Nom donné* invites me. When the propositions offered on stage are transparent, because they allow their construction to be noticed, then the stage and the spectator are equal. The spectator emancipates.

Emil Hrvatin: As far as I understand, you are applying a certain kind of emancipatory dimension in this dispositive, which establish in your performance: Why do you, politically speaking, establish this situation where you need to leave a space for the audience?

Bel: Well, I didn't go so far – but just to find more equality between these two spaces is something. This means that I always – not always, but most of the time – use the process the performance is built on in my research. I start with the first things I was thinking about during the rehearsals, and then I follow the time of my research. So the audience can share the process and then make the piece. We make the piece together in a way. And what I also try to use is transparency. I give you the rules in the beginning, and then we play together. And of course sometimes later on, I change the rules just for fun – but I mean I try not to hide anything of the work and not to say things that did not happen. Is that ok? That is the only thing. Not to dominate is my favourite political statement till now. I recently made a piece for the Paris opera, I wanted the worst dancer of the company because I wanted to give her the stage, the possibility to speak about her work. The stars have the possibility to give interviews on TV and in newspapers, but not the corps de ballet's dancers …

Ritsema: … you are a social worker.

Hrvatin: What I wanted to ask is that you probably have a certain understanding of a political subject of today which in your opinion can communicate in the performances we are talking about, comparing the political subject, as it was constituted in the sixties for example.

Ritsema: I don't know if this is an answer but I have the tendency to answer with Rancière again. It's from an article he wrote about the politics of aesthetics: A performance is not political, because the subject is political. A performance is political when it tries to give space to voices that were at that moment invisible or not heard. You have to see this as a very wide way, a voice can also be a way of looking at something. A typical artistic event is to make a proposition that people look at in a different way than they were accustomed, used to.

That can be a social situation, a theory or a visual arts piece. You should be aware of how much space you give. Think about in what way you share the space which is given to you, with the people you are dealing with. With this kind of performances one cannot avoid self-referentiality. When you want to be transparent you always refer to yourself. So the subject always is the performance and the performance situation, too. And this position can be political, it is like Jérôme's quote of Godard: "The way I do travelling is political".

Bel: The way we are doing this, for example, by choosing not very beautiful people, no costumes and things like that.

Ritsema: Frederic is beautiful.

....

Jérôme Bel / Jan Ritsema

Bel: Frederic is not beautiful. Frederic – and we have been working together now since 10 years – is medium. The medium thing is a good thing for me. It is closer to everybody, the most beautiful boy and the worst. Because if I take someone very beautiful, the one who is not beautiful won't identify with him. This is just to create links. For example, in *Jérôme Bel* I had the chance to find this lady of 60 years who the audience could identifiy with; usually dance performances are with young people. With an old woman on stage I realise that many old people were happy, I mean they were more involved as spectators …

Cvejić: All the examples that you give, the ideals of transparency of the rules of the game and the control (given) over the spectator.

Bel: I don't have control over the spectator. I give him time.

Cvejić: That means that the political objective of your theatre is to emancipate a 19th-century bourgeois spectator, who goes to theatre to be represented by identification or recognition of the sublime event presented.

Bel: No, because they get mad because there is nothing sublime.

Andrea B. Braidt: Excuse me, can I just … maybe it is a little late in the discussion, which is already charged emotionally and politically. Which comes of course from using terms like repression, emancipation, freedom, dominance, but I want to link my state-ment to the very first words you said when you described the roles of the performer and the audience in the performance we saw last night. For me what I heard was a very accurate description of a performative speech act. Because what happens in the perform-ance is, I think, a performative speech act in terms of that the roles of the speaker and the audience are very clearly defined, they have a very clear context. And the freedom, the participation of the audience comes exactly from the role that the audience has. I think this is freeing the emancipatory experience that one has, just like in a wedding ceremony. You have witnesses, you have an audience, they are important, because you need the audience for the performative speech act, so the performative speech act can be successful. This is the link and this is the difference to the other kind performance you described. The kinds of performances you described, when a product is produced and you don't need an audience. I really share with you what you said when describing the roles and the effect and the context of the audience of last night's performance.

Bel: But there is a limit, which is also the limit of my work, because there are still those holy things like a wedding. I keep this little holy sacred space which is the theatre. And this is still a problem for me. People say "go and make it in the street" but nobody would watch it in the street. Do you see what I mean? You are talking about the wedding … for the performance we need this context and for me it is still a problem … Do you follow me, or am I wrong?

Braidt: The difference is that it is not about meaning but about successfulness. You are not an agent, you don't propose a message but the message comes from the conventions, citations, from the relationship of the agent to the objects and from the interaction and the role of the audience. And this is the difference. A performance where you have a performer who proposes a message and who says "I want the audience to agree or disagree"? I got a very different feeling with your performance and that would be the difference. And that would also be the kind of political force of it.

Veronica Kaup-Hasler: I just wanted to add something to Andrea B. Braidt. I think it is very rare that a performance makes you think about your role as spectator and as an audience. We have a notion of "the audience", as if it was a homogeneous mass of people, but it is also a fact that this audience is formed by a certain quantity of individuals being in the same space at a very special moment. So I wonder if there is a relation between spectator and audience that could possibly be considered as equivalent to being a citizen and being part of "le peuple / the people". Let's take an example – *The show must go on* by Jérôme Bel. It is a really intriguing performance because it deals with memories and emotional reactions you have hearing this kind of pop music. But the critical point is the point of silence. Sometimes you go with the audience, you recognise things, you feel as part of a community, you feel comfortable hidden in the mass, in this faked community, and suddenly when it comes to the point of silence, you really hate the one beside you laughing and you start hating the audience, because it cannot be silent. It makes me reflect on my position in the audience. And that is the political point. It is also like the effect when I see performances by Tim Etchells.

Bel: In some performances, everybody keeps silent. It happens. Sometimes everybody loves each other, or they start to dance together, but very quietly. Sometimes they fight. But it is not always the same thing. That is why it is interesting, that is what I like. Every time it reveals a political situation of … sometimes a country. This is just an anecdote from when we did the piece in Brazil, in Rio de Janeiro. It was in 2002, two days after the election of Lula, the new president, when we put on *Imagine* from John Lennon, which for me was a criticism of the 1970s' idealism (the theatre is in total darkness during the whole song). At that moment the spectators all started to scream together out of joy. I thought, oh, they don't understand anything. And then I realised that I was the stupid one, of course. Because for them, two days after the election of this man, a former factory worker, from the left, something was possible. How stupid am I? My idea was: *Imagine* your best performance (because I was not presenting anything, because the whole theatre is in a total darkness) … this was the first layer. Now I am more free with this and I accept that people smash each other, and that they do what they want. But at the beginning I was like "shit, shit, shit". Of course I have a dream. I am a director, it's paradoxical but I'd like to direct everybody, at the same time I'd like to give space to think for the audience … but I will learn.

Katherina Zakravsky: I would like to add a comment to the show which I saw the second time yesterday. Connected to issues brought up before – the issues were repression and less mature treatment of the audience. These are issues that can be very well illustrated with yesterday's show. I would not talk about repression, which is a strong psychological term, but about manipulation. And in this sense I even find something sublime in yesterday's piece because for me it is a lot about sublime manipulation; and in this sense – this

Jérôme Bel / Jan Ritsema

isn't a criticism – it is such a clever piece about the modes of manipulation we are living in now. Because it is about transparent structures, rules, rules being changed. But I was lucky to hear a lecture you gave on *Self-Unfinished*, Xavier's piece in Leipzig some years ago, and I was so amazed that you found a world myth in this piece. It was all about huge issues like death and so on, the white room, it was very sublime actually, but also correct. When I think about the piece yesterday, it is a little bit like a boys' room, with those ten everyday objects, but at the same time it is also like playing god, like "okay, lets create a world". These objects are very banal, but they are also extremely symbolic. They have their complementary relations, there is the light, there is the book and so on. And I want to add a little question about a tiny detail, a question about the one element of manipulation. I was wondering about the miracle of the salt box. The salt box was a writing tool and so on. And there's another question about the money bill. Is it real or not? (Bel: Yes.) In the end it was divided. I am sure that there were two salt boxes involved. You just brought the second one from the back of the stage.

Bel: There are two salt boxes. At one point I go out, taking the salt with me, and then I come back with another one. This is the only trick in the performance. And the last one of my career. No, for sure, there are many (…), of course I manipulate. But I say, "Look how I manipulate you".

Pristaš: Just one more thing, then I will stop talking. Just to go back to the performance in Zagreb. It was in the bourgeois theatre, in the National Theatre. But the audience there never goes to that kind of theatre, I think that the performance produced something similar to what happened to Brecht when he had the premiere of *Beggars' Opera*. He also expected that everybody would hate the performance and go out, but people liked the musical. In a way that performance produced a kind of jouissance. People celebrated the quality of the performance. We sometimes don't believe in a serious laughter. There are people who are laughing, we become too serious considering them, how do they dare. That kind of joy I was witnessing in Zagreb. Knowing the audience, for me it was a serious joy, a joy which was not a bourgeois joy. A joy about something that people really liked and understood. They enjoyed your proposal. But it is sometimes like that, that "dead end" might produce that kind of jouissance.

Bel: No, no, hopefully it is very funny. The piece is a good joke. I want the spectators t o act, as they should act. We have to do our job. As we do our job in the performance – *Let's dance* by David Bowie, so we dance, we are dancers. And they expect dance. There is light, music, some people dancing, so I did my job. I want them to do their job, too. Their job is not to dance, but to watch other people dancing. If they dance there is no more theatre, no more representation. They need to be passive, passive physically. Not intellectually of course …

Tomislav Medak: I think we can push the idea of jouissance a step further – and this is maybe also self-reflection. You might expect people to enjoy a performance, not because they enjoy watching a musical, but rather because they enjoy recognising the divestiture of the authorising element. What they enjoy is the fact that they recognise the rules of the performing dispositive. That is basically the consciousness and habitus of the late-twentieth century intellectual – consciousness that you're someone who recognises the rules, and you enjoy it. It's a cynicism, in a way. And in Bel's work, where the rules of performance are made evident, that presents, in yet another step, the opportunity for reflection on this cynicism produced by the self-reflection of those who have insight into the evidence he stages, but who are not emancipated by seeing the rules that they are obeying to when they go to theatre – unlike the bourgeoisie. So for those who are not bourgeoisie, they are cynicists.

Ritsema: There is also something else. You understand a rule but you also understand the offering of being able to understand. That's very important, that is also an emancipating and equalising aspect.

Medak: I think that there is a step of emancipation from this consciousness where you are enjoying the fact that you recognise. Maybe there is some emancipation in the sense that you recognise your own cynicism.

Ritsema: I don't think so. I don't know. But I want to say that the performance is not only an enigma and a challenge to know if you understand all the propositions that are offered. It's explicitly about movement, and the joy of looking at movement in a completely different way. Like the movement of thinking. And discovering that. It is an invitation to make combinations in your brain. It is a proposition, it is not when you say "do you understand the rule?", it is almost a stupid game that is being offered. And it is also a more complex thing because there is this movement …

Bel: Sorry – it is just to give a rule so they know what will happen, so they won't be surprised and so we can think. Nothing special will happen. Especially in yesterday' performance. You don't expect anything, so you can be free just to be there and watch what's happening and not be expecting/desiring.

Ritsema: You expect that there is an audience that walks away, so there is an audience that doesn't like it – and if they don't like it is because it doesn't suit their expectations.

Medak: Those who stay, who want to stay, who enjoy it, they stay because they recognise what the author or director is putting forth. They recognise this game of rules – I'm insisting on this just to reflect that there may be another jouissance than the one where you have an impulse to dance, maybe you have impulses to think and to identify your thought, to create an identity of your thought, that might be another danger that one should reckon with. I am not contesting that when you recognise that there are rules put forward, an entire field opens for the perception. I don't claim that this is not happening. I am just claiming that there is another level of jouissance, that may be happening outside of this moving field.

Ritsema: Of course there are all kinds of dangers, like the danger of the sublime manipulation that you want to prevent. Happily enough Jérôme had lots of problems with his last performance. So he had lots of reasons to think and rethink, and those problems happen, because you want to rethink what you are doing and you want to try and pick other entrances and not go into the same trap. We are dealing with this all the time.

Jérôme Bel / Jan Ritsema

Bel: The last two questions.

Boyan Manchev: I want to react to this shortly. I think that there is no presupposed rule in this play and I think the enjoyment comes from the experience of the interruption of the presupposed idea and logic order. What is at stake in this play is the "surprise of the event". People are laughing exactly when something really unexpected happens, and this is not a negative thing, this is not a manipulation, it is an interruption of conventional order and representational frame, which opens a free space. And laughter is precisely the experience of this open space. It provokes a reaction. So I do believe that there we are facing this opportunity to step out of the rules. Happiness? This is another story…

Cvejić: How specialised is the spectator these performances are addressing? Because of course it is the Western spectator, who enjoys practicing the protocol in his/her role. According to the speech acts theory, this would be the fourth intention of the performative which reasserts the tautological charater of convention: the performer intends that the spectator recognises his/her intention as an intention intended for recognition. There can't be an act of rupture or opening to the unknown, "surprise of the event".

Ritsema: Are you asking if there are any special facilities needed from the audience to enjoy Jérôme's performances?

Cvejić: I think there are degrees of jouissance.

Bel: That's the reason why the show is a success. There are people enjoying it, dancing. This depends on the piece; the one from yesterday, *Nom donné par l'auteur* has been touring for ten years now. Today even if it is boring they stay. Usually dozens of people were leaving the auditorium. Now it is different. But in the beginning I realised – also with the piece called *Jérôme Bel* – that the people who didn't have any expectations for the performance followed it. I was doing simple things on stage which everyone can understand. And then the choreographic field and the theatre field supported us. The people who left were the bourgeoisie which is sure of its values: "I know what dance is". After a few tours I could tell you when people came into the theatre who was going to leave, just by the outfit. Couples, groups of women … you have to understand, a few colleagues in the office, they like dance, they decide to go to see the performance. I mean the one you saw yesterday, and I can understand them. They like dance and they go to see this and also because they are a group. A social group always is a problem for my performances. Because they don't accept that they could be interested in this. For them there is not only the relation to the stage – which is why I later did *Jérôme Bel*. I realised that if this was public, the auditorium, the stage should be private. Nakedness. That was my experience. You know my dream is to have Bourdieu next to me. During the performance, I would like him to explain to me why they laugh, why they are leaving … But I have to learn this by myself. I try to know, I improve and that is why I now can manipulate more, and I have a bigger audience. But the larger audience is a problem now with *The show must go on*, because I have more and more misunderstandings. I don't know what to do.

Ritsema: Ok, shall we stop now?

Bel: Yeah.

Ritsema: Can you put your lighters on, can we sing together and be happy? Thank you very much.

Bel: I would like to thank the girl who is going around with the microphone (Marlies Pilhofer). Jan, thank you so much.

39

Communication and beyond:
"Conceptual dance" in Belgrade

Ana Vujanović

The title of the text was transformed, changed and re-shaped several times, from the head of the panel's first invitation over the abstract of my paper and then the exposure in Tanzquartier to the final text. What made or at least helped the confusion I have tried to resolve by the re-namings was my wondering whether the congress – which itself changed its name, as well as the panel in which I took part – was to be on contemporary European choreographic dance, known as conceptual dance, or on the inventory or inventories in the contemporary dance field in general, or on various performing practices or performance art practices. Or, perhaps the focus was to be on the inventory of the recent relations between contemporary dance and performance, or of the recent relations between contemporary dance and performance in "the former two halves of Europe". Or, it could be on inventing contemporary dance and performance or their actual relationships. After reading the project descriptions for the n-th time I finally realised that I could not be sure ever, as I was not an "insider", familiar with all potential references, implied streams, involved people, and their positions. Then I also realised that this communicational break at the edge of the context – in the situation when the context is not closed by an authoritarian gesture – was what was the important question of / for both contemporary dance and performance, no matter whether conceptual or not, Eastern or Western etc., and their economies of exchange.

So I'm dealing here with the exchange between performance and audience, called "communication", and focus on its economy in contemporary performance situation. Therefore I shall combine a broader and more abstract theorisation of the exchange process and differences in communication of the traditional theatre and ballet audience and nowadays' performance and dance spectatorship, and some concrete notes on the case of the Pro Tools festival of contemporary European choreography, held in Belgrade in 2004.

First of all, I put performance in the economic circle: production-exchange-consumption, and consider it with all its aesthetic categories, functions, features, and surpluses within the frame of the circle. I find it the basic one – since performing is, from my point of view, basically nothing else than a social practice of specific production, which produces something (performance, as knowledge, experience, symptom, event…) and offers it to the consumers' (audience's, spectatorship's) consumption. The exchange in a performance situation is between the two: production and consumption. While consuming a performance, the audience takes the offer and gives something to it, in a way pays for the consumption. I would like to put the meaning in the centre of the exchange, in order to emphasise that the central point of the exchange therefore always-yet is – failure. When I talk about the meaning I'm not just talking about the pure and abstract semantic level of performance as it was seen in structuralist semiological theories of text, with their category of the "constant semantic skeleton" put within the frame of the theatre by Anne Übersfeld. Instead, I'm rather talking about the fact that all of a performance's features are meaningful; even the feature itself is a material medium – the performance's aesthetic, emotionality, its energy, "eventness", and the most material physicality that appears before the audience's eyes. By considering them (as) meaningful, I try to avoid seeing and leaving them innocent, literal, directly accessible, non-mediated, as something that could be taken as such, that could precede or avoid the discourse and thus exists by its nature before or without entering social discursive networks.

In the light of the meaning put in that way, I am interested in the communication (the meaning) in a performance situation; that is the situation that always has to but never can achieve the unique and continual context requested by and for communication. In the case of most of the contemporary productions, rejecting the unification of the context even happens on purpose. The influence of Jacques Derrida's re-reading speech acts theory and theory of the performative (as they are put within analytic philosophy and ordinary language philosophy in particular – e.g. in John Austin, Peter Strowson, and John Searl's work) is significant for the thesis. I would just mention Derrida's text *Signature, event, context*, where he undertakes a radical deconstruction of the very conceptual system that enables, as it is presupposed, a unique continual communicational context, and happy realisation of a performative utterance in the frame of it. Thence he achieves a replacement of the elements in the binary pair "literal (original) – parasitic (mimetic)" performatives, deconstructing common sense propositions of the "seriousness" of communication in ordinary life as opposed to the stage situation. His re-reading already entered the field of performing arts, where it became integrated in its basic concepts and practices, such as the concept of performance itself. Thanks to the shift, new paradigms and strategies of the performance's performatives in its cultural and social context replaced former (neo-avant-garde) naïve beliefs and intentions to direct impact and interventions by means of saving and delivering meaning produced on the stage. But the question of communication and it's failure still remains.

So the topical subject here is in fact the process of performance miscommunication, asymmetrical exchange that emerges as a necessary effect of two partitions. The first one is the partition of the field of performance situation into the contexts of producing / performing and of consuming / seeing, listening, comprehending the performance. There is no smooth continuity between them, but a break, gap, radical cut that could never be bridged. The removal of the fourth wall (as the traditional border between the two contexts) and the destruction of the "black cube" as emancipatory performance gestures from the last decades could not achieve the uniqueness of the communicational context, but only replaced the old tendency one-way delivery of meaning with the new tendency to mutually share meaning. This failure is linked with the second partition in the per-formance situation – the partition of the field of the audience into a relatively supposed, expected and directed but always endless public space as a common communicational ground (audience), and numerous relatively unexpected, undirected, and exclusive individual spaces (spectatorship) that would be finite if only the performerwould be familiar with all of them and their actual structure, which is virtually impossible. (The analogy can be made with the difference between communicational processes in electronic mass media such as radio and television that tend to one-way information, and in new digital media such as the Internet which tends to interactive sharing.)

Ana Vujanović

In order to make the partition process more precise, I'll recite some "frequent questions". In fact, there are two relatively simultaneous positions / lines of questioning that are important in the exchange process:

1 The performer's: How can I (my act, word, gesture, performative, etc.) communicate? How can I save and deliver the meaning I produce, since I cannot (or even do not want to) control the whole audience space as the context of getting the meaning?

2 The spectator's: Is the meaning I get that which is produced by the performer and supposed to be got, or is it constructed by myself after the breaking of the communication context? To what extent should I be familiar with the context of producing the meaning in order for me to be sure that I really get it?

The passing by / encounter of the positions in the performance situation is constitutive for the economy of exchange and its failure, since both of them are needed and, which is important, asymmetrical at the same time. The process explained in the speech acts theory and its further elaborations are analogous to the psychoanalytical process of subject constitution; but to explain the approach would need more space and concentration than I have here.

Within the frame of the problematic I would like to mention the Pro Tools festival, organised in Belgrade (in the Centre for Cultural Decontamination) in 2004, by TkH (Walking Theory) – centre for performing arts theory and practice (edited by Bojana Cvejić). Although I would rather like to say something else – being familiar with all the difficulties we had while organising the event, and especially with its significance for the local scene – the Belgrade audience simply missed the works by Xavier Le Roy, Tino Sehgal, Mårten Spångberg, and Mette Ingvartsen, performed within the festival. I shall emphasise the difference I noted in reception by the "competent audience" (critics, theorists, dancers, performers, choreographers, etc.) and the "common audience", trying to articulate it from the aspect of this problematic. It is clear that the audience is not a homogeneous mass, but I think it is possible to mark some symptomatic characteristics. According to the critiques and reviews published afterwards, as well as talks with the audience during the festival, the presented works present mostly unknown references to both of them (with the exception of a small number of well-educated and "up-to-date" persons there, who travel abroad and / or read recent literature). The basic problem is that there is no tradition in dance and theatre history in Belgrade that could be the point of departure or should be extended with the newest achievements to provide a platform for understanding the works. So the critics chose either to support the event euphorically or to contest it resentfully, depending on their a priori ideological (artistic) attitudes – pro-innovative and -Western or pro-traditional and conservative. The polarisation culminated during Spångberg's work *Powered by Emotions*, when many members of the "competent audience" got angry or left the venue, being irritated by his amateurish movement and terrible singing of pop songs (from *Buena Vista Social Club*), while others were amused with Spångberg's scoffing at the high art institution (dance). The reaction of the "common audience" (which is not so "common" taking into account the profiles of the venue and

TkH, who attract very specific audiences) was similar. In brief, many of them enjoyed the work, and joined in it singing, laughing and dancing at their seats with lighters in the air. The reaction was benevolent and not too naïve, but with a cynical distance to the pop-cultural trash and even the belief that Spangberg asked for this kind of reaction to succeed in his "provocation". Those reactions shaped the field of (mis-)understanding the work in Belgrade, and all (other) problematics that the author involved in the work (authorship, proprietary relations, capitalisation, etc.) were simply missed. No phenomenon could close he gap in communicational context, except one which verifies itself through a master-signifier that fixes the context. And almost all contemporary performance and dance production is far from the kind of verification known from drama theatre tradition.

The example I emphasised is not exceptional for contemporary performance or dance and their exchanges with spectatorship. What is important here is that it is symptomatic, and demonstrates clearly what is often neglected when the exchange is discussed. And that is the fact that what is really exchanged in the exchange process of contemporary performance is neither the meaning nor any other value than the exchange itself. As money has become a meta-value of exchange, the value of all values, and therefore value itself in the context of capitalist society, as it was put by Marx, communication becomes – paradoxically at the first glance – the only value that is really communicated in the communicational process of contemporary performance. In a way it becomes an empty signifier; which does not imply that it is abstract, non-material, and free from the discursive structure of the society. Instead, it manifests the deeply material social structuration of the very concept of communication, which is based on an implicit social consensus allowing its signifier to cover all miscommunications that in fact are only what is realised in nowadays' performance practice. So, the communication of performance as, in Althusserian terms, relatively autonomous but necessarily inner social practice, first of all is an uncertain illocutory act of its discourse in the network of social discourses. And its politics is therefore either frustrating failure when it resists the consensus, or communication of oh so wanted communication when it complies with the consensus.

The conclusion could be brought to the ultimate instance: *There is no such thing as communication in a performance situation!* The conclusion is especially important in the situations of contemporary dance and performance, where communicational context – I will repeat, on purpose – is not used to be framed, limited, and ended in its totality by a master authority. Is there still something that should be focused in an exchange process of that kind? It must be. Otherwise, the conclusion would be almost unbearable.

I said "almost" because, to be honest, this relates mainly to the common sense meaning of the word ("communication"). Maybe you can find out another one … Moreover, perhaps you already have found it. And … maybe everything is perfect with performance communication … And perhaps I am wrong about everything I said … being entrapped by common sense … So … it probably has a chance … Perhaps you are still able to follow me, although I do not refer to any master authority to verify my speech …

....

Ana Vujanović

Maybe … you are really familiar with what is happening in my head … and perhaps with its relations to my theoretical framework … Which one? Possibly you know … But perhaps you cannot be absolutely sure … Perhaps, I said … But … perhaps … you anyway can get the context from what I am saying … But you probably cannot frame it entirely …

45 Maybe you can always re-open it again to add some new details, … to re-read it by means of new lateral facts that you discover afterwards … Probably you are just missing something of the context … It could be something extremely important for the entire speech, who knows … Maybe you always miss something … maybe only to some extent … Perhaps the point is that you cannot stop the context, ever …

Wording – conceptual dance,
laboratory, research

To end with judgment by way of clarification...

Xavier le Roy / Bojana Cvejić / Gerald Siegmund

Xavier Le Roy: Because we cannot escape this terminology any longer what is your understanding of conceptual dance? What is it in relationship to dance? In relationship to conceptual art? When have you read, heard the terms "conceptual dance", "non dance" or "anti dance" for the first time? How do you think these terms are understood in the field of choreographic art? in other fields? What is your understanding of these terms? Or why do you think they where chosen?

Bojana Cvejić: The term "conceptual dance" has never been theorised, introduced in a programmatic way by the makers, i.e., the choreographers who are attributed the label, nor has it been elaborated theoretically in the European or American discourses of performing arts who would be following the so-called conceptual dance practises today.

So far I have been convinced that the term is so inappropriate that it should be dismissed, its usage being more harmful than supportive of the development of these practises. But as the term stubbornly recurs, and more and more with the negative intention of closing a paradigm down, perhaps it is important to use this panel as the last opportunity for contesting the grounds on which the denomination "conceptual dance" with regard to Conceptual art has been made. I would very systematically and concisely divide the arguments in two: what makes the content of the concept "Conceptual art" – the grounds for "yes" (which are definitely not the reasons why the term conceptual dance was coined, because the usage of the term shows that it isn't informed by knowledge about Conceptual art), and the grounds for "no".

Grounds for "Yes"

1 Conceptual art developed the new aesthetic of *the speech act* in the late 1960s. The artist representative of minimal sculpture, Donald Judd best exemplified it with the statement: "This is a work of art if I say so". Indeed if some recent dance practises use the performative of "this is choreography, this is, this could be dance" to constitute their novel propositions on dance, they nevertheless move away from the aesthetic of declaration and intention.[1] The proposition "this is choreography" is never neutral and arbitrary, for it is devised to meet the resistance of Dance in singular, the dominant essential views on dance, the institutional resistance to not only proposing other propositions, but to the form of proposition as such.

2 When a work of dance or choreography is considered a kind of proposition presented in the context of dance it issues a comment on dance. Here we have to reconsider how *the proposition "this is choreography"* relates to Joseph Kosuth's definition of artwork as an analytic proposition. In dance there has never been a determination of analytic critical conceptualism of the kind of Kosuth, which would analyse the types of propositions using positivist logic, or linguistic or semiotic models, and replace the matter of performance with a metalinguistic discourse on the nature and concept of dance. However, the propositional form of the so-called conceptual dance practises shares with conceptual art self-reflexiveness, much less discursive or epistemological and much more perceptual/antiessentialist, thereby working mainly with the materiality of dance and the perceptual

experience and interpretation of the spectator. Self-reflexivity in conceptual dance is directed towards the dispositif of theatre, the conditions, roles and procedures whereby a spectator is presented something as dance, which becomes the object of its own performance. Such a re-orientation promotes a radical stance: if dance tries to tell us something about the world it is bound to fail … it can only represent representation, in other words, its means, mechanisms and ideologies of producing meaning and status in contemporary culture.

3 The self-reflexiveness should better be replaced by *spectatorship,* when it addresses the frame of perception, and in some rare cases, receivership, when it requires that the spectator discursively engages in the understanding of what the work proposes as choreography. Meaning is created in structural relationships between the work and the field of dance and choreography, the conditions and roles of the author and the spectator.

4 Does conceptual dance share with Conceptual art the *institutional critique*? Only with regard to critiquing the ideological fetishism of the status of object and commodity status. Nevertheless, the so-called conceptual dance participates in the institutional distribution; there is a necessary collaboration between the programmer and the choreographer to a certain degree; some programmers strive to co-create concepts or rather contexts of festivals which will support the propositions of conceptual dance.

Grounds for "No"

1 The work of so-called conceptual dance isn't based in *the withdrawal of the perceptual*. It doesn't map the linguistic onto the perceptual, even if it is influenced by the so-called Duchamp effect; the word does not prevail over the movement. There is no dogmatic prohibition of physicality (like it was the case in Conceptual art that the art object was replaced by the theoretical object). On the contrary, the practises are based on configuring other materialities of movement and body expressivity, which would no longer rest on the Romantic notions of the ineffable and unfathomable, the speechless anonymity of the body etc.. (I'll return to these notions with regard to Dance in singular.) The fear of the ugly words "tautology" and "self-referentiality" associated with Conceptual art and used against the so-called conceptual dance comes from relying on the entrenched hope in Western culture that dance would be the event of thought before it acquires a name. This is where Western philosophers like Alain Badiou, theorists and intellectuals take pleasure in dance, and become complicit with dance practitioners who aim to preserve dance as a medium-specific practise of the sublime and ephemeral self-expression of a free individual. Badiou confirms Mallarmé's definition that dance is poetry emancipated from the writing tools. The practises called "conceptual dance" approach dance as writing in Derridean sense, which doesn't and cannot reiterate the writing of a text in the domain of theory.

2 No utopia: Conceptual dance cannot be seen as part of the historical project of Modernism, as it was the case with Conceptual art. It doesn't belong to the same lineage of abstraction which would make it the last instance of abstraction (Merce Cunningham –

Xavier le Roy / Bojana Cvejić / Gerald Siegmund

Yvonne Rainer – Xavier Le Roy, Jérôme Bel or Tino Sehgal; Marcel Duchamp – Donald Judd – Joseph Kosuth) or reductionism and self-reflection, where the use of language substituting for movement would be a form of dematerialising the object and the commodity dance. There is no goal in transforming the format of presentation (theatre performance of dance), audiences or institutional market. These practises operate from within the institutions, emphasising a critical use of the theatre dispositif.

3   However, the practises bundled under "conceptual dance" propose a plurality of configurations of movement, body, subjectivity, cultures, beyond self-referentiality and homogeneity that could be associated with rational self-reflection only from within the medium. We couldn't speak of an artistic movement or formation, we would even have difficulty to make one paradigm that would include Bel, Le Roy, Boris Charmatz, Vera Mantero. This proves two things: the heterogeneity points to a hybridity of different influences, strands, disciplines, media and genres (hybridity against the purity of the pure modernist dance) and an openness of differences, many not only concepts, but conceptualisations of dance beyond Modernism.

The next step in this discussion would be to consider how a concept is formed: how it emerges, starts to regulate a practise, projects itself onto a practise. My thesis is that conceptual dance was so ill-named for it proposed an open, unbounded concept of Dance as Choreography, which contradicted or showed that choreography was used as a closed concept of Dance. I will explain the difference in the following paragraph.

Le Roy: Do you think – and if yes, then why – that dance always needs to be defined in a binary mode? There used to be Ballet / Modern, Modernist / Postmodern or Postmodernist, or Modern/dance theatre. Or was it Ballet/dance theatre (*Tanztheater*), and how is it now: conceptual / pure dance? Is binary logic specific for dance? Do you think that it can have something to do with the fact that choreographic art is not a well-established or recognised art practise in comparison with visual art or music for example?

Cvejić: Until the 1990s, one could get away with talking about dance performances by way of asking what kind of object "dance" a performance is: what is its dancing "matter", body-instrument-technique-style, and then, perhaps, some subject matter, what the performance tells by way of a metaphor. In the 1990s, this question was no longer sufficient, and another approach settled in. Not what kind of object a dance performance is, but what kind of concept of dance is performed, or put forth in the performance. This entailed that the new practises could not be defined essentially, by grasping and reasserting the same properties or distinctive traits which constitute the work. The work of, say, Vera Mantero and Jérôme Bel, or Jérôme Bel and Xavier Le Roy, can never make a perfect community of aesthetic properties, but can belong to a family of resemblances, properties which appear similar but in fact configure the work of each one differently. An example. We can speak of transparency or clarity of procedures in the case of Bel and Le Roy. In the case of the former, the clarity of procedures comes from linguistic operations and speech acts (cf. *The last perfomance, Shirtology, The show must go on I & II*), and with the latter, it is the means to provide a direct access to the body materiality, a posthumanist vision of what a body can do (cf. *Self-Unfinished*, *Giszelle*). The wrong conclusion to draw is to make this feature (transparency) essential, to treat it as an aesthetic ideal.

What was so different in the works of the aforementioned choreographers is how they conceived the concept for each performance. Now, concept has become either an over-rated or an inflated term: hated by those practitioners, critics or programmers whose ethic of work implies a non-reflexive studio craftsmanship or degraded by those proposals and applications for subsidy where a certain theoretical or political agenda is expected in the written proposal (not always making it to the work). This only shows that concept is a poorly understood term in dance.

Every work of dance has a concept, of course, because it is founded on a conceptual order of ideas, beliefs, values, procedures and meanings even when they are generated by intuition. However, from the 1990s on, concepts are being thematised, and discussed for every choreographic work of the new practises. So it was no longer understood that the choreographer – her style, language, technique, represented themes – is sufficient to stand for her object dance with her concept of it. Choreographers began to conceptual-ise choreography as the object of work. In other words, they don't treat it any longer as a self-evident notion, a concept that is closed. A close concept defines choreography as composition, and identifies composition with inscribing a form or structure, but in any case a notion of a whole, by bodily movement in time and space. Inscription of movement in time/space is rather a vague, empty signifier, but vagueness is exactly how regulative concepts function. They fulfil a normative function, especially because their content is elusive. So such a closed concept of choreography rests on an agreement ("whatever your composition is, it necessarily has to pertain to bodily movement and parameters of space and time") and a hierarchical apparatus of production (choreographer transferring knowledge to dancers by show-copy model or material molding).

The choreographers in the 1990s contested the idea that choreography is the writing that follows, resembles, represents the speech of dance, like the written following the spoken word. They insisted on the separation between dancing and choreographing, so that writing may precede dancing. Writing isn't only language for action, movement, thought, reflection, consciousness, unconsciousness, experience and affectivity; it is all that, but also the totality of what makes it possible; in other words, it can include a deconstruction of the assumptions, rules and values which guide writing.

To claim that choreography is an open concept implies that the notion of choreography (composition) be expanded and modified. In order to derive itself, choreographic practise starts using other tools than the so-called immanent, but actually inherited beautiful forms of eternal value. So far, the new tools have been: language and theory, history and historicity, sign communication, visual arts, secondary effects of other media like film (cinematic technologies), music, digital medium, then the theatre dispositif in relation to popular culture, the spectacle in both senses of the society of spectacular commodities and the spectacle of performance.

....

Xavier le Roy / Bojana Cvejić / Gerald Siegmund

So when we speak of the concept as unbounded as a language game (Wittgenstein), it implies that a performance sets serviceable rules given for the present case. An open concept of choreography accounts for an unforeseen situation to arise and leads us to modify the understanding of it. This is not an academic sterilisation of the process of concept formation. If we behaved according to the politics of this argument, then the simplifications of what conceptual dance is and why we should disregard it would not s tand a chance.

One more charge to consider. We too often hear that the practises under the name conceptual dance are the result of a belated influence of the Judson group of choreographers in Europe, mediated not so much via Steve Paxton or Trisha Brown, but more indirectly via Yvonne Rainer who stopped doing choreographic work already in the early 1970s. Sitting in this panel here with Christophe Wavelet and Xavier Le Roy who worked on reinterpreting works of the Judson choreographers within the project *Quatuor Albrecht Knust*, of course, we cannot deny this influence. However, we have to be careful when pronouncing the judgment that European dance only now experiences the influence of the American so-called postmodern dance and therefore, is somehow a bastard child of the 1960s.

There is something more to understand here about the open, unbounded concept and its temporality. Prior to the point at which we would say a concept has emerged, it might be that many if not all the threads of what becomes the content of the concept already exist. This is why the new appears as much continuous as it is discontinuous with the old. So it is a case of transformation, and not repetition. Continuity is crucial to the functioning of open concepts, weaving through a living and changing practise. Modification, continuity and expansion suppose that we cannot make paradigm examples, which we would treat as ideal types for an aesthetic, and we have to give up the so-called "monster-barring" (excluding difficult borderline examples), because all cases become more or less monstrous, connecting unreproducible connections. What does Thomas Plischke have to do with Juan Dominguez, Christine De Smedt with Alice Chauchat, Mette Ingvartsen with Antonia Baehr? Not much, except that their work stands outside of a closed concept Dance. In other words, it betrays an essentialist view that has dominated dance since Classical Ballet up to the still Modernist established practises of the choreographers who emerged in the 1980s and who are desperately clutching to the idea of Dance as the invention of body. And to illustrate this view I will quote an excerpt from the infamous essay *Dance as a Metaphor of Thought* by Alain Badiou.[2] It offers a philosophical sublimation of what is the doxa haunting contemporary dance: "It is a new beginning, because the dancing movement has to be such that it finds its own beginning again. Dance is innocence because it is a body that didn't exist before dance. It is oblivion in so far as it is the body which forgets its own force, its weight. Dance is also a play which liberates from every social mimicry, every seriousness and every appropriateness. Dance radiates the disappearance of the negative shameful body".

This view favours two notions:

1 Presence: The meaning of being, captured by the interiority of the subject; by virtue of hearing oneself speak, by virtue of feeling oneself dance, the subject affects itself and is related to itself in the element of ideality. The frequently asked question about how one experiences one's own dance solo.

2 The ineffable sublime: Dance shares the same cultural destiny as music. The ideal that music was for art and its culture in the 19th century, dance is at the end of the 20th century and today. The ineffable, inexpressible, universal, infinite in the finite form, transfigure in the values (Romantic illusion) that dance promises in the age of liberal capitalism. Defying these assumptions is what connects the non-similar practises of these choreographers. Calling them conceptualist choreographers means subtracting dance out of their practises for the simple mistake of overlooking that their procedures only target the body, the materiality of performance calling for sensation inasmuch, or inextricable from communication. In other words, their work isn't conceptual because it doesn't dematerialise the concept from its object.

Le Roy: How and why, at the same time that the terminology of concept dance, non-dance, anti-dance etc. appeared, could we observe focuses on other terms such as: "process", "laboratory" and "research"? If you agree with this, when did you notice that in your environment? Would you relate this to the word or questions about collaboration? What is research?

Cvejić: Investigation is a set of procedures of discovering, developing, describing, explaining and interpreting the functions, methods, values and sense of art. This term was introduced by Giulio Carlo Argan for Neoconstructivism in the 1950s, but it also applied to a branch of Conceptual art that focused on addressing the question: what is an artwork, how is it being made and how does it function in the art world. Art as research presupposes the following:

1 That art has a cognitive power – to produce knowledge, specific to that art; and a power to theorise, to produce a problematic and resolve it.

2 That art based in research doesn't find its purpose in the artwork as the final result of the process of making or producing, but in the process of investigation. The result of research need not be achieved, or isn't worthwhile mentioning or is overcome the moment it has been achieved. The process of research shows itself as a thinking model, a model of working and behaviour of the artist.

3. That there need not be any homology between the scientific methods and the methods of producing an aesthetic object.

But what is the specificity of research in dance, especially with regard to the currency of research, process, laboratory or collaboration nowadays?

4 Here I would give an opinion, or an estimation. It seems that work came to be represented (not necessarily conceived so) as research in the 1990s with the growing

Xavier le Roy / Bojana Cvejić / Gerald Siegmund

number of so-called independent artists. Entertaining that development, a new model of venue emerged, where the programmer undertook the role of a patron of research, not always of a curator. With patronage I mean parenthood, the programmer authorises a work as a process of research: (s)he first invites artists who (s)he thinks need the support of a so-called independent venue, then (s)he talks to them in order to find out whether their topic, concept of work or model of thinking smells like searching for something (not that it has to pertain to a particular area of research that the programmer is curating), and finally (s)he decides on the format of presentation, which often needs a festival or another kind of special manifestation: "opening-doors". When a parent-patron, the programmer takes the responsibility of the shown process or product (usually, it is presented as a work-in-process, promising and postponing the final result). As the presentation likens the performance, it doesn't offer an insight into its research methodology nor its objectives of research, or to anything that would make it different from a product. It differs from a performance-product only in the degree of completeness. The work seems to finish the process of making when it acquires the satisfying looks of searching for something. Ethics of research, experiment and critique transfigures into an aesthetic of indie-work, foreclosing further development when the outlook of research is achieved.

However, there is an entirely different usage of the term research and laboratory, much less specific and contemporary than what I outlined here, but maybe more general and common for contemporary dance practises in Western Europe. Research is understood as the process of inner necessity of the dancer searching for her proper authentic body movement and language in self-expression. The studio seems an indispensable site of the reinvention of the human body through dance. This shows that the ideology of Expressionism has been negotiated into a kind of hidden matrix, or mode of production in dance, similarly to what happened to the conversion of Romanticist 19th-century music into pop music or 19th-century opera to Hollywood film production. But to say that dance specifically requires a search for the original, authentic movement of an individual body is to romanticise the basic definition of poetics as the principles of making which always entails a process of searching for something. The condition of art since and after Modernism presupposes that the artist searches whenever she makes work. [1]

If we consider the concept of art as research as introduced in the visual art theory by Argan and explained above, the common use of research in dance as we know it is inappropriate. We still may need to discover which practises in contemporary dance have developed problematics, methods and techniques in the mode of investigation and not poetic search for the means of expression.

[1] Cf. Benjamin H. D. Buchloch, "Conceptual Art 1962-1969: From the Aesthetic of Administration to the Critique of Institutions", *October*, Vol. 55 (Winter, 1990), 105-143.
[2] Alain Badiou, "Danse comme la métaphore du pensée", the proceeding from the International Conference on Dance and Choreographic Research "Danse et pensée, une autre scène pour la danse", held in Paris in January 1992.

Footnote

Dear Xavier,

Thanks for sending this text. I feel that Bojana has been so exhaustive with the topic there is really very little left to say. She maps the faultlines out neatly, so off you go printing it. There is one thing that keeps coming back to me everytime I read the text. Its definitions of modernism all seem to refer to American modernism (Graham, Humphrey, Cunningham) but have very little to do with what happened in Germany which is in spirit at least a lot closer to what you are doing today. Wigman and Bausch (and the others …) also had no fixed dance language but a set of questions. I mean, Bausch was hated in the 1970s for her non-dance pieces! Gerhard Bohner resurrected the Bauhaus ideas. Does that sound familiar? The question of spectatorship: there is hardly any of Bausch's great pieces where the audience isn't taken on board either by breaking down the fourth wall by dancing through the audience or by the emotional content of the songs: the Show Must Really Go On. I don't want to sound like the last defender of *Tanztheater*, but high american modernism a la Greenberg and Fried has been done away with since the 1970s on both sides of the Atlantic! Which means: there must be something else that is at stake with the misnomer "conceptual dance" than a critique of so-called modernism. For me, it has to do with the idea of the body as an image, as a performative formation and not as a stronghold of emotions and individuality. It's the "naturalness" and the "realness" of the body that is being questioned and which a lot of people don't like.

    This is just a little footnote to the discussion and Bojana's text.
    Love,
    Gerald

Xavier le Roy / Bojana Cvejić / Gerald Siegmund

57

The doing of research

Mårten Spångberg

The complexity of the establishment of research and related discourses into the field of performing arts has taken the course of an avalanche. From the product and image intensive period of the 1980s, following a period of politically orientated work, the 1990s and early 2000s will most probably be remembered as the era of research. Overnight, research was established around 1997 and already consolidated with the now legendary exhibition *Laboratorium* in 1999, which also included a small number of contributions from the performing arts. The reasons for this development would need a thorough analysis addressing the phenomena also from perspectives of economy, ownership and social / political justification, as it is my belief that the actual interest in the community of makers and programmers was and is rather exaggerated.

It is fascinating to return to the mid-late 1990s and experience how dancers, choreographers, set designers and even the production manager in a microsecond grew an obsessive passion for research. Artists who had never shown interest in process orientated investigatory strategies transformed into first-rate researchers and with production phases of more or less a year the laboratorial rat had found its place in the performing arts. With the introduction of the r-word, a truckload of firmly established terminology exited the stage. Somebody defining his work as experimental was looked upon as the plague, and even only a vague hint towards avant-garde equalled immediate banishment from the entire scene. As much as research caught performing arts with the intensity of a hurricane, it was – and is also far too often – superficial in content and consistency. The lack of frames made whatever one called research into research.

The difficulty however is to what extent this is a positive or negative quality? Any field of research carries out the research it deserves, and it is always necessary with a super-contextual shift to manifest a change in a field of research. Epistemologists have examined how paradigms emerge, consolidate and dissolve as regularly as the sun rises, but since we know this we must conclude that, e.g., performing arts executes the research it desires. But it is also possible that what performing arts consider research in fact is something entirely different, something that will become apparent within the next few years when the flood of research turns tide and another current is building up. To initiate a crusade against the inconsistency of research in the field would therefore be to shoot one's own leg, independently of the ambitions of the field. The engaged believes in research and will continue to do so until he doesn't believe anymore, and at that moment it will seem as impossible to have believed, as it is natural today. A critique configured in this manner would inevitably position itself outside the field, which would propose a new or other fundament, or institution, which in its turn would need a thorough investigation. Addressing the field through negotiations vis-à-vis governmentality however could offer interesting observations about what research, so to say, has done, or produced in respect of the performing arts.

Before starting, a brief detour into the state of the belief in research. Ten years after I first heard the word in the performing arts context, it is clear that the believers are already doubting, if for no other reason than the very fact that research today is as trendy as

Dixieland jazz or t-shirts manufactured in sweatshops. What once was a close to hysterical migration into has over the last couple of years turned into a slow but unstoppable stream of defectors returning to more classical templates of production. Moreover, the belief structure has changed; it is no longer the creators or programmers that praise research, but rather a mixed group of theoreticians, who in addition are late converts who have moved in rather than initiated the field's topology. The high-end ambitions of research platforms have too often, in accord with academic writing on the development of a field of research, turned into a retreat for individuals that either can't reach or are prohibited a position in a conventional frame of production, or are considered a threat to a common frame of production.

The orientation of research in performing arts initiated an expansion through a series of politically correct tactics that emphasised inter-disciplinarity and culturalism, quite in the same way as performance studies, and it didn't take long before research was hijacked by enthusiasts with the only mission to find themselves a place to belong to. The third step in the development of research in performing arts, after establishment and expansion, implies redefining the field and rehabilitating its symbolic value. This process is inevitably painful as it implies exclusion and closing doors; but it is necessary in order to define, not only a territory, but most of all topological and methodological consistency. What research in this sense has done to the field of performing arts is in fact not an auxiliary elaboration of its intra- or inter-relationships, but has rather undermined its status and exclusivity in general.

The field's resistance and even aversion against methodology is strong evidence to the state of research being considerably weak, similar to the phenomenon that anti-intellectu-alism normally indicates stasis or the decline of a field. Research in performing arts has yet to establish an accurate set of tools and a thorough methodological protocol in order not to perish in the climate of late capitalist research production. Tools and protocols that cannot be appropriated from other fields but neither can be autonomously produced from within the field, as both would result in a corrupt discipline due to personal, relational, economical and image reasons. Tools and methodology should be created in consensus with well-established ethical checkpoints combined with a thorough analysis of the field's specific conditions, in this case, e.g., notions of temporality and the impossibility of, or not, repetition.

The common consideration is that methodology is an obstacle to creative and artistic potentiality, or with another wording: freedom. But if that is the argumentation, we have made a fundamental mistake in making artistic work or processes synonymous with research, when in fact those protocols are oppositional, and in so being to no extent competitive. It is urgent that the field make distinctions between engaging in artistic processes and research, hence a thorough apparatus of definition also would clear up any hierarchical misunderstandings. There is no higher or lower value in engagement in research processes; it is simply another practice whose aim is to produce other kinds of knowledge and artifacts. Without methodological accuracy and consistency, it is impos-

Mårten Spångberg

sible to evaluate the quality and importance of a certain work and keep processing outside the domains of taste and individual desire, which in the case of research implies that its knowledge economy remains passive and consolidating instead of active and potential. Instead of producing restriction, a thorough methodological framework would enable the field to validate work for what it is, and moreover produce a platform for an active criticality that would grant a critical reciprocity between providers of research platforms, economical frames and researchers, creators and users of research results. It is important, too, that methodology under no circumstances here is related to science or academia but simply is a set tool and protocols that offers opportunities to identify, compare and differentiate a territory of research and hence produce autonomy based on production rather than heritage or charisma.

The lack of accurate methodological protocols manifests power in the provider of research and platforms to the extent where research, instead of expanding and emancipating the field's knowledge production, consolidates it and furthermore places an unacceptable emphasis on success, especially in respect of representation and efficiency. Only through the establishment of an accurate methodological frame can research free itself from the superficial demands of capitalist economy.

What research has produced relative to the field up until today, instead of a surplus and hence a lateralisation of knowledge, is a hierarchisation of processes and practices that in a larger perspective homogenises the momentum of the field's endeavours.

At the time when research first appeared, it was due to a need to change the strong product orientation of the market and its subsidy systems. Questions were asked to what extent, e.g., a choreographer could, so to say, update his or her practice when there were no economical or physical frames for other kinds of work than production. Only in rare educational frames could research activity be considered, and a dominant part of workshop opportunities were at that time directed towards the passing on of established skills such as release technique, or a choreographer's individual perspective into dance and performance. Research related activity at that moment appeared as a means to shortcut those manifestations especially in relation to result and representation. A number of projects and processes were initiated by individuals or small communities on an often idealistic basis, but with the institutionalisation of research in performing arts an opposing momentum occurred. Everybody engaged in research practices at that time was of course enthusiastic to all expansive opportunities that appeared, as the formulation of a field is precisely when and where active and vivid knowledge production is most potential. The field's territory also stakes out a grid for what kind of research and activity it can muster, but as the distance between creators and managers is distinct in the field of performing arts, this development was rather soon appropriated by venues and festivals and taken out of the hands of the researchers.

Instead of releasing performing art practices, the introduction of institutional research frames resulted in further consolidation, and today it is clear that rather than an emancipating movement, research has institutionalised the practice even more.

When an autonomous artist in the performing arts field today receives a research grant, he or she actually is not at all free to engage in an open process but is instead inscribed to the extent where individual creativity is being institutionalised. Prior to the institutionalisation of research every individual was free to engage in whatever process of thinking, practicing and experimenting, whilst today those activities have also been mapped and applied to a, however vague, protocol of authorisation.

In this respect what research has done to the field of performing arts is not to emancipate it from the circulation of exchangeable commodities, but has instead also commodified work, understood as engagement in some kind of research process.

Research was implemented in a mode of production due to proprietary licensing which stratified its discourses and immobilised its capacity of any deterritorialising radical knowledge production.

It is telling to return briefly to the recent history of performing arts in Europe. The circulation of what is conventionally called contemporary dance, performance and theatre takes place in institutions and venues that, at least as a model, were established around and just after 1980. At that time, a young generation of artists and managers detected and worked for a new system for presentations of a new kind of work. For a period of ten to fifteen years, these venues were established and consolidated as sustainable economies. Systems of exchange, networking and production were elaborated, and often quite clear hierarchies of circulation grew strong, something which a "general" audience reacted to and favored in respect of expectations and reliability. When research appeared in the mid-1990s, it could generally be understood as a counter-reaction to known of frames, initially as a creator- and doer-based initiative. A heterogeneous group of independent new players appeared on the market with new needs and desires, players that to a higher or lesser degree did not wish to be inscribed in the established market or simply were not welcome. Process orientation, research and a kind of ad hoc production basis appeared to be an attractive mode of production, but with the incorporation of the mentioned modes of work in venues and festivals modeled in the 1980s, research instantaneously turned into precisely the opposite. Instead of opening for a new platform of circulation and ownership, research-based work became inscribed as a means of maintaining the power of established venues, festivals, companies and makers. A choreographer or group identified with research was – instead of being a potential, and I would argue, positive threat, or opportunity disarmed and classified in a way where it could never grow out of the, so to speak, small format. There certainly are exceptions but it is easy to detect what kind of artists is identified with research – and it certainly aren't those who are engaged in larger institutional frames, even though these are perhaps the ones that most of all could need a break from the obsession of production.

What research has done to the field of performing arts is not to open for the elaboration of new and alternative modes of production, of new and alternative kinds of work. It has actually made it largely impossible for young and progressive initiatives to elaborate and obtain sustainable economies and audiences. In other word, research has been incorpo-

Mårten Spångberg

rated in "conventional" models of the performing arts field in order to maintain the hierarchies created already in the 1980s. This consolidation of power has increased the identity of the artist over a romantic set of protocols purporting individuality, oeuvre and calling on the one hand, and precariousness on the other.

The unique opportunity and complexity of performing arts that the expressed and the expressing often, if not as a rule, coincide, offers a minimal distance between invention and expression. The choreographer dancing has always been a hands-on researcher, or in other words, his/her own guinea pig, his own frame of experience and sensation. Such relations, implementing their own, individual and common-sense methodologies which to the same extent intensify regressive strands, which enter realms of execution for the simple sake of pleasure or economical winning and inventive capacities that, often using intuition as methodology, encourage differentiation in the field. A strong example is Alexander technique, but these inventive practices more often take place in informal settings over years of hard work, and rarely in unorthodox circumstances. With the introduction of research, the relation between creator and executor has changed where the formal awareness of the process has been institutionalised. Research has, spoken with a light hand, made it difficult simply to go and dance, to use one's imagination and make it happen. Research proposes certain hierarchies of process and production, individual and group processes and work, and most of all formalises relations between the validity of a process and work-relative sets of discourses active in the contexts at a certain moment. With the introduction of research, performing arts has not been offered enlarged opportunities for inefficiency or processes dealing with extreme topics; on the contrary – what research has done to the performing arts is to make it trend- (who today would make an image-based work with an extremely elaborated light design?), format- (collaboration is everything and a pseudo-lateral working process imperative), discourse- (bring some books without pictures like S, M, L, XL to the studio and work as you always did), media- (show a video at the end of the piece where you are instructed in doing something you can't really manage and speak about knowledge production on a personal level) sensitive, and hence has homogenised its expressions.

This litany could go on forever engaging in what we thought was doing well but turned out to be doing exactly the opposite. But has research then only been negative to performing arts? Certainly not. On the contrary, the expansion of the field of performing arts with the realm of research has been imperative for the field's survival and as performance and performativity in the 1990s became a buzzword for any intellectual with dignity, it is rather encouraging how open the field has been to the engagement of, and in, other kinds of knowledge production.

In fact, initially there are only two issues that need to be raised in respect of how to change a possibly negative development. But there is of course a slight problem with those two – which is that they both demand the format of a PhD to be thoroughly discussed. What follows here is in a sense comprehensive but tries to formulate, in brief, some perspectives.

1 What adjustments are necessary to approach after ten years of working under the criteria of research?

2 With the institutionalisation of research, what has occurred in respect of distribution of responsibility?

It is today ten years ago since Hotmail was globally released. In 2006, Hotmail has approximately one billion hits a month. It is also ten years since SMS appeared in conventional private-user mobile phones. The world-wide volume of SMS was in 2005 estimated to be more than 300 billion messages. Amazon and Ebay similarly were created in 1995. Google was released in September 1999 from a garage in Palo Alto. In the spring of 2006, Google CEO's mention 150 million queries per day, or more than 50 billion per year. Skype was registered as a domain name exactly three years ago, on April 23, 2003. At this very moment there are 5.5 million users on line, out of more than a 100 million downloads.

Considering that research in the performing arts has the same ten years long history, and that Skype was invented two-thirds into that brief history, it is quite easy to conclude that adjustments might be small in perspective but enormous in proliferation. There is of course the danger of rushing to the next base while forgetting the kids in the shopping mall, but new modes of communication and production do not imply a homogenisation of results nor an arrogant relation to the history of research; but there certainly are no reasons to evaluate research that jump over classical resources as less prominent. On the contrary, if research in the performing arts nourishes a desire to be something more than a tiny field for the already engaged, it is obvious that all opportunities must be explored.

Generally speaking, the field can choose to confirm research as it is established in and through strong and historically prominent fields, or bring forth the specificity of the field and explore it as something that other fields could gain momentum from. Good examples are Doris Humphrey's book *The Art of Making Dances* that largely is a defense of dance in regard of the classical treatise producing an expression as specific due to its universality, and on the other hand Yvonne Rainer's No-manifesto and adjoining texts, where instead the art of making dances dissociates itself from expressions constituting sustainable artifacts. Humphrey is easy to cancel out and to be asked to get a grip on and start painting or writing poetry, as she also necessarily confirms classical, male representational orders. Yvonne Rainer instead differentiates and potentialises dance in respect of all other expressions, and in this act, at least announces that dance and performance only can be "inscribed" in representational orders we are familiar with, but, precisely in this "forced" translation produces itself as ontologically critical.

The setup of research in performing arts is based on modes of distribution and circulation that today are largely outdated. Ten years ago is basically closer to J.S. Bach walking to Lübeck to listen to Buxtehude in 1705 than to the ease with which we move over Europe today. So why is it still important to work on research on the basis of discussion, exchange and same-room-organisation, when time and economy allow us to meet in the sushi bar of

Mårten Spångberg

the Ryan air terminal somewhere? – And that's only for those of us who don't communicate over digital platforms or group chats.

The communicational tools that the field utilises naturally influence the result of its endeavours, and it is precisely in producing distance between, e.g., new communicational tools and the position of the body and movement that conventional dialectics are maintained and further consolidated. If the body and its movement are in one or another way fundamental to human life and consciousness, it is not likely that Skype, PDF or P2P (peer-to-peer networks) will affect it any more than central perspective, combustion engines or moving images, but on the contrary could offer the potentiality to understand and utilise the body and its movements in new and alternative ways. These are certainly issues that directly concern research in the field; also this publication which I hope will be available on the net to download for free, so that interested persons who have different opportunities of accessibility can take part of our research and thinking.

Is it a good or a bad sign that there are almost no video clips of contemporary dance and performance work available on the internet, when on the other end of the line it is obligatory to send videos to venues and festivals? It is surprising that however the performing arts has been engaged in collaboration, collectivity, processes of orientation and research, that material is not made available on the Internet, as it is a platform that would increase, e.g., the possibilities for visibility in a decentralised way, give individuals and groups living and functioning outside urban contexts the opportunity to familiarise with contemporary dance, and open the quite homogeneous formats especially of dance performances. And most of all, give a larger group of researchers access to material produced here and now: not only performances, but interviews, lectures, presentations, rehearsals which would not only be extremely vital for the scene, but furthermore would increase mobility and a decentralised, lateralised, user-innovative climate. As Erik von Hippel has shown in his recent *Democratizing Innovation* (Cambridge, 2005) economies that stimulate user innovation obtain significantly enhanced heterogeneity and versatility in product development. It is not as often believed that users are keen on keeping their innovations to themselves but an allowing climate where sharing is stimulated instead creates responsibility for the situation's or product's quality, status and place on its market. Open source like licensing increases a client's identification with a product; responsibility increases and abuse decreases. When Ebay experienced a need for prohibition due to abuse of the platform the company, instead of creating complex sets of legislation turned to the community of users that subsequently innovated self-regulatory monitoring systems.

The common mode of engaging in research in performing arts is behind a closed door and without an attached web page, live streaming, wiki or blog. Why does research in performing arts that wishes to place itself inside the contemporary urban mosaic desire to be closed off, locked away instead of in the middle where it happens and where today's movement practices are communicated and produced?

The body always moves. Blood pumps through the veins, stimuli flow into the brain and responses shoot back to keep whatever is going on, going on. At some moment, quite often, the body starts moving through space, or its spatio-temporal coordination changes. Sometimes we recognise these changes as dance, at other times as walking or being hit by a car. Still, these movements are recognisable precisely as movements framed by a context which is continuous. Is the body actually moving, or does it remain immobile? Its domain has been enlarged but it is still under control.

With a glance back into the 20th century we might find that the body perhaps only moved a handful of times. That it passed out of coordination without anybody noticing, and moved into the light, into the recognisable again with – for those who were willing to see and sense – an enormous power, and on second thought had always been there, always already. Only when expanding or exterritorialising itself and its conditioning has the body really moved. It is not the exterritorialisation that is the movement but the reterritorialisation, recoordination or recoding. One could say that the body moves without traces, imperceptibly, and that movement is representation catching up. Those movements that are moments, however always on the move, are the rare instances when the body is truly mobile.

Research functions in quite the same way: intrinsically it is always moving, or better yet is remixed and re-recorded. Sometimes, it is set in motion, shifting its co-ordination, but it is still a matter or repetition, or better seriality. The known moves, but how often is it that the unknown moves into the known? Always – however imperceptibly. It is only in those instances when the known catches up that the unknown appears. Those moments are the rare cases when research is truly mobile.

Space is striated. Its continuity is dividable, and its parts are consistent. It is this consistency that provides us with the opportunity for orientation in time and space. The striation of space, literally and metaphorically, produces a sensation of security but when enhanced turns into some or other kind of prison.

In an early film by George Lucas, *THX 1138* (1971), a futuristic world is shown in which the humans are inscribed in an absolute control society. Their lives and environments have been turned into an inescapable striation. A small number of individuals however rebel against the situation and are imprisoned; but instead of putting the prisoner behind steel bars, George Lucas offers a brilliant solution: the prison is represented as an endless absolutely white space, without beginning or end. Space has become smooth, without horizon and therefore deprived of co-ordination or orientation. Simplified, one could say that striated space equals knowledge or reproduction and that smooth space constitutes the unknown, i.e., territorial and exterritorialised, respectively. In the extremes of both versions, one is imprisoned.

Brian Massumi developed the concept of phasespace, which is a space composed by incompatible entities. It is discontinuous but undivided, i.e., it consists of incompatible superimposed phenomena that offer an orientation, however unreliable. Or better yet, a

Mårten Spångberg

multiplicity of becoming orientation. Phasespace is those instances of true mobility where knowledge appears and the body really moves.

Translated into frames of research, striated space equals a set-up where the co-ordination between research and institution or production is static and immobile. Smooth space, on the other hand, could be identified as a situation where the division between researcher and institution or production has been completely abandoned. What the two set-ups have in common is that neither research nor the body can move. On an abstract level, a research set-up aiming to make knowledge move is one that offers itself as phasespace. Such research frames thus are those where the engaged is continuously shifting from being a researcher and representing an institution or product, a receiver and producer, a staff member and guest. Where a multiplicity of orientation is possible as long as the engaged is willing to negotiate the validity and ontology of each and every decision and its process of emergence, i.e., according to what mode of production a decision can be taken. Therefore, the question is not if we need positions such as researcher and institution or product, but how it is possible to produce a frame in which engagement in any position is the result of a particular negotiation. Needless to say, the downside of a phasespaced research platform is one of sustainability and initiative, but on the other hand, the upside is the opportunity for a radical heterogenisation of knowledge, ability and desire. Is it possible to rethink research not in the sense of what it needs but, on the contrary, through what it doesn't need? What are the fundamental needs of research in performing arts?

Secured needs and allocated resources inevitably produce striation and decrease the opportunity for the mobility of knowledge and its agents. Research in performing arts is not in need of further stability, grants, institutions, structures and labs, but of mobility and versatility. It is in the cracks between the implicit striation of methodology and epistemo-logical accuracy, and the smooth terrain of radical mobility that research can intensify prosperity in the field.

How does research in performing arts identify its user? Does the field itself actually need users, and if so, how can it be its own client without becoming a self-indulgent territory which produces closer and closer family relations? Since there are very few traces in respect of publications, video material and ongoing discussions (I have, e.g., not found any blogs related to the field) it is not evident whether the field wants to have users at all. It is not easy in this field to detect the user – but thorough methodological consistency will certainly give the opportunity to clarify who he or she can be, which when the basis of research is individual and, in a negative sense, project-to-project based, will be far more complex, and it will therefore be difficult and energy intensive to create a community of interest. If the field identifies the user as already initiated and active in the field, the current climate is quite effective and productive in the sense of creating a clan-like circle, or better a small number of competing circles whose opposition is based on negative critique and exclusion which in the long run only can create a vicious circle.

If research projects would be evaluated not only due to the topic but perhaps also due to what presentation format in respect of which user group, it would be possible to measure the success of a research project from a multiplicity of perspectives. In contrast to how today it often is connected with how "cool" the topic is estimated to be, and how inspiring, i.e., successful and understandable the presentation of the project is with regard to a general user who is always supposed to be satisfied within ninety minutes.

Such an approach could also open opportunities for complex and mature research into a wider field of performing arts practices, such as work related to children, reception, learning processes or disability, and for more conventional approaches it would similarly expand the capacities to relate to larger frames than what has been made popular by other fields of research in relation to different performatives such as gender, colonialism or identity politics.

In the initial phase when research in the performing arts was first established, it was important to make many and different individuals participate. Research, as we have seen earlier, needed to grow as a field and it soon became connected to participatory activities especially in relation to inter-disciplinary and cultural practices. But however much somebody participates – it implies that one leave one position and engage in another. When participation, when the research period was over – in our field normally spanning from a couple up to twenty–thirty days but very rarely longer – it was easy to change the costume and forget about research. It is not the activity of researching that is important but how processes activate individuals, and how many. An example from history could be Dr. Ignaz Semmelweis, who in 1847 through empirical research found out that it was a good idea to wash one's hands after handling dead bodies. The factors were many but Semmelweis, even though he managed to convince other doctors to participate in his experiments, did not manage to activate in them the results of his research. Consequently, Semmelweis' research was forgotten and he died in a mental hospital at the age of forty-seven. In the same year, Joseph Lister started a series of related experiments, and it was through his research that medics were first activated to start disinfecting hands and instruments when passing from department to department.

This anecdote brought together with the communication technology we today can use easily and at a cheap price, can perhaps assist research in performing arts instead of working on participation to emphasise how its research is distributed, circulated, and to activate individuals and groups to be involved and use research results in their daily practices.

In order to activate a larger group of users and doers, it is also important to look further into how research results are being licensed, something which is complex in our field as most creators earn their living by transforming their research into circulating products. However, it is clear that proprietary interests often, on a long-term basis, tend to create much less feedback and innovation, as well as responsibility. Open-source-like licensing instead tends to increase responsibility and grass-root initiatives.

....

Mårten Spångberg

Internet publishing, e.g., will not only create activation but also a faster and cheaper mode of publishing where material output is less stable and therefore can be rewritten and updated continuously.

Furthermore, open-source-like licensing is an opportunity for not striating the field of research but can – instead of how research conventionally has functioned via permanent membership, often via an oath – allow for more fluctuant concepts of ad hoc association where a differentiation of expertise can lead to higher specification rather than suffer under the concessional regime of interdisciplinary practices.

I would like to mention a related issue in respect of institutional organisation connected to research. In any academic, medical or other public research it is unconditional that the head of an institution has merits in research. A professor is assessed on the basis of his / her research rather than on the basis of being a good boss, even though that isn't a bad thing. This construction places the head of an institution in a healthy paradox where the research and the infrastructure, or economical basis balance each other as the head of institution has to keep up negotiation in two directions. Corporate research, on the other hand, is naturally dependant on economic expansion, placing the researcher under the oath of efficiency.

Looking into the performing arts field there exists an unclear framing in respect of leadership. It is not the current situation that directors of research platforms are themselves engaged in research or have the necessary knowledge in the field to evaluate the projects together with the research teams. In scientific research it is also common that a research project should be further evaluated by, e.g., an ethical board. The lack of such procedures can easily lead to confusion of interest and consequently to less accurate research projects.

This leads over to our second question concerning responsibility. It is very easy to blame institutional frames and their inherent inefficiency, but we also know that no institution is better than its researchers and it is only when the two resonate together that the result can be innovative. In the case of research in performing arts it is my experience that researchers rely to a large degree on the capacities of institutions and platforms, and often act in passive and demanding ways. As research has no market outside itself, has no or very few engaged users, it is often understood as something doers and creators engage in between production periods. If this would be the case in, e.g., medical research, doctors would be surgeons during the week and do research in the weekends. It is clear that such a division will not win anybody a Nobel Prize, nor innovate medicine. If an executing doctor takes an interest in engaging in his work also in the weekends, this is all positive – but we shall perhaps, also in our field, make a difference between being interested and proper research processes.

When it come to research in performing arts, this problem is not easy to solve due to the market share for research being relatively small. But it is only if the researchers produce a demand and argumentation for its share in the budget that it can grow. It is, however, also interesting to consider that in corporate business the conventional amount of money spent on research is approximately 3.5% of the total budget, and in high-end fields up to 7–8%.

Since performing arts considers itself a high-end field, it is surprising to notice how few the institutions, venues and festivals are that allocate any budget at all to research and development. It is therefore my belief that only if the researchers themselves devote time and economy to research we can experience a renaissance in quality. In short: it is today, and in the near future, time to look into what responsibility the field's creators and researchers claim.

Only through a collective engagement in a consistent methodology and specific epistemology, a thorough and ongoing analysis of what research has produced in respect of the field both when it comes to its aims and its users (and due to that, elaborate proper licenses), in combination with an individual responsibility with regard to what processes we are actually engaged in that we can look forward to a research climate that will enable the field to expand and create research, as well as performances that add something radically different to our expression and the world.

Mårten Spångberg

71

Dance studies and desiring bodies

73

"Stocktaking" in the realm of dance
Scholarship on dance: theory and practice

Gabriele Brandstetter

Historically, discourses establish different orders of knowledge – in daily practice as well as in the arts and sciences. Thus, in the course of a contingent procedure a continuous stocktaking occurs of that which possesses discursive value (*Bestand*) and is recognised as being worthy of tradition (*überlieferungswürdig*). Dance and performance, too – as indicated by the programme text of this congress – are situated in such a discursive field.

How can we meaningfully speak of *Inventur* in such a context? *Inventur* – so the dictionary tells us – is a process of stocktaking. In the commercial sphere, such a stocktaking yields information as to the "assets and debts of a firm at a specific time". What kind of "stocktaking" could an *Inventur:Tanz* produce in such a context? What kind of commercial undertaking is here in question – and how can "assets" and "debts" be set off against one another? Perhaps a glance at the prospectus for this conference may enlighten us. According to the preliminary summary entitled *Point of Departure* the object of our "stocktaking" is: "a new and diverse field of artistic work with the body" that is said to have developed since the middle of the nineties and that is supposed to be responsible for the upsurge of "interest in the expansion of the borders of the genre of the art of dance and performance". Parallel to this "a new interest in theoretical reflection on dance and performance" is alleged to have come into being, "which, supposedly, has set itself clearly apart from postmodern dance theory in the Anglo-American mode". – Linked to this point are my own thoughts, which are directed in a general sense on "stocktaking" and the connected paradox questions concerning the relation of theory and practice, science and performance: An *Inventur* in the sense of a "stocktaking" could not be carried out in this "enterprise". Not only because what is in question is a "new" and "diverse" field of artistic endeavour so that there can be no "genre", no conceptual apparatus, no systemic locus for this kind of "dance"– but also because the "stock" itself – which would have to figure in any such inventory – lacks *in principle* the requisite concrete existence. Dance, movement, the ephemeral quality of any performance simply does not let itself be preserved as an object, as a document in a filing-system. Of course there are gestures in this direction: notations, documentations in image, script and other media – hence the movement of transposition into an archival scenario and the storage in memory of "what once was". But these are not "dance", not the performance as event. Rather, they are traces, incomplete and defective ones at that, which stand for an absence: an inventory – if you like – that lists the possessions that cannot be possessed. If, then, there is no "stock" that can be inventoried, so neither can there be a corresponding theoretical locus. If with regard to this the orientation towards theory of the new modes in dance and performance, and an interest in their being "embedded in theory" is mentioned in the preliminary outline: is that not repeating and reproducing a conception of "theory" according to which theory and performance are considered discrete entities? Theory then appears as the framework, the "bed" within which dance and performance occur? On the contrary, it is – I suggest – more fruitful to think of dance and theory as both being equally in motion. In this motion, both what is perceived and its perception are moved simultaneously – but in an asynchronic process which is indivisible from the spatio-temporal displacement between an event and its perception.

"Kinaesthesia" would thus not mean the perception of movement, but rather perceiving *in* motion.[1] In such a constellation, dance and performance cannot be fixed as an object, as a *fait accompli* that can become part of an inventory. Were such a stocktaking to occur, then it would of necessity be confronted with what was missing from the stock, what had somehow been "pilfered". "Assets" and "debts", the absence of that quintessential fleeting quality of dance, would together produce double inventories that could not be reconciled with each other.

What are the implications, for scholarship concerning itself with dance, of this resistance with which dance opposes a process of "stocktaking"? I ask this especially in the sense that the study of dance is a component of theatre-studies, of performance-studies, indeed of the humanities in general – hence of disciplines, that file away knowledge in archives and thus by definition construct filing-systems of the "stocks" of human culture. These are all branches of learning that are skilled in making lists, when they take stock of what they study and of their own history as disciplines. François Jullien illuminates in his essay, *The Art of Drawing Up Lists*[2], the ambiguity of lists as such: on the one hand there are "authoritarian lists"; on the other, there are "inventive lists": "In cultural terms, no action appears more neutral than drawing up a list. The succession of instances, the operation of the tabulator: the process scarcely seems to be one at all, as it has the appearance of being summary and discreet". (p. 10f.) But then we have those lists as well, that obey the heterogeneity of a different logic, chance, the delight in "what does *not* belong together" – in short, the inventory, that still encompasses the sense of *inventio*, of the topos of discovery. It is precisely this ambivalent status of lists and of their heterogeneous, gap-ridden seriality that not only accounts for the recalcitrance in whatever we subject to a process of stocktaking, but also makes the action turn on those who "enact" it. A register, as "the most elementary way of shaping knowledge" (Jullien, p. 17), points to what can never be included in an inventory, to an excluded remainder, something superfluous which, in turn, reveals that there is an "inherent indebtedness" of the "scholarly discipline" *vis-à-vis* its object of study. For it is precisely where science clings to the phantasm of an ideal, given object that it lags behind the essence of dance: movement, the irruption of the body. It cultivates the element of control – not in the act of dancing itself and of the physical labour this entails, but in the mastery of lists that register competence.

I suggest that any profitable reflection on the relationship between dance and the discipline that studies it (or performance and performance studies) must begin from this pivotal point between the "study" and its object – a point beyond any *Inventur* – in a stirring of irritation, in which the apparent sovereignty of list-making exposes itself for what it is. It is that moment in time when "stocktaking" applies not only to "dance and performance" in a novel form of artistic practice, but also to those lists which have political relevance: lists of those missing in wars and natural disasters, lists of the dead; the lists of a bureaucracy of terror: Eichmann's list of those to be deported – lists whose logic obeys the imperative to complete a series. "Authoritarian lists" mark the extremity of a process of stocktaking, which, as an enterprise of dominance, expunges the distinction between debts

....

Gabriele Brandstetter

and assets, between obligation and potentiality. But dance and performance – and here I follow Jacques Derrida – can only be conceived as the promise of the possibility of an event. *Inventur* in the sense of *inventio,* meaning the discovery of a new event, stands in contradiction to the expected completion of a series, the registry or filing-system. I should like to quote from Derrida's address in Stanford on the "university without constraints": "To link belief and knowledge in a particular manner, namely to integrate belief into knowledge, means blending movements one might call performative with those best designated as perceptual, descriptive or theoretical".[3] Here he refers *not* to those discourses, which articulate something known already, but rather to the production of events, which are then articulated as discourse. But this presupposes, in turn some irruption or explosion, which shatters the horizon of expectation, interrupts conventions and all discursive complicities. The "assets" side of an *Inventur* conceived in the sense of *inventio* – one that could never be accounted in lists – would thus be the potential of the unexpectable event – which Derrida calls "thinking the impossible possible" (p. 73).

The Berlin dance and performance festival Context #2[4] was titled *Traumatised Bodies?* in dance and performance. If, in psychological terms, "trauma" designates an "invisible wound" that is marked by a gap in memory – how can such an invisible wound be made visible in dance, in performance? And how could this inaccessibility be represented by the body? *Who's Afraid of Representation?*[5] is the title of a performance by the Lebanese artist Rabih Mroué. One might describe it as the performance of a stocktaking. And, at the same time, it takes stock of performance: an accounting of the historical resources of Western (that is: European and American) body-art. This recapitulation proceeds from a particular attention horizon, and has recourse to specific time-clips of performance since the seventies. Quite literally: lists are presented in this work in such a way that the inventories of "events" are manifested as a filing system whose two "lists" are placed in opposition to one another so as to enable a process of "double accounting": events from the realm of art (performance art, that is) and events from historical reality are set in counterpoint to one another – evoked by mechanisms of chance and placed in a historically asynchronous series. Both series of events tell of pain, of physical violence, of wounds. The performance-artist, Lina Saneh, recounts in the first person, and yet in the laconic diction of an encyclopaedia, the actions of wounding and self-wounding entailed by body-art. Language, projected script (in translation), video-projections of the body-tableaux of the performance-artist standing calmly before a gauze-screen – these "represent" excerpts from the "self-productions" of such performance artists as Chris Burden, Gina Pane, Marina Abramovic.

From time to time Rabih Mroué appears before the screen, "playing" a man running amok, whose tale of violence is inserted into intervals in the series of performance artists. This Lebanese, so Mroué reports (in the first person), has shot eight of his colleagues and wounded four. During these horrible episodes, minutely described as if in an action of body-art, Saneh outlines behind the screen the bodies of the dead, whose shapes remain visible on the screen, as if in police diagrams of crime scenes. Interspersed between these narratives are short reportages of events from recent Lebanese history. All in all, this results in a double scenery of this performance: In this way two separate, narrative lists are staged –one of art, the other of politics. They are counterpoised against one another and, at the same time they mesh with each other: the *artistically contrived violence* of Western artists performed on their own bodies is juxtaposed with the *socio-political acts* of violence in the Middle East. The stages of this thematic interweaving raise questions as to the legitimacy of art, its relation to reality and its precarious ways of dealing with violence and pain. Questions which performance art itself has always raised from the outset, but which acquire a fresh relevance by their confrontation with limits and a quite different history of violence. Keeping the question: "Who's Afraid of Representation?" a genuinely *open enquiry* forces performance and theory to share one common space: not an arsenal of *Inventur*, but rather a space of *inventio*, if we may understand by this a topos of discovery. I see this in the sense of finding a possibility, a potentiality or prospect of what may be possible, which – in the words of Derrida – "demands a transformation of our way of conceiving, experiencing or speaking of the experience of the possible and impossible".[6] The possibility of an *Inventur* (in its twofold sense of inventive and archival activity) can only be conceived – as an "irruption" – in terms that presuppose its own impossibility. Rabih Mroué, when asked in an interview what it meant to him to live as an artist in Lebanon – given the state of Lebanese politics and violence that is part of everyday life – and also what it meant for him to stage his performance in Berlin, in a "peaceful" country, simply replied: "I do not believe Germany to be a peaceful country".[7]

We could thus see the task ahead not as an *Inventur* in the sense of a stocktaking of what is already given and present, but rather as working within a zone devoid of topoi, in a border region where perception and knowledge interpenetrate each other. It would not be a task that could ever be "completed", but it would be one that replaces the concept of *Inventur* by the actions of a "ReMembering" as a *possibility*; a ReMembering as a task of memory and as witness (*Bezeugung*) of the political body dismembered by violence:

> Permutations between thresholds of horror and thresholds of the socially acceptable are: imaginable but impossible; unimaginable but possible; imaginable and possible; unimaginable and impossible. When all four are in operation, it is the thresholds themselves that require revision – not because they have gone beyond their own conceivable limits, but because the limits have been introjected into the system's core. In the case of violence and horror, it is clear that a revision of their 'exterior nature' to the boundaries of society is in order – for their 'unimaginable impossibility' is nothing but the masking of the quiet routine of the system.[8]

[1] Bernhard Waldenfels, *Phänomenologie der Aufmerksamkeit*, Frankfurt a.M., p. 172.
[2] François Jullien: „Die praktische Wirkkraft der Liste: von der Hand, vom Körper, vom Gedicht", in: ders. (ed.): *Die Kunst, Listen zu erstellen*, Berlin 2004, S. 15–51.
[3] Jacques Derrida, *Die unbedingte Universität*, Frankfurt am Main 2001, p. 22. (= edition suhrkamp 2238).

Gabriele Brandstetter

[4] The festival took place in February 2005 in the three HAU (Hebbel am Ufer) theatres.

[5] "Who's Afraid of Representation?" To the memory of Edgar Aho. UA: 24.2.2005, Hebbel Theater Berlin (HAU 3).

[6] Derrida, p. 41.

[7] Interview by Miriam Ruesch and Verena Brehm, in the framework of the seminar "Tanzdramaturgie / Trauma und Tanz", WS 2004 / 05, FU Berlin.

[8] *ReMembering the Body. Körperbilder in Bewegung*, ed. by Gabriele Brandstetter and Hortensia Völckers. With STRESS, a pictorial essay by Bruce Mau with texts by André Lepecki, Hatje Cantz Verlag 2000.

The desiring body in dance

Gerald Siegmund

Let me begin with a question. It is an old and even trivial one: Why do we watch dance at all? Why do we sit in a dark room night after night to watch dancers engaged in some kind of choreography, moving across the stage creating the special rhythm and the atmosphere of a dance performance? The answer is simple: Because we enjoy it. We go to the theatre to bring our love to the stage and those ghostlike creatures that inhabit it. Raised on a platform they are elevated, they are separated and removed from us, acting in a sphere distinct from ours. And yet the two realms are bound together by this institution we call theatre, where those up there expose themselves and give us something to see while we watch from down there. But what do we desire to see and experience there? How is this enjoyment channeled and structured? One answer, albeit a rather general one, and one that gives rise to even more questions, is, of course, the Other. We want to enjoy the Other. Which Other? Some life-affirming force that is often associated with dance? The energetic presence of the dancers who share time and space with us for the duration of the performance? Their rather special, sometimes even erotic bodies that are able to perform all kinds of tricks we would not even dream of trying?

In my brief essay I would like to throw some light on what I call the desiring body in dance. The concept of the desiring body enables me to develop a line of theoretical thought on what is at stake when they dance and we watch. First, let me approach the question of enjoyment and the Other on a more basic level. The founding principle of our Western theatrical experience is the split. We as members of the audience hand over knowledge, expertise and even our bodies to some specialists called "dancers". They perform for us and in front of us. They thereby articulate and to some extent mirror experiences from the superior vantage point of what we cannot do, while simultaneously channeling our desires in the legitimate form provided by the theatre. They dance for us in another space and time; they are our alibis in the literal sense of the word "alibi" meaning "in another space". In his essay on dance *La passion d'être un autre*, Pierre Legendre traces this fundamental split back to the Judeo-Christian roots of our culture.[1] The split is the result of the Christian prohibition on dancing. Dance from the 5th century onwards was excluded from the liturgy and replaced by the singing and speaking voice. Christian moral law, which regulates the subject's relationship towards its body and therefore also to dance, has condemned the body as sinful and in need of being saved by the soul. The prohibition of dance functions as a kind of castration, which cuts the desiring body from itself and, of necessity, inscribes it into the laws of culture. Dancing as stage dancing therefore represents the desire of the human being, which is made to speak on stage. Because it is forbidden for the body to dance officially, professional dancers have to find a way to make the soul dance. The symbolic law takes possession of the body by cutting it to pieces and reassembling its parts according to the principles of reason, which is granted to human beings because they are different from animals as the only ones who can walk upright. The human being's erectness (in the double sense of the word) enables him or her to see the heavens and the face of God. Dance technique as dance language ensures that it is the soul that dances and not the body, because it fabricates a second body that speaks truthfully.

After a detour via the European courts of the Renaissance, which were organised socially like stages representing a secularised model of political-religious worship of the king or the duke, the prohibition of dance eventually gave rise to the institution of theatre as a split space. In the theatre, we legitimately and safely participate in the desiring body of the dancer by watching him or her dance, which is equivalent to dancing ourselves, because we see the soul in the dancers' eyes mirroring our own gaze. The graceful and dignified dancers, think of Heinrich von Kleist's puppet on a string or Edward Gordon Craig's notion of the *Übermarionette*, speak truthfully because it is only the soul that dances, and not the body that is overcome by principles of elevation and lightness aspiring towards heaven. Viewed from this anthropological perspective, there is no difference at all between ballet and modern dance, between Isadora Duncan and Mikhail Fokine, between Martha Graham and George Balanchine. They are all, as Graham put it herself in her autobiography, "an athlete of God".[2]

Legendre's thinking gives rise to a somewhat more structural model of dancing bodies, which includes those bodies that simply watch others dancing: they are all desiring bodies. In his book *Le corps et sa danse*, the French psychoanalyst Daniel Sibony draws a triangle explicating the fundamental relation between the constituent elements of stage dancing.

> There was the viewing body or spectator – the mass, you – and the dancing body (singular or plural, including the choreographer who forms one body with the dancers and extends the limits of his body with their dance), and there was the pole of the Other, which is evoked by the holy dances, but which is there all the time; it is the heated and glowing hearth from which creation springs, the spring of alterity … And this triangle is set in motion, it vibrates: the dancing body invokes the audience in search of the other pole, the Other which does not have a palpable body but which is a presence: the presence of the original being that is, as the trigger of language and of memory, the support of that which exceeds everything that is, and, most of all, exceeds the body.[3]

The dancing body meets the viewing body during the spectacle, both of which present themselves in front of a third body that Sibony calls the Other. Derived from the religious function of dancing, this Other is surely not God any more in our secularised societies of today. Its function, however, remains with us. The idea of the Other remains the source of creation, because it is capable of producing language and memory, because it describes the cultural horizon in front of which there is dance, in front of which we watch, understand, and interpret dance. Dance in this sense gives rise to cultural and individual memories. It carves out a space for our desire, a space in which the dancing and the viewing subjects meet and miss each other. I miss the performers while I watch them and I miss the performers after they have left the stage.

....

Gerald Siegmund

What do we make of this on a more concrete level? Dance takes place on three levels simultaneously. It belongs to the levels of language, of the image and of the body. This body, therefore, can never be a unified entity. The dancing body as a desiring body is always already threefold. According to the Lacanian model, it belongs to the three registers of the symbolic, the imaginary and the real. It articulates a certain relation to the symbolic order presenting a utopian sense of community or *societas*. At the same time, it produces images of the body that lure us into believing that other bodies than the ones we produce for everyday life are possible. It makes us believe in potential bodies. Lastly, it reminds us that bodies are made of flesh and blood, they consist of energies that may eventually lead to the collapse of meaning and symbolic codes during the performance. The materiality of the body cuts through the symbolic to produce a kind of auratic presence of the remains of the body.[4]

Based on this model, a line of analysis arises that tries to produce questions with regard to a dance performance, questions rather than categories that have to be identified by the scholar.

1 On the level of the Symbolic, questions with regard to theatrical representation have to be asked. What are the stage conventions inside which the performers work? What is the visual apparatus of the theatre, what are its perspectives? How are gazes organised? If dance technique functions as a language of dance, how does it regulate the access to the stage? Who is allowed to dance and to stand in for us as our alibis? In the 17th century, the French king Louis XIV had a simple answer to that question: by means of a unified pedagogy under the auspices of the *Académie royale de danse* founded by him in 1661, the Law creates subjected bodies, which in turn represent and make evident the order of the absolutist state that has produced them in the first place. More pertinent for our debates today would be the question of non-professional dancers. Why is critical opinion so skeptical about them? Is it because we fear that it might only be their social bodies that *move* rather than their souls that *dance*?

2 On the level of the Imaginary movement, gaze and the body have to be conceptualised differently: not as language, perspective and subjected body, but as image and desired object. While moving, the dancer creates an imaginary body by looking at himself with a little help from cultural images, other media images that may either be used on stage or may be incorporated in the gaze of the dancer already. Think of Isadora's love of images from ancient Greece or Michael Laub's incorporated filmic gaze that structures the bodies in his performances. As a desired object, the gaze functions as the scopic drive. It projects the body into the void, thereby creating a negative of the body which is simultaneously absent, yet also present out there on stage, where it encircles "object a" which is movement. Or the other way round: it is not movement that is encircled by the gaze, but the gaze of the dancers functions as "object a" that is desired by the moving gaze of the audience. In both

cases, dance oscillates between movement that hides the object – because it is always already somewhere else – and inactivity that kills both movement and the object it desires. The imaginary "object a" stands in for the void that is the original phantasmatic object of desire, which is the mother's phallus. On this level, the dancer's body functions as a fetish that covers up the absence of the original object.

3 On the level of the Real, movement can be conceived as *jouissance*: as that which is more than sense, that which exhausts sense in movement. Because it will always be more than meaningful and readable, I can enjoy the moving body. I can become fascinated by it, love it, hate it, be appalled yet drawn into its doing. It functions as a link with that which is excluded from the symbolic, but which returns, for instance in Meg Stuarts physical tics and twitches, or in Boris Charmatz's bursts of energy from under the skin. The body as a fetish works as a *sinthome* of the Real.[5] It is both a site of fascination, which results from its materiality, as well as a site of horror, which, as in Jan Fabre's performances, threatens to break down the symbolic by sheer physical exhaustion. Consider William Forsythe's research into the abject possibilities of classical ballet: movement as abject that haunts the borders of ballet's identity until – in his most recent productions such as *Decreation* and *We Live Here* – the system breaks down and is transformed into some kind of undefinable "other".

To conclude: On all three levels the idea of absence plays a crucial role: on the level of the Symbolic absence of the Other as an entity that can be represented (since neither God nor language may be represented in their entirety: Language has no way of verifying itself, as Roland Barthes once concluded in *La chambre claire*. It has no means to turn around and look at itself.[6] It can never get a true or full picture of itself – and this is where the function of the Imaginary gets in, "Ye shall make you no idols nor graven image", as God said to Moses in the Old Testament, for God, like language or the code, or the *Matrix* in the film of the same name, is ubiquitous.); on the level of the Imaginary, where the absence of the object as maternal phallus *produces* a sequence of desired objects; and finally on the level of the Real as the absence of meaning and meaningful movement as well as the trauma of the collapse of the body and the entire performance.

As desiring bodies, we are moved by what we see as spectators. But the site of this moving and being moved is not the phenomenological presence of the dancers. *L'(é)mouvant, das Bewegende*, as I would like to call it, takes place in the absence, that is to say in the interstices of the Symbolic, the Imaginary and the Real. Moving and being moved is a question of that which is not present, but given as negative space, as a *volume* of bodies and the phenomenologically empty spaces in-between the dancer's bodies. This volume includes my own body as a spectator as a negative imprint. I am carried away, ghostlike and ghosted, to where I am not. The same holds true for movement: the negative space of movement is that which is not performed but given as a mere potential, a potential that functions as barrier and friction towards the movement that is performed. The absent as the site of watching und understanding dance is what motivates my final observation. It allows for a theoretical view on dance that takes as its basis that which

Gerald Siegmund

cannot be captured, that which escapes – and by doing so implies the spectator's subjectivity and his or her desire.[7]

[1] Pierre Legendre, *La passion d'être un autre. Etude pour la danse*, Paris: Seuil, 2000.

[2] Martha Graham, *Blood Memory. An Autobiography*, London: Macmillan, 1991, p. 3.

[3] Daniel Sibony, *Le corps et sa danse*, Paris: Seuil, 1995, S. 114.

[4] Vgl. Dieter Mersch, *Ereignis und Aura. Untersuchungen zu einer Ästhetik des Performativen*, Frankfurt / Main: Suhrkamp, 2002.

[5] Slavoy Žižek, *The Sublime Object of Ideology*, London: Verso, 1998, p. 55ff.

[6] Roland Barthes, *Die helle Kammer*, Frankfurt / Main: Suhrkamp, 1989, S. 96.

[7] Gerald Siegmund, *Abwesenheit. Eine performative Ästhetik des Tanzes – William Forsythe, Jérôme Bel, Xavier Le Roy, Meg Stuart*, unveröffentlichte Habilitationsschrift, Justus-Liebig-Universität Gießen, 2005.

The need for the dancerly study of dance

Isa Wortelkamp

A dancerly academics does not seek, it finds. And it finds by chance. Whoever seeks to find requires a certain degree of composure towards the things he will encounter along the way. He has to wait until they come to him. The eye needs to be active, the gaze should glide, not stopping for too long, not fixing itself on anything. The finder needs to lose sight of his goal before the finding can occur. He waits. He is open to what will come and what will slip away. In contrast to the seeker, who is fixated on an object, the finder moves around in a state of heightened awareness, ready to pause or continue onwards at any time, not knowing when he will find something. He who seeks does not find. Whilst the seeker lacks something he feels he needs or has lost, the finder receives. The chance-find – if it is indeed to be found – demands movements that can at any moment turn around and go back, movements that open up a space for chance. The finder's movements are not premeditated and not fixed. They are themselves movements of chance – unpredictable and indeterminable. Whereas the sought after object crops up within the premeditated field of knowledge, the chance-find occurs unknowingly.

An academics that does not seek but finds, moves in the knowledge of its lack of knowledge. It is prepared to relinquish what it knows and wait for the unknown to occur. In this sense it itself is in motion. The dancerly study of dance opens up a space for chance, in the knowledge that it will always lack the object it seeks. It moves within this space, well aware, but also unaware, of what will slip away and what will come to pass.

If we focus our attention on the *invenire*, the *inventory* then exhibits a moment of finding which always encompasses the unfindable. An inventory turns up what is in stock as well as what is missing, constantly moving between what is there and what is not. In its stocktaking, the *inventory* opens up a space for the absent, making it present as absence in its catalogue. Applying the concept of the *inventory* to dance and Dance Studies means focusing on their handling of knowledge's blind spots. In its fleetingness, dance is almost unique in its perpetual questioning of academia: it has always questioned the traditions of its own transcription. But where does the moment of withdrawal lie and with it the loss that is experienced in the dance of knowledge?

Dance makes its own study difficult, difficult to describe as movement alongside its socio-cultural history, its visual images and linguistic metaphors. Dance – fleeting movement through space and time – destabilises the ground on which knowledge stands, it undermines and disturbs, resists attempts to make it stand still. In this sense it performs a *subversive* movement. Dance circumvents the strategies of an academics that attempts to make its movements legible, via an observable and objectifiable system, and, through this legibility, repeatable.

In its fleeting movements dance eludes the gaze and with it the written language of description. The fact that it is tied up in the moment of its performance makes it impossible for the gaze to rest. Dance demands that the gaze move with it through space and time. In place of engagement with the object and continued observation, dance draws attention to its movement and to the movement of one's own perception – a continuous process of creation and evanescence. With every movement that fades before the eyes of the observer, dance evokes both the memory and the forgetting of the event. Just as the movement of dance circumvents the gaze's attempts to make it stand still, so too does it evade the writer's intention. Any attempt to record its performance at the very moment the dance takes place hinders one's perception of the whole – writing dance as it happens means that one will miss it. The postlude follows after the event – in another time and in another space.

In the constant creation and evanescence of its movement, which ceaselessly erases the traces of its own being, dance stretches the taut relationship between academia and movement, between writing and fleetingness, to its very limits. In its embodiment of fleetingness, dance is present and absent at the same time. The dancing body does not stand still, it evades the present and therefore the act of imagining, drawing attention to its own transience with a smile. Always a moment ahead of itself and always reaching back into its own past, dance moves between times.[1] The dancer and choreographer Saburo Teshigawara describes his own dancing as follows: "In dance, I get the feeling that time is not yet here, that time is not ready for me. I'm always touching the latest action with the new thing I'm doing. But the stream is not a line that you draw behind you as in skiing. That's in the past, whereas our stream in dance is already in the future."[2]

In contrast to the skier, the dancer does not leave behind any traces. Always already past, the movements are always already caught by the movements that follow and overtake them. The body of the dancer does not carve its traces into space, rather it carries them within itself. Dance remains traceless within this movement – refuses to be written down to a place and a time. The tracelessness of dance makes the memory's work difficult, according to Eva van Schaik. Tied to the moment, dance is "the art most to be pitied":[3] "What chiefly remains of dance is a trace drawn in the kinetic memory. The dance itself has cut and run, however. Dancers, dance creators, dance consumers: they are all looking for traces, participating in virtual dance even before it has been invented".[4]

Without leaving a visible trace, a trace that can be read and written down, dance carries the search for its traces along with it, in the form of the history and study of dance. This search pursues the past movements of dance, striving to collect and order them in writing. Writing on dance attempts to trace the movements of dance, to lend them traces that can be read and written down. Talk of dance has always been accompanied by the question of its textualisation, writings on dance interpret dance's disappearance without a trace as a loss. That a loss is experienced, however, seems grounded within dance's textualisation. Already in the 18th century, the dance master Gasparo Angiolini attributed the imperfection of dance to the lack of perfection in "choréographie".[5] The roots of dance's imperfection lie precisely in the absence of choreography in its original notational sense, according to Angiolini. Similarly, at the beginning of the 20th century, in 1925, the dance theoretician Böhme believed that the independence of dance would only be recognised alongside the development of its "graphic representation".[6] Up until the present day, the establish ment of a universally applicable system of notation has attempted to balance this deficit – to dissect the complexity of dancerly actions into linear-logically ordered signs, to sort them and make them legible.

It is this search for dance's traces that creates the fleeting peculiarity of dance as something that passes by the sought after object, which is not in fact an object, which is always already absent where it is present. In the search for what is lost, the tools for textualising dance always step in at the point where dance no longer is, and attempt to pin down what cannot be pinned down – movement. In the search for what remains, the eye misses precisely that which is peculiar to dance. The movement only appears fleeting when one attempts to make it stand still and only seems lost when one longs for something to remain. That a loss is experienced is rooted in the expectations of another.

If we abandon the search for what is supposedly lost, then that which is sought after becomes visible in a different way because we are moving towards it in a different way. Beyond the search for a means of textualising dance, its fleeting and fading movements are themselves revealed to be a trace – a trace which can be remembered as well as forgotten. The movements of dance, their constant creation and evanescence, by pointing the observer towards his own sensual experience, lead what has been perceived to be saved and recorded in memory. The movements of dance, in their fading state of becoming and in their present absence, lead to a heightened awareness. Movements which appear to pass us by *without a trace* can be traced through one's own body and remembered, as Saburo Teshigawara suggests:

"The body already has a memory. Especially the joints. Skin and muscles already have a memory even if we are not conscious of it. In my opinion every joint or bone has a strong memory …

Of what?

Of a sense of possibilities. When you hear a sound, your body reacts. Even if you don't want to, you will move automatically. (…)."[7]

The bodily perception described here is close to what Merce Cunningham calls "muscle memory", where dance structures itself during the period of movement as a "sequence of movement events".[8] But even without the sensitive motor feeling for time possessed by a dancer, one can speak of a kinaesthetic perception[9] through which movements of the bodily memory are set free and write themselves onto the body of the observer. Eva van Schaik writes of memory in the *Theaterschrift*: "one cannot simply wipe out invisible traces, one cannot simply forget memories".[10]

Made aware of the body's own existence and perception in the presence of dance, the observer too is induced to save and record what he has perceived within his own self. The more fleeting the appearance, the more strongly the memory is induced to commit the movements to memory. There is an inversion of the relationship between the remaining and the fleeting, each becoming a condition of the other. This is a *torsion* in the sense of a change in the loaded relationship between writing and dance, a change that itself becomes visible through the observation of movement.

As well as designating the "turn", *torsion* literally describes "the change of form undergone by solid bodies twisted in opposite directions". The bodies of writing and dance do indeed appear to distort themselves in opposing turns: dance becomes visible as a trace in the memory and writing becomes visible in its own movements. Dance uses this memory to avoid being tied down to the fleetingness that seems to characterise it, a fleetingness which could be made to stand still by writing it down. Similarly, the image of the eternalising text, a text that conceals its own movements and its own fleetingness in the service of making dance stand still, relativises itself. But it is precisely here that a Dance Studies writing style seems able to approach dance – as movement towards movement. Like dance, always a step ahead and a step behind, the text writes after and beyond. Both dance and its textual academics seem perpetually "next to the trace" – detached from their own textual and dance bodies. In both traces a space reveals itself between the body as bearer of text and the body as bearer of dance. It is in this space between that the movement is located, the movement that always reveals itself differently and always reveals something about the other – without encroaching on the other's field, which it does not cover but discovers – finds.

If one strips the seeker of the lost object, the search itself appears baseless and begins, in its movements, to circle around itself. Made aware of one's own movements, they, even in missing, become aware of what is missing, as a postlude to the impression of loss from somebody who was present. If we move beyond the attempt to pin down what is sought after to a place – the place of knowledge as well as of text – another approach to movement opens up. An approach that displays the openness of the person who finds without seeking – on the lookout for the movements of that which will be found and for the movements of its own self. A movement towards movement has to give itself over to chance in order to find. In contrast to an academics that seeks, an academics that finds opens up a space for the unfindable, it gives this space over to it. It carries out its inventory of dance in the spirit of *invenire*, continually on the move between the present and the absent, without replacing one with the other. It tries to take into account what is not there – to do justice to it as autonomous space, space that belongs. Such an inventory would gather what is not there in the knowledge of its return, record and remove it, discover it without concealing it. In its harmonising movement the inventory would retain the awareness of the finder – ready to pause or to continue onwards at any time, not knowing when something will be found or not. Dance Studies requires the mobility of the thing it devotes itself to in the space between presence and absence. In this sense it is necessarily *dancerly*. Open to chance as well as to what is not there, it dances by moving between knowledge and lack of knowledge – ready to find and to fall.

And where could we find this dancerly movement other than in dance itself? Being in awareness of they who find, without seeking,– Jérôme Bel together with Frederic Seguette showed on the second and third evenings of the congress *Inventur: Tanz und Performance* in Vienna his performance *Nom donné par l'auteur* from 1994. – A play with chance, in

....

Isa Wortelkamp

which nothings remains by chance; an invented chance, which only seems to occur by chance, which plays its own occurrence.

A vacuum cleaner, a carpet, a packet of salt, a pair of skates, a ball, a pocket lamp, a dictionary, a hairdryer, a chair. In this inventory of objects the chance is found in between. Between dictionary and ball, in between skate and chair, vacuum cleaner and hairdryer, begins a dance of association. In a continuous changing of place, meetings and movements between, next to, upon and under the things arise – things which find themselves again and again, in a different way.

Without allowing things to flow or to pass by chance, this play of things, in the precision of any movement at any time and at any place, opens up a space for chance in the perception of the spectator, who will take in what he finds. In the passing of time and things, the seeker becomes a finder: aware of the movements of what is found and of his own reception, he lets happen what occurs before his inner eye. He stays active, always ready to see in a different way and to see different things. In coexistence of things, images develop perceptively – move forward in perception, blur, stand still and retreat only to be completed, displaced or overlaid by other images. With a knowing reference to their own objectivity, in *Nom donné par l'auteur* things gradually seem to set themselves in motion, setting in motion the perception.

We don't see the things, we see with them and through them and, between their relations, movement occurs. – Chain reactions of staged chances. In *Nom donné par l'auteur* things start to dance in perception – are dancing out of line.

It's this line (or order) in one's mind in which things compose themselves continuously, taking up and giving up relations, changing places and roles. Always moving, they evade the attempt of order and arrangement and thereby a definite classification. Found meanings are changed, given up, are relinquished, are left up to chance. Known is overtaken by unknown and unknown is overtaken by known. Between knowledge and lack of knowledge the order of things begins to move itself, while having to do over and to reflect and invent itself again and again anew. *Nom donné par l'auteur* releases a movement and mobility of view and, over the duration of the performance, produces an awareness towards the things which doesn't seek, but finds. The play with chance forgoes the fixation on an object that would led inventoried and recorded itself and instead of that invites– all in the sense of Michel de Certeau – a mobile reading that selects, reminds and forgets.[11] *Nom donné par l'auteur* brings to mind what may be a dancerly study of academics: an academic that would invent its lists always anew, movable and fleeting like dance itself – in so far as it would, in the knowledge of lack of knowledge, help maintain space for that which is not seen and not found.

[1]   See Isa Wortelkamp, „Flüchtige Schrift / Bleibende Erinnerung. Der Tanz als Aufforderung an die Aufzeichnung", in: *Tanz. Theorie. Text,* Gabriele Klein, Christa Zipprich (ed.), Münster 2002, 597-609.

[2] Saburo Teshigawara, „Ein Gespräch mit Saburo Teshigawara. Der unsichtbare Moment", in: *Theaterschrift*, 8 / 1994, 202.

[3] Eva van Schaik, „Das kinetische Gedächtnis", in: *Theaterschrift* 8 / 1994, 172f.

[4] Ibid.,182.

[5] Gasparo Angiolini, *Lettere di Gasparo Angiolini a Monsieur Noverre sopra i balli*, *Mld. 1773*.

[6] F. Böhme, „Materialien zu einer soziologischen Untersuchung des künstlerischen Tanzes", in: *Ethos* 1, 1925 / 26, S. 274-293; Repr. des 1. Teils in: *Tanzdrama*, no.9, 1989, 23-26.

[7] Teshigawara, „Ein Gespräch", 198f.

[8] See Merce Cunningham, „Zeit / Raum und Bewegung", in: *Zeit:Räume*, Leipzig 1991, 298-304, hier 300.

[9] See *Klinisches Wörterbuch*, Pschyrembel, Berlin; New York 1994: *Kinästhesie*, f: (engl.) kinaesthesia; perception of movement as quality of depth sensibility.

[10] Eva van Schaik, „Das kinetische Gedächtnis", in: *Theaterschrift* 8 / 1994, 190.

[11] Michel de Certeau, *Die Kunst des Handelns*, Berlin 1988.

....

Isa Wortelkamp

93

Performativity or else

95

"I do"
Some considerations on performativity and agency

Katherina Zakravsky

Performance vs. performativity

The obvious kinship of performance and performativity can prove misleading if not abysmal. These words which surely belong to the same semantic fields and grammatically derive from one another are perhaps very different – if not downright contradictory – conceptually. We can start from semantic proximity, leading to conceptual difference and ending up in the possibility of strategic competition.

Proceeding from "performance" to "the performative" to "performativity", grammar becomes more and more abstract. Of course the large frequency of more or less naive usages of "performativity" in today's cultural industry might indicate that "performativity" is simply the big happy overall universal family of all the individual items of performance – "a single performance" being the individual organism, "performativity" being the species. But, to take another example, is activity the actual total sum of all acts together? Or does the enthusiastic use of performativity as some sort of universification of performance not rather point to a latent inclination to perform? In this sense the transition from the concrete act of performance to the abstract concept of performativity does not indicate an enlargement but much rather a potential, an inclination, a general probability that performances take place. As "performance" already displays a hybrid family of meanings reaching from the most concrete meaning of a single theatrical performance to the specifically English and already abstract meaning of economic etc. "performance".

"Performativity" as the latest craze of the cultural industry would point to ever heightened levels of overall performance. The overall sum of performing has become so high that performance becomes latent, invisible, abstract, performance becomes performativity. This analysis shows to which extent a poorly defined concept becomes a powerful symptom. Performativity taken as a concept with the meaning just explained would be – another familiar term – a performative self-contradiction. If in relation to all sorts of cultural, linguistic and symbolic systems "Performance" can only claim a clear meaning as the actual carrying through and realising of these codes, this "langue" that is in itself a potential and latent system that can never be actualised as such – if this by now archaic definition of performance –a term, by the way, which has nothing to do with "form" – is still the best starting point of definition, then the turning latent of a term that only means actuality does not make any sense. In this sense the complementary term to performance has to be competence in the narrow linguistic context, or constative in opposition to performative in Austin's speech act theory.

If performance means the most obvious act of doing something in relation to a complex system of social and symbolic structures that stay latent, what shall we make of performativity as a general tendency of doing something without reference to the actual act of doing it? Either this meaning gives the field of the performing arts a lot of reasons to cheer up because it can profit from a general inclination to perform called "performativity", or the self-contradictory term indicates a major crisis of the cultural activity of performance. In general those who make use of the term "performativity" do not go through the pains of a general definition; they immediately turn to the topical usage some authors have made of this term. And the citation of these authors replaces a general definition – ironically I am talking about authors who are well-known for their theories of citation, topicality and their general doubt of general theories. Within this little family of authors, Judith Butler's theory of performativity is so hegemonic that on one web forum discussing the meaning of "performativity" it simply is defined as a term used by theorists of gender and sex – a very pragmatic sociolinguistic cocktail party style strictly contextualist shortcut of a definition. Without myself having to comment on the complex relation between gender (as seemingly one application of performativity or else the one example that generates its own generality) and performativity, I want to make one thing clear: Butler certainly destroys all hope that the performativity boom in the cultural field would be a good sign for performance as a professional artistic discipline.

In the chapter "Critically Queer" in *Bodies That Matter* (1993) Butler states that: "Performativity consists in a reiteration of norms which precede, constrain, and exceed the performer and in that sense cannot be taken as the fabrication of the performer's 'will' or 'choice'." (24) There is no "one" to take up the norm. The agent behind the performativity of, say, gender is not a subject that is nothing but its after-effect, but the general discourse of gender. As this statement is already a classic there have been a lot of answers both theoretical and practical to this dilemma. A smart bridging of the activity of performing and this theoretical approach to performativity seemed to be parody – the excessive, hyperbolic displaying and performing of the otherwise unconscious processes of engendering performativity. The fact that the subversive potential of parody has meanwhile faded is not only due to the normal erosion of history and fashion but an effect of the built-in paradox of parody itself. If performativity in Butler's theory serves as an anonymous, discursive, normative machinery of subjectivation that simply has no performer to execute it, it would be a classical logical mistake to think that the exaggeration of something invisible and abstract would make it visible like a magnifying glass. If Butler is coherent in her definition of performativity, parody makes performativity visible in one item of performance. Butler's performativity, properly understood, in short created jobs for a lot of academics, but it renders performance artists unemployed; not because the disempowered subject of Butler's universe lacks the minimum ability of will that is necessary to rehearse and perform a piece of theatre, dance or performance; but much rather and more tragically because of the opposite reason: the general menace of the engendering machine renders everyone an impostor, a comedian, a cheap entertainer of his / her sex and gender. Society simply hasn't needed professional performance artists ever since each single social agent is a performer. The strict divide between performativity and performance in Butler indicates that the performing subject cannot voluntarily perform the performativity that made them what they are; they much rather perform the symptoms of their history of subjectivation. In this sense, the mere idea of being a professional performer of the real social mechanisms of performativity is an illusion so idiotic that it equals the idea of playing God – professionally.

....

Katherina Zakravsky

<u>Agency after all</u>

"I do":

So let's become familiar, for a moment, with some examples of idiotic agency. The medial framing and re-framing, the historical layering and re-layering allows for the re-significa-tion of seemingly simple speech acts – only within complexity simple performatives can be read. This reading which at the same time is a performance shows the emergence of an agency that is neither the good old almighty willing subject (even though it might appear on stage) nor an abstract discourse machine grinding behind our backs but a flickering event of intelligence that is activated between agents, between ages, between stages.

So let me set a good example through the lens of another example, and the example itself will break a mirror which by the way will also invoke and revoke Lacan's "stade mir-roir". "I do" is an idiotic phrase. It is the reply to the famous Austinian quote of the priestly performative speech act "I declare you husband and wife" – the mother of all speech acts. And it is untranslatable in German. "I do" in all its idiotically concrete emptiness does not do at all what it says. It says "I do" whatever, but it stands still, stupefied in front of this overwhelming rite of transition. This seemingly neutral subject saying "I do" surely does not do anything at this very moment. Even though we just learned that such a thing cannot exist this surely looks like a performance of performativity. The pure will to perform it, this act of marriage, over and over again till death will do us part, an act of promise, the prom-ise to "perform" in yet another very concrete sense of the word – performer is the brand name of a condom – "I do" wants to open up a fertile future through this narrow passage of one futile self-contradiction of an utterly inactive will to performance. Each single mar-riage, as a performance, has always already been a performance in drag almost everyone has the right to perform.

"I am free":

Let's now turn to the one example I want to give, the mother of all shampoo commercials. There are some scenes in Ken Russell's film version of Pete Townsend's Rock opera *Tommy* (1975) that almost make me cry when I think of all the bad aesthetics it has engendered ever since. Going back to this first site it is an encounter with one condensed node of agen-cy and performance. In Roger Daltrey as the first autistic and then messianic pin ball hero Tommy, usually in white jeans and naked from the waist up, we meet the epitome of a re-gime that is not patriarchy but the kingdom of the son. The son that rebels against the fa-ther, in fact rebels against the law, the code, the explicit system of obligations and prohibi-tions, already is the winner in the age of performance. Daltrey in all his tanned muscular health and idiotic smile that only so slightly changes in the otherwise dramatic passage from autism to messianism appears like a transvestite of masculinity today; the good or puzzling news is that this does not really disturb the spectacle. And the spectacle is as fol-lows: Tommy's very desperate or rather hysteric mother confronts her autistic son in an all white very sixties swinging London bedroom. She performs a mad dance in an orange dress to lure his attention away from his own mirror image that appears quite small and helpless in a huge round glamorous mirror – a revocation of Lacan's stade mirroir as his mother does not show Tommy his own image but wants to be seen in her own flesh in place of his reflection. Finally she grips Tommy by the shoulders and throws him into the mirror. Much to his surprise, Tommy falls through the cracking glass. What should actually lead to death becomes a powerful performance of a rite of passage. The breaking mirror gives way to the swimming pool below the room. Tommy sinks into the water, at this moment right between autism and messianism, but as his face emerges from the surface of the water, with his first draw of breath, his expression has changed and he sings "I am free". Seeing him running through all four elements in front of all that national geographic imagery of volcanoes, oceans and geysers shot in a blue screen technique that is so childish it might even have been outdated then, what should we make of this late pop star heir of Jesus, Prometheus and Dionysos, expressing and promising singing "I am free", and obviously performing what he is saying? It is a tiny, overdetermined monument of the inaugural speech act that opened up the son's kingdom. Here we witness the birth of exactly the illusionary, narcissistic, wilful subject that Butler bids good-bye. In whichever abyss of history this subject might have disappeared – what stays is this filmic trace of agency, the evidence what it actually looked like when this speech act was performed. There also are the light hues and fashion styles of this concrete item of film and musical performance; unrepeatable in a way in all its potential repetitions. Each time it is shown, watched, performed, it resignifies something else. This might be something to work with, professionally.

For a strategic use of "performativity"

To conclude: If the relation of performativity and performance that Butler has pointed out is the only correct definition of these terms, performance artists are rendered unemployed. By close inspection we do not face the strict alternative of a desperate restoration of the classical individual agent or the unconscious discourse machinery. There is a lot of interference between individual and collective agency. If this is true, though, we might end up abandoning the overrated term performativity altogether, or pin it down to a narrow but precise use.

The case is not closed yet. In Jon McKenzie's *Perform or else* we encounter a very elaborate effort to "rehearse" a "general theory of performance". McKenzie's approach is a very complex theory that takes the semantic kinship between cultural performance and performance in organisations seriously.

McKenzie quotes Marvin Carlson who speaks of " … the futility of seeking some overarching semantic field to cover such seemingly disparate usages as the performance of an actor, of a schoolchild, of an automobile", and answers " … what's at stake in our general theory is not an overarching semantic field of performance, but rather an underworldly stratum of performative power and knowledge, a pragmatic formation upon which all this contesting of performance unfolds".

....

Katherina Zakravsky

And to do so, McKenzie proposes a systematic conceptual vocabulary that differentiates between performance, the performative and performativity. In this sense "performativity" has to be conceived within a systematic conceptual framework.

We might also stick with Sybille Kramer's claim that performativity is in fact only a productive term in relation to media. In this sense performativity is not the exaggerated tendency to perform but on the contrary a surprising side-effect or disturbance within the symbolic processes of media and machines. So instead of making us lose all grips on agency the latest turn (or performance) of performativity leads to the discovery of the agent in the machine. And this leaves me with a result that always served my performative practice well: "There are more things in heaven and earth, Horatio, Than are dreamt of in your philosophy". (Shakespeare: *Hamlet*)

Literature

101   · J. L. Austin, *How to Do Things with Words*, Second Edition, Edited by J. O. Urmson, Marina Sbisà, Havard University Press 1999
·   Vikki Bell (ed.), *Performativity and Belonging*, London 1999
·   Judith Butler, *Bodies That Matter. On the Discoursive Limits of "Sex"*. New York / London 1993
·   Jacques Lacan: „Das Spiegelstadium als Bildner der Ichfunktion wie sie uns in der psychoanalytischen Erfahrung erscheint", in: Lacan, Jacques (Hg.): *Schriften I*. Bd. 1 Ausgew. und hg. von Nobert Haas. 3., korr. Aufl.. Weinheim / Berlin 1991: Quadriga, 61-70 [Report for the 16th International Congress for Psychoanalysis in Zurich, July 17, 1949].
·   Jon McKenzie, *Perform or Else, From Discipline to Performance*, London / New York 2001
·   Moya Lloyd, "Performativity, Parody, Politics". In: Vikki Bell (ed.), *Performativity and Belonging*, London 1999
·   Sybille Krämer: Introduction to Sybille Krämer (Hg.): *Performativität und Medialität*. München 2004

Film
·   Ken Russell: *Tommy*. UK., 111 min., 1975

Transformance: the body of event

Boyan Manchev

If we are living a radical transformation of the experience of event, implying redistribution of the dispositions of power, representation and actualization of experience, the demand for ontology of performance is urgent. It is not a demand for a reduction of the event – the uncontrollable irruption of contingency – to the archaic matrix of ontology, but a critical necessity, which we experience today more physically than ever: our prostheses are going ahead of us, sensitive and senseless like a skin, or a screen.

The aim of the present text is to propose a theoretical perspective for future reflection on the possibility of an "ontology of performance", in relation to the broad political meaning of the notion of performance, considered as an inherent quality of contemporary society. In fact, its thesis could be resumed in one verbal substitution: starting the discussion with the notion of performance, I will propose a new concept, alternative to it – the concept of transformance. My first hypothesis, concerning the broad political dimension of the problem, is that in the last decades, especially after the end of the bipolar world model, a fundamental transformation of the social structure took place, introducing the image of global capitalism. If the "postrevolutionary" era between 1968 and 1989 radicalised the tendencies of what Guy Debord was calling "société du spectacle" (I would suggest to translate it by performing society), then today we are witnessing on the one hand the radicalization of this model, but, on the other hand this radicalization touches upon the very limits of the model, and thus becomes its own destruction. I would suggest calling the new model emerging out of this radical transformation, the society of perverted capitalism. I can only briefly remind here of the etymology of the word "perversion"[1], which does have a lot to do with "performance". Perverted capitalism is the capitalism pretending to step beyond the conventional roles and agencies, beyond the oppositions concerning labor force and power, beyond the rigid frames of economical, social, and cultural production etc.. This is a situation in which the subject-object opposition of producer and agent of the producing process is replaced by the proliferating heterogeneity of universal production-consumption, including and not excluding all traditionally considered as playing a liberating role in fields such as art, hedonistic autonomy of the body etc.. To sum up, transformation appears as the main quality of contemporary condition.

This transformation is radical and in some sense unprecedented. One could say, referring to the Hobbesean-Rousseauean opposition between nature and culture, that it affects not only culture but the very nature of the human being. I'm not even thinking of the development of biotechnologies, which became able to intervene in the biological definition of the human species. I'm speaking rather of the transformation of the experience of cultural and "natural world" in the fluid sphere of the new sophisticated prostheses (biological, medical, cosmetic, of daily life, social, cultural …). The "tools"-prostheses are replaced by inorganic pulsations, by the fluid and indifferent sphere of the inorganic. The pulsations, or the inorganic flows, are possessing us, and not the opposite. We have entered the era of the fluid panic of globalised prosthetification.

103

For the purposes of my argument, I would briefly refer here to *The sex-appeal of the inorganic*, a book by one of the remarkable philosophical voices of our time, Mario Perniola. The book ends with a chapter entitled *Perverse performances*. In this chapter, Perniola establishes a direct relation of the problematics of performance (in the sense of "performance art") to the contemporary condition. He presents an alternative critical position to that of Judith Butler: if we accept the assumption that the theory of performativity implies a specific conceptual attitude towards performance, then performance is considered not as the way of creation of stable, rigid identities but as a way leading to the neutral sexuality of the inorganic, which is beyond any identity and which, according to Perniola, defines the core of the contemporary condition, implying a radically new experience of the things and the world. Perniola's work is undoubtedly inspiring or even, if I may say so, exciting; but at the same time I wonder whether his original approach to the neutral sexuality of the inorganic, to the sensible thing, according to his formulation, is not a kind of unconscious ontologization of the basic contemporary (neoliberal) myth of flexible technological capitalism, creating the image of a global society based on the fluidity of relations, institutions, networks, productions, goods, capitals, values etc. Indeed, it seems that such a position, all its critical potential taken into account, is still inscribed and in a way over-determined by the imperatives of the contemporary condition. Because, as it was said before, fluidity, transgression of borders, destabilizing of conventional social structures and roles, including traditional identities, is the very rule – and not at all the irreducible otherness of contemporary condition. All this means that we are facing an urgent demand for a critical reflection concerning performance and dance, because in this situation they find themselves in the position of being, unconsciously, we could say against their will, the privileged figures of performing, or perverted capitalism (and this is indeed my second hypothesis): as the perverted performance became the new myth of the social contract, based not on distribution of relations and agents but on flows of neutral intensities and fetishistic fixations. Then the question is how a radical critical position is possible in this situation? And is it possible at all? And what about the critical potential of artistic practices today? How could they react to the described radical transformation – and do they have to?

Evidently, the artistic practice of performance emerged in the era of the performing society as a reaction and critical disclosure of its rigidifying force. Nevertheless, in the society of perverted capitalism, the main characteristic of which is the constant transformation, performance in its classical sense could no longer fulfill its inherent critical function, which had brought it on stage few decades ago as a leading artistic practice. At the same time, in the last decade we have been witnessing the emergence of new tendencies in performing arts and contemporary dance. I would suggest designating these tendencies as "transformance". Let me first make a brief etymological comment. Evidently, the word transformance comprises two elements, Latin trans "across" and formare "to form". Latin *transformare* means than "change the shape or form of". Let's now confront it with the etymology of performance. It comes from *per-formare*, which means that its first

Boyan Manchev

meanings would be to "bring to completion", to achieve, to fulfill the form. The meaning "to represent", "to act", "to play" is only the third meaning of "to perform", which still comprises the first two. No doubt that there is a conceptual gap between the two terms. In contrast to performance, transformance would then mean not fulfilling, executing the form, but constantly destabilizing it, stepping beyond its borders, changing the very condition of its actualization, suspending its limits in the unlimited potentiality (here I use the term "potentiality" in the sense of the Greek *dunamis* as opposed to *energeia*, to the actuality, which in the Aristotelian line of metaphysics enjoyed an undisputed ontological priority and superiority). Transformability is the other name of potentiality. If the theory of performativity proceeds, perhaps unconsciously, from the Aristotelian premise for superiority of act or activity, energeia, we claim here, in contrast to the Aristotelian metaphysical tradition, that potentiality precedes activity[2]. Consequently, the act should be thought of as the act of the potentiality itself, and this act of potentiality is precisely transformation.

But then, the next fundamental question would be: how could *transformance* resist the transformed society of perverted capitalism? Wouldn't this be the same relation as that of performance to the performativity of performing society? The potential answer has clearly pronounced anthropological, or I should rather say, anthropotechnical perspective[3]. Not surprisingly, this perspective goes back to the debate on "human nature" and it could be resumed as follows: There is no human nature which precedes culture; the opposition nature-culture is the fundamental speculative tool to project the idea of origin onto the essentially a-natural figure of man. Consequently, the inorganic represents the prosthetic substance of the substantially insufficient human being. One could even say that the human is the being with whom the inorganic has entered the world. Homo sapiens is originally a technical being. *Tekhné* (in the sense of ability, skill, art, technique) originally fulfills *phusis*: the anthropological is originally techno-logical. The prosthesis is the non-substantial substance of man. In other words, we are forced to conclude that the described qualities of contemporary condition should not be defined at all as transformation of the human "nature", because transformation is the very nature of man. In that sense the futuristic theses about the emergence (after the post-humanistic) of the "post-human" world, seem to be not so original if not lacking real sense.

In that perspective we could claim that, anthropologically speaking, dance originally served as an opening of the properties of the body, or rather as an experimentation of the techniques of the body, that is to say, the de-monstration of the body as the *tekhné* par excellence, the techno-logical becoming of the body. That means that dance, and performance as well, provide an open space for body experimentation, for experimenting with its techniques, but also for elaboration of, so to speak, counter-techniques of resistance to the different attempts, existing in all historical contexts, for appropriation and reduction of the unlimited potential for transformation of the body and its sensibility. For, if the present socio-cultural transformation is unprecedently radical, it is because perverted capitalism appropriates the potential for transformation, the potentiality itself. (That is why dance is of primary importance for contemporary philosophy: it is the place where what I call a transformed ontology, or ontology of the body, could begin. Philosophy and dance today are in an inspiring proximity. We should all be ready to dance, as the contemporary transformed Zarathustra.) *Transformance* would then be the new form (stepping out of the form) of dance and performance, which defines the modes of resistance to the transformed condition of perverted capitalism, which exploits exactly the technical transformability of the human condition. But if the main characteristic of the contemporary condition is the opening of the inorganic world, then how does this opening relate to the opening of transformance? What is its relation to the way out in the opening of the radical modifiability, which affects the very conditions of living (I'm thinking here of biotechnology, genetic interventions etc.)?

We are facing a striking paradox at this point. If the human originally is a technical being, wouldn't the resistance against technology and 'technologisation' imply a resistance against "human nature" itself? This question has obvious political implications, which address the reduction of artistic creation to a technology of production, inscribed in the system of cultural industry and institutionalization. And how could we resist without promoting visions of an archaic body of vital power or romantic ideas of poetic excess, which also imply ambivalent ontopolitical figures? How to go out of the pitfall of (re)productibility and technologization, preserving at the same time the original potentiality for transformation of *tekhné*? The paradoxical answer is that the only way through which we could try to cease the continued productivity – or performativity – of technique, is to reveal its "original" being. What I tried to call transformance is doing, in its general orientation, precisely that. Thinking of the capacities of the body, contemporary dance and performance oppose the preconceived ideas of its functionality. We could find a remarkable example for this operation in Xavier Le Roy's work *Self-Unfinished*[4]. In this piece Le Roy shows a metamorphic body possessed by the power of the radical exterior in contact with which it is getting dehumanised; it touches the inhuman, or, in other words, discovers a breathtaking power "inside" itself, which makes it step beyond the limits of "human" in the direction of some archaic morphologies as well as in the direction of the transformation in a machine, in an automaton. Becoming dysfunctional, being disorganized, suspending the functional organics, this body also annuls the systems of identification, the esthetical, social, political, gender or even biological codes projected on it. In that way the body detaches from the order of representation and functionality in order to reveal itself as a space of the possibility, of the potential for metamorphosis, for transformation, for event. The resistance of this body against the fixed state of the final product, that is to say against the logic of production, related to the Hegelian logic of work, reveals an "original" potentiality, a potentiality which is opposed to the fixation in actuality, and in this way preserves the capacity of the body to take on other forms of life, to seek experiences which are never its own. Perhaps this idea of the inappropriability of the body could propose a possible perspective to think about "what is body" as the original site of event and transformability.

....

Boyan Manchev

The performance has a signifying rhythm: the body of "Xavier Le Roy", the human body on stage is distracted, slow, one may say, hanging around. This slowness is the speed of resistance of potentiality against the impetuous logic of the project and the fixed functional form, corresponding to it. Of course, this radical experience of the unknown necessarily leads to the rejection of all known techniques of stage representation, including the techniques of contemporary dance (which in a sense represents an ecstatic study of technique which sounds the capacities of the human body, transforming it in that way into a super-instrument, an instrument of still non-existing functions). Perhaps, it also leads to a radical attempt: the attempt to renounce technique in general (that is, in an etymological sense, "ability" and "art"). But if *tekhné* is thought of as originally proper to the human being, then to know if on stage a dancing body is abandoning technique probably isn't so important. Because in the end it means that going out from a technique, it is already entering another one. And at the same time, the way in which it seems this continued productivity of technique, this incessant search for prostheses, for substitutes, that which is perhaps our only substance, could be paradoxically interrupted, is by demonstrating the "original" technicity or power of transformation of the body.

However, Le Roy doesn't try to step beyond the anthropotechnological conditions by going back to some mythical visions of the body as immanent organics, as the Thing itself, which escapes from the performative technique and representation, and reveals a profound "substantial", onto-biological body. This is an important remark to be made because such an impression could be created from the apparent return, the transformation of Le Roy's body in sort of archaic morphologies, primitive forms of life. But I have the impression that rather some of the big figures of Flemish dance, such as Jan Fabre or Wim Vandekeybus[5], are running this risk. In many of their spectacular works they experience, in the line of Artaud and Bataille, bodily excess, the radical risk of the body's erupting passions. However, it seems that this radical attempt also discloses a nostalgic longing for archaic states, for an original organicity of the body. It implies some intuition of an original state of vital power, and the obsession with animal life in particular is symptomatic exactly for that, to the extent that animal life remains a privileged figure of vitalist myths. What about Le Roy? Let's look attentively at *Self-Unfinished*, where the incompleteness of the self goes so far as to erase not only the "self" but to efface any animal morphology. As if we were witnessing the opening of an abysmal power of the body to transform itself into primitive forms of life. On the stage appears an acephalic figure – not a superior organism without a head, such as in the icon of the legendary group Acéphale made by André Masson, but a morphologically primitive form, without distinction, without organs – nothing but torso and tentacles quivering like agonizing, apparently expressing a completely different logic of interaction / reaction to the exterior. One may say that this is the image of bare life: a minimal, vegetative life. But this is not so much an archaicizing nostalgia longing for the primitive, up to the vegetal realm; on the contrary, it is the exploration of the conditions of life in the metamorphosis, the traffic (a word launched by Le Roy) of intensities, of forms and rhythms – this is the body as the opening itself and not as a frozen figure, even if it would be the figure of a monster.

In this sense the *transformed* performance, or the *transformance* steps beyond the risk of archaicizing vitalist myths by showing the body precisely in its permanent transformation, which is always the transformation of certain techniques. The body thus appears as anything else but the potentiality of metamorphosis: the power, for instance, to become a primitive inert acephalic bodily form, or an automaton, a technological body in such an explicit way that it becomes comic (at this point the confrontation of Le Roy's automaton and Henri Bergson's theory of the comical related to the automaton seems to be promising). In other words, in order to step out of the bad infinity of transformation, the transformance shows the impossibility of the way out. Undoubtedly, this transforming operation is at stake in Xavier Le Roy's *Self-Unfinished*. The resistance against the techniques then, or, more strictly speaking, against the techno-logies, consists of the "revealing" of the primary technological condition (or rather of the transformation as the only origin). Nevertheless, this "original" transformability, revealed by – or rather through which transformance takes place, should not be understood as a simple fluidity, as the contemporary unlimited permeability and speed of the global market; on the contrary, the potential (or transformability) implies an inherent resistance, a resistability, even a state of inertness, in which resides the gravity of experience.

The metamorphosis relates to potentiality, to the singularity of the body, which takes place only in the confrontation with other singularities. The opening of the potentiality of the body is the pure manifestation of its freedom, without any end.

[1] Pervert comes from the Latin *pervertere* "corrupt, turn the wrong way, turn about" from per- "away" + vertere "to turn".
[2] This statement follows the line of the radical ontological critic advanced by Maurice Blanchot with the notion of inoperativity (*désoeuvrement*), developed further by Jean-Luc Nancy, Antonio Negri and Giorgio Agamben. Inoperativity is not simply a sort of passivity: it is the power of transformability, which negates the substance and form division.
[3] For a more elaborated presentation of this issue see Boyan Manchev, "Proteus and the Prostheses" in *Sociological Problems*, 3-4, 2004.
[4] The following remarks develop further some of the arguments raised in the frameworks of the discussion on contemporary dance and performance, with the participation of Xavier Le Roy, Franz A. Kramer and Agnès Izrine, and moderated by the author. The discussion was held in the framework of the project *Crossing the Borders* in November 2004 at the Goethe Institute in Sofia, on the initiative of its director Peter Anders.
[5] In relation to this topic I would like to call to your attention the issue of *Janus* on Animal & Man (13/03), where one can read the following quotation from an interview of Wim Vandekeybus: "I do think that we shouldn't humanise animals, as often happens these days. It is much more necessary to animalise people". See also Alena Alexandrova's

Boyan Manchev

article "Furious Body, Enthusiastic Bodies. On the work of Wim Vandekeybus", *Performance Research*, 8, 2003.

Terms and tribulations:
Performativity, performance and film-hip hop

Andrea B. Braidt

Fifty years after John L. Austin's "performative speech act manifesto" *How to do things with words,* which the philosopher delivered as the William James Lectures at Harvard University in 1955 and which was published after Austin's death in 1962 it seems to be time to reconsider how his theory of the performative has flourished in the humanities, in the studies of the aesthetic, in social sciences and, of course, in philosophy. "Performativity" has become a key term, a leitmotif some argue, across the disciplines, especially since Judith Butler adopted the concept for thinking about gender. In the early 1990s, the "performative turn", a consequential follow-up to the "linguistic turn", initiated a definite departure from the notion of an essentialist, stable, semiotic, pre-discursive and humanist-enlightened body, work of art, subject. In the following I will sketch out the initial Austinian concept of the performative speech act and its deconstructivist – Derridaen and Butlerian – development, and will then demonstrate how performativity can be connected to performance in the analysis of a scene from the movie *8 Mile* (USA 2002, dir. Curtis Hanson).

111 John L. Austin devoted his life's work the single project of showing that the traditional philosophical assumption that sentences are always some kind of statement which in some way or other *describe* some "state of affairs" either truly or falsely can not be upheld. He found that there are speech acts which do not describe anything but rather "do what they name". These performative utterances – as opposed to the descriptive, constative utterances – cannot be true or false, but they can be happy (successful) or not successful. The classical Austinian example for a performative speech act, the formula at the wedding ceremony "I do (sc. take this woman to be my lawful wedded wife)" illustrates how *saying something* at the same time implies *"doing" something.* "I name you Queen Catherine" at a ship christening ceremony; "I bet you sixpence" at the horse races; "You bloody idiot"; these sentences do not describe, but they do: they effect a name on a ship; a possible transaction of money under certain circumstances; an insult of a person. (Austin 1994, 5)

What is crucial here is Austin's insight that all performative utterances, in order to succeed ("be happy") must be regulated by conventions. These conventions can be linguistic conventions (something that Austin calls "use of language": the grammatical, lexical, idiomatic knowledge about language) (Austin 1995, 104ff.), but also conventions concerning the various social functions of those who speak – and those who listen. Performative utterances need an audience, they must be heard in order to work: the groom needs to stand opposite his bride (or groom?) when he declares "I do"; the player needs a hand to shake when saying "I bet you"; and the insult, in order to be effective, must be heard by the person insulted.

But sometimes it is difficult to say whether a speech act is a performative or not, whether a sentence is a mere description of something or if it implies "doing" something. "You bloody idiot" can be an insult, but can also be a mere description, either true or false, of a person. Austin thus introduces a terminological triad: every verbal utterance is, as Austin dubs it, the performance of a locutionary act, a simple use of speech. And every locutionary act implies a distinctive function, which may or may not be performative. For example, the utterance: She said to him: "You marry me". With this utterance, we do not know whether "she" was *asking* him to marry her, whether she *issued* a warning, or whether she was trying to *force* him to marry her. All functions are possible. An utterance which explicates the communicative function of the locutionary act Austin calls an "illocution", for example: She urged him to marry her. The locutionary "force" behind the utterance is clear now: She tried to persuade him to marry her. What we do not know yet, though, is what consequence this illocution had: was the performative implied successful or not? In the case of the "perlocution" this becomes clear: She forced him to say "yes" to her. The perlocution thus explicates the performative consequences which, in the illocutionary utterance, are only implied.

According to Austin, the performatives need certain circumstances to be successful: they must be uttered within a certain conventional procedure which gives certain persons the role to utter these sentences within the procedure; persons and circumstances must be appropriate; the procedure must be executed by all participants correctly; and completely; the persons must have the appropriate feelings and thoughts and conduct themselves accordingly; and they must conduct themselves accordingly in subsequence. Again, think of the wedding ceremony: the conventional procedure entails standing before an altar, witnesses to each side, and a priest before the couple (role of persons); the couple to be wedded must not be married (appropriateness), the priest must be of a certain religious confession; to the questions of the priest, the couple must give "correct" answers, and they must stay through the whole ceremony (correct and complete execution); the couple must really "mean it" when they say "I do take you to be my lawful wedded partner" and must act as if the partner, after the ceremony, is their lawfully wedded one. Whereas the first four prerequisites for a successful performative deal with social conventions, with the proper roles of those who speak and those who listen, the last two points deal with the "good faith" that must be implied with the utterance of the performative: for a performative to work it must be accompanied with the according "feelings", it must be uttered in sincerity and with the proper *intentions*. And it is these intentions that make the performative successful.

This last point is taken as the point of departure for a deconstructive remodelling of Austin's theory of the performative. In his influential text *Signature, Event, Context*, originally published in 1972, Jacques Derrida argues that it is not the intention of the speaker which makes the performative speech act a successful one but the fact that the performative is always a *citation* of a speech act uttered (and heard) before. (Derrida 2001) The power of the performativity of "I do" lies in the fact that this utterance is a citation of many similar utterances before: there is a whole history of this utterance, and this history and citationality makes it powerful. It is thus not the singular performance of a speech act which gives it the power to do what it names but the history of the speech act as a performative, the sign chain which makes an utterance a citation. But the singular performance of the performative speech act makes its own history invisible. This absence of the history of discourse – produced by the presence of the speech act – is, according to Derrida, the main prerequisite for the successfulness of the performative. Austin's intentional *repetition*

....

Andrea B. Braidt

of certain performatives is thus remodelled into citational *reiterations* of utterances which render speech acts performative. The speech act becomes a deed without a doer, gaining its power from its own discursive history. It is not the authority (the feelings or intentions, the will, as Austin formulated) of the speaker which makes the performative successful – quite on the contrary: it is the performative which produces the speaker and his or her authority. (Derrida 2001, 30f)

This interpellatory power of the performative becomes central for Judith Butlers extension of the concept into the realm of the social, into the realm of subject construction:

> Where there is an 'I' who utters or speaks and thereby produces an effect in discourse, there is first a discourse which precedes and enables that 'I' and forms in language the constraining trajectory of its will. Thus there is no 'I' who stands *behind* discourse and executes its volition or will through discourse. On the contrary, the 'I' only comes into being through being called, named, interpellated (…), and this discursive constitution takes place prior to the 'I'. (Butler 1993, 225)

The performative utterance is thus not a product of the speaker. The speaker is, according to Butler, an effect of the discursive power of the performative, the "I" of the performative utterance is always already constituted by former speech acts, by a discursive history. This interpellatory power (Althusser's term) lies at the core of Butler's concept of "performativity" – be it in regard to gender performativity (as opposed to gender performance), or in regard to sexual identity and the potential to subvert essentialist notions of both. Butler's argumentation concerning gender is easily demonstrated by the first sentence after the birth of a child, uttered by the doctor or the midwife: "It's a girl" or "It's a boy" does not work as a constative (descriptive) statement, but is the first in a never-ending series of performative utterances which constitute the subject as a gendered subject. But it is neither the intention of the speaker, nor his or her will or good faith which produce the power (the success) of the statement, it is the discursive history of the statement itself which effects, through iteration, a gendered subject, gendered subjectivity. The deconstructivist potential lies in the possibility to draw attention to these citational powers of the performative and thus to render the discursive history of the performative utterance visible.

Let us come to a halt for a moment here and recapitulate. Austin introduced a definition of the performative speech act which does not describe something, but "does" do something by being uttered. This theory of the performative was taken up by postmodern philosophers like Derrida, who went one step further: the performative utterance *does* not *do* what it names because of the *authority / will / intention* etc. of the speaker, but it derives its power from its own history: the performative is always a citation and never a singular event. It bears the trace of other performative utterances, said and heard before. The performative thus always refers to an absence. Philosophically, this insight was extremely important as it would change the whole notion of the authority of the speaker: also, of course, of the possible or rather impossible intentionality of the speaker, and also, of course, of the impossible intentionality of the philosopher. In her formulations about the performative Judith Butler radicalised the status of the speaking subject: according to her, it is the performative speech act which constitutes the subject. The "I" which utters something like "I bet you" is always already interpellated by other speech acts which gave the speaking I the necessary discursive history, "the discursive condition of social recognition precedes and conditions the formation of the subject". (Butler 1993, 225f)

This very crude summary of the main points concerning the concept of performativity should make clear what far-reaching consequences the embracing of this theory would have on thinking about the human condition: if it is the performative speech act that constitutes the speaking subject and not the other way around, and if every utterance – locution – has the potential of a performative – illocution, perlocution – then every utterance – be it in politics, in the arts, in philosophy, on the theatre stage, on the movie screen – can be analysed in terms of its power in subject formation. If every utterance derives its performative power from the absence of its own history which renders it a citation, then the study of this absent history of every utterance becomes an issue. And indeed, across all disciplines the incredible range of possibilities which lie within the application of the concept of performativity have been realised. I will demonstrate with the analysis of some aspects of a short scene taken from a narrative fiction film how the concept of performativity can be used as a tool for performance analysis. As I see it, the concept is especially fruitful for the heuristic distinction of certain levels and aspects of a performance, especially concerning its mediality, its employment of the audience and its discursive (cultural, aesthetic, social) situatedness.

The film *8 Mile* (USA 2002, dir: Curtis Hanson) is a fictionalised biopic[1] of the white rap artist Marshall Mathers, called Eminem. Eminem stars in the movie playing the character of Jimmy Smith, a white trash youngster coming from a dysfunctional, abusive family and dreaming of a career in rap music. The film begins with a scene where Jimmy (called B-Rabbit) seems to be far from the fulfilment of his dream: he completely fails in a rap contest, being unable to even start the song out of nervousness and insecurity. The rest of the film depicts his long way overcoming his inability to perform, culminating in a final scene which marks his success, the last rap battle of the film. Battles are rap performances where two rappers face each other on stage and perform their raps "against each other", whereby the goal is to win the audience's approval. An "MC" (Master of Ceremonies) functions as moderator and referee, and a DJ provides the hip hop music. In the scene I want to analyse here (the final battle scene[2]) we see how B-Rabbit (played by Eminem) wins over his black opponent called Papa Doc, who is the leader of the HipHop gang, The Free World, a gang which claims to embody the prototypical "gangsta qualities" of HipHop stars. After tossing a coin Papa Doc is chosen as the one who can decide the order of singing, and he decides that B-Rabbit should start ("let that bitch go first", he says). The DJ starts the music, and after a few moments' hesitation, B-Rabbit starts rapping:

....

Andrea B. Braidt

Now everybody from the 313,
put your motherfuckin' hands up and follow me
(here the crowd starts cheering for the rapper and follows his instruction to move their
hands like he does)
Look, look,
Now while he stand tough,
notice this man did not have his hands up,
This Free World's got you gassed up,
Who's afraid of the Big Bad Wolf,
One, two, three and to the four,
one pac, two pac, three pac, four,
Four pac, three pac, two pac, one,
You're pac, he's pac, you're pac: none!

This guy's no motherfuckin' MC,
I know everything he's got to say against me.
I am white, I am a fuckin' bum,
I do live in a trailer with my mum,
My boy Future is an Uncle Tom,
I do have a dumb friend named Cheddar Bob,
Who shoots himself in his leg with his own gun,
I did get jumped by the six of you chums,
And Wink did fuck my girl,
I'm still standing here saying "Fuck tha Free World".

Don't ever try to judge me, dude,
You don't know what the fuck I've been through,
But I know something about you:
You went to Cranbrook, that's a private school.
What's the matter dawg, you embarrassed?
This guy's a gangsta? His real name is Clarence!
Clarence lives at home with both parents,
Clarence's parents have a real good marriage.
This guy don't wanna battle, he's shook.
'Cause there ain't no such thing as halfway crooks.

He's scared to death,
he' scared to look in his fuckin' yearbook.
Fuck Cranbrook.

[a capella]: Fuck a beat, I go a capella.
Fuck a Papa Doc, fuck a clock, fuck a trailer, fuck everybody.
Fuck y'all if you doubt me, I'm a piece of fuckin' white trash,
I say it proudly.
Fuck this battle, I don't want to win, I'm outtie.
Here, tell this people something they don't know about me.

After finishing his performance, B-Rabbit passes his microphone to Papa Doc. The DJ starts the music again, and Papa Doc tries to rap, but seems to be so shaken by B-Rabbits lyrics that he is unable to start. After several seconds, he surrenders and B-Rabbit is announced winner of the contest.

In her analysis of the pimp figure in rap lyrics, Eithne Quinn identifies performativity as the major principle of this artistic practice: "The convention is for the rapper to embody and then, without explanation, to drop the chosen character and comment on that embodiment". (Quinn 2000, 126) The chosen character always in some way references something like a pimp figure, a trickster who derives his potency persuading other people, e.g. "hoes", to work for him, a man whose linguistic ability has the power to make his talking into doing. This pimp / trickster figure has its antecedents in African-American folk culture, especially in animal types like the "Signifying Monkey" (signifying meaning cursing) or a type called the "Brer Rabbit". (ibid., 125f.) In the scene described above the process of this performativity is shown in the following way: in order to win, B-Rabbit must expose the insincerity and uncredibility which lies behind the chosen pimp / gangsta character of his opponent, Papa Doc. B-Rabbit thinks that the strategy of his opponent will be to humiliate him with the narration of certain anecdotes from his own life which will make him definitely not look like a pimp / trickster figure / potent mack: he still lives with his mum, his girlfriend has been cheating on him, and his best friend shot himself accidentally because he could not handle the gun. So what he does in order to counter this strategy is, first, to use his opponents "arguments" himself, in order to establish himself as an even tougher guy because he is not afraid to admit all these humiliating facts, and to expose his opponent as the son of an intact, upper class family who attends a private school and only performs to be a crook whereas he, B-Rabbit, really "is" a crook: B-Rabbits performance derives its power from its (rhetorical) performativity, whatever he says is exposed as "citations" of a gangsta background, whereas the (not yet realised) performance of his opponent could only be a description of an identity which not really exists, it would be a constative utterance about a pimp character which is "false" as the speaker behind the utterance derives his ability to speak from this private school education, and not from his underdog existence. B-Rabbit does not embody the gangsta figure in his rapping, but he prefigures a discursive history which his opponent would have to cite but leaves him before a paradoxon: as opposed to being a history for reference, the discourse established by B-Rabbit leaves a deconstructivist space for his opponent, who is unable to turn history around, so to speak. Thus Papa Doc is left with an almost impossible space for the embod-

....

Andrea B. Braidt

iment of the pimp figure. B-Rabbit, on the other hand, embodies what he is: a contestant in a rap battle, talking about the bad starting position he has. And commenting upon his own embodiment in rejecting it in the last lines of his rap: "Fuck this battle, I don't want to win, I'm outtie". A statement which is – only a few seconds later – proven to be made in insincerity: B-Rabbit is absolutely happy and proud when he finds out that he is the winner.

The important aspect in this process of embodiment and performativity (embodying the contestant, pre-figuration of the performative's discursive history) is that the film narrative has firmly established B-Rabbit's underdog-existence in showing his trailer home, his alcoholic mum, his stepfather as wife beater. What the narrative has not established is the insinuated upper-class background of Papa Doc. Thus, when B-Rabbit accuses him of being a "false" pimp, the film audience does not know whether this is – diegetically spoken –"true" or not and in this sense has the same epistemological position as the battle's audience in the film scene: they also don't know for sure if B-Rabbit speaks the truth, but with their clapping and cheering somehow make true what B-Rabbit says. B-Rabbit does not win because the audience believes what he says about Papa Doc; he wins because the performative of his performance is successful.

All of Austin's circumstances for the successful performative are in place: the utterance is performed within the conventional procedure (the rules of the battle) where certain persons fulfil certain roles (the contestant raps, the MC moderates, the DJ plays the music); the persons and circumstances are appropriate (the way all persons behave is the way one behaves at a rap battle), the procedure is executed correctly and completely (the battle ends with the announcement of the winner); the persons conduct themselves according to the situation and also in subsequence (the scene following the announcement of B-Rabbit as the winner is the final scene of the film: the star leaves the scene of his success in a Charlie-Chaplin-ending). The particular rhyming pattern of the "outing" of Papa Doc also seems to add to the successfulness of the performativity of the utterance: "This guy's a gangsta? His real name is Clarence! Clarence lives at home with both parents, Clarence's parents have a real good marriage." The name "Clarence" does not rhyme with "gangsta", but it does with "both parents" and it shifts harmonically to "good marriage", two qualities in life that a real gangster does not have – according to the role-model of the pimp. Rhyming of course has long been established as a rhetorical argumentative strategy and thus it is not surprising that the Clarence-both parents-good marriage list of three marks the climax of B-Rabbits destruction of his opponent.

Another aspect of performativity can be derived from the study of the physical gesture in the clip. B-Rabbit frames his performance by a dramatic trick: he makes the audience imitate his rhythmical gesture of moving the arm above the head to and fro. Papa Doc of course does not imiate the gesture, as he does not want to be included in the group of the affirmative, cheering audience. B-Rabbit then claims that those who move their arm in a certain way belong to the real HipHop, whereas those who only stand there still do not belong. ("Look, look, Now while he stand tough, notice this man did not have his hands up.") This trick functions as the perfect introduction to his rhetorics of exposing Papa Doc as an outsider and works as a performative in the following ways: it is a performative utterance as it implies: those who move like me (B-Rabbit), *are* like me. And I move like you, because I am like you. The gesture and the immediately following meta-commentary on the gesture works as – and at the same time shows – the interpellatory power of the performative act: the act produces the subject as it points to the absence of the history of the gesture via the sheer presence of it. Moving the arm the way the audience members do furthermore establishes them as members of the audience: they need to hear – and acknowledge – the rhythm of the lyrics in order to be able to move their arms. Thus B-Rabbit establishes the necessary – social – context for this performative practice: every performative utterance must be heared in order to gain its performative force. And the listener must act according to the protocol of performativity, as Austin held.

But the problem with such an identification of the performative in an artistic practice is the notion of intentionality. Every aspect of this performance we have just seen is an effect of artistic decisions, made by the director of the film, by Eminem, by the camera-man, etc.. The sheer choice of the stage name "B-Rabbit" for the protagonist indicates an awareness of the whole sign history behind the performative utterances involved in rap practice (the similarity of the name to the African-American trickster figure could hardly be a coincidence, but who knows) that it seems highly problematic to talk about the deed without a doer. But of course, we must not forget that we talk about a media practice which forgoes certain distinct medial qualities. The media theorist Andrea Seier has developed an inventory to differentiate between the performativity of the medium (mediality), aesthetic performativity and gender performativity, and to talk about the various relations that these performative levels form with the performances absent at the time of viewing. (Seier 2004) The particularity of films' performative mediality lies in the absence of the prefilmic instance at the time of projection (the filmic instance works as a perlocution as it shows the consequence of the presence of the person Eminem on a Hollywood filmset embodying the character B-Rabbit) and in the absence of the single image (in order to suggest movement, film needs to hide the single frame by projecting in a speed which makes it impossible for the human eye to discern the single frame). (cf. Seier 2004, 48f) According to Seier, the film can now form various relations with this performativity, either ignore it or, on the other hand, expose it, comment on it. The various levels of performativity (medial, aesthetic, gendered) help to differentiate heuristically and make it possible to distinguish how the performance interacts with the performativity.

In my example from *8 Mile*, the gesture of moving the arm in the rhythm of the rap lyrics, links this performance to the level of media performativity: the fictional figure of B-Rabbit is played by the rap star Eminem, whose trademark gesture when performing in a concert is this particular gesture with the arm. Like every film, *8 Mile* needs to hide the apparatus of its production (fictional characters are characters, but not actors), but the use of this particular gesture in the scene exposes a trace of Eminem's presence as a rap star. The success of B-Rabbit is thus partly due to the performance of Eminem as B-Rabbit, the performance exposes the performativity of the medium. And these are some of the ways

Andrea B. Braidt

in which the notion of the performative can work in the analysis of media performance: Although this demonstration worked on the mikro level of a media instance and performed only a fraction of a detailed insight into one exemplary usage of the concept rather than giving an overview of the many theories and applications which are "around", I hope my example is suggestive in terms of the implied theoretical frameworks: one a first level, one can describe artistic practices in terms of their use of performative utterances (performativity in rap lyrics in my example; performative speech acts in theatre performances); on a second level, we can talk about the performative utterance within an artistic performance in relation to its social function, to cultural, gendered, ethnical habitus: the analysis of the gesture with the arm has, although only cursory, pointed in that direction. And on a third – and most important – level, we can discursivate the performances with the notion of media performativity. With Andrea Seier's heuristic distinction of media, aesthetic and gender performativity[3] we arrive at a complex analysis of the relationships of the performance and the performative.

[1] As a genre, the artist biopic could be seen as a performative act in itself: the narrative fiction shows how a musician becomes a star and thereby works as a star vehicle for the film actor, who is also a star – outside the film, a fact which is reiterated by the fiction.

[2] min. 94:17 – 98:52, in: *8 Mile*, dir. Curtis Hanson, with: Eminem, Kim Basinger, Mekhi Phifer, Brittany Murphy. USA: Universal International Pictures, Imagine Entertainment, 2002. Quoted Version: DVD *8 Mile*, Mikona Productions GmbH&Co KG, o.O. 2002.

[3] In her dissertation (forthcoming), Andrea Seier uses the notion of re-mediation for her analysis of media performativity.

Performing politics

Performativity and processuality

Marina Gržinić

How should one go about re-writing the recent history of performance in the East / West axis, as the title of this panel *Performance agency: East / West* suggests? I will make references to the philosopher and queer activist Beatriz Preciado's text *Gender and Performance Art. Three Episodes from a Feminist Queer Trans Cybermanga …*, published in 2004, where she tries to develop such an inventory reflecting on the history of performance art in the West in relation to the American history of feminism and post-feminist as well as queer practices and writings.[1]

I will try to do a similar move for the East European space, more precisely for the ex-Yugoslav space. In the last instance, my task is to present through a certain new genealogy (this includes what is perceived as the Second World, i.e. the former Eastern European space) what I call the gesture of re-politicisation of the space of performance art and its history, and likewise the gesture of re-politicisation of (post-) feminism through queer optics.

Why start a genealogy of performance art in the East European context with connecting performance art with feminism? The relationship between performance art and feminist activism is, according to Eleanor Antin, constitutive for performance art: "practically, it was the women of Southern California who invented performance". (Antin in Preciado) The Western genealogy of performance, as an effect of feminism, says Antin, has its roots in guerrilla theatre and in the university and street riots of the American women's movements of the 1960s and 1970s.

Deviating from what Antin suggests, in the context of ex-Yugoslav territory, I can state that performance through feminism has a deep connection to art practices as body art and the conceptual and post-conceptual tradition of the 1970s and 1980s, and to the alternative or underground movement of the 1980s and 1990s in Ljubljana in ex-Yugoslavia. What does such a change imply? It is clear that the public space in socialism and post-socialist times belonged to the political elite, and that it was necessary to find another space, precisely to develop and re-appropriate the space within contemporary art and culture in order to develop a public space. Therefore, another space had to be brought up and contested as a public space. The history of performance and as well the history of feminism and queer politics is actually a history of battles; it is not given, and it must not be taken as granted.

I do not see performance only as identity politics, but as a practice and as a theoretical framework that today opens the perspective of activism, agency and interpretation in the arts, culture and the social realm. Today, performative politics is one of the most important re-articulations of the field of fine arts that emphasises processuality and auto-reflectivity in arts and the political. The notion of performance therefore paradoxically finds its productive meaning in the area of aesthetics and in drag culture in connection with political activism.

Beatriz Preciado in her newly rewritten genealogy of performance within the Western context introduces three levels of dramatisation of the feminine, sexuality, and, I will add, of performing politics in relation to (post-) feminism and the queer. My thesis is that not only we can detect, we can draw and read, a similar genealogy of dramatisation as it is presented by Preciado in socialism and in the post-socialist context in the ex-Yugoslav space as well, but moreover we can learn about changes in the paradigm of queer strategy in our contemporaneity. It presents a further developing and activating of the new political subject and its forming of alternatives for not only art and culture, but as well for clear activist and political acting within global capitalism.

It is time to draw a new genealogy of forces, actions, thoughts, politics and experiences, and to include new strategies toward new forms of labour in art, culture and society in order to strike back at the fortress Europe also with subverting new forms of enslavement and new forms of proprietary relationship of bodies, histories and rights in the territory of new Europe.

Preciado talks about the dramatisation of sexuality as a three-stage process that is developing from heterosexual to drag and in the end enters the queer space.

In the 1970s in Zagreb and Belgrade, we witnessed *the dramatisation of heterosexual femininity*. In the 1980s, within the underground or alternative movement in Ljubljana, we witnessed *the dramatisation of femininity in gay culture*; and further, in the 1980s and 1990s in the post-socialist context (under the influence of media art, and new performance), we witnessed *the dramatisation of masculinity in the queer context* of the east of Europe. Therefore the specific genealogy of performance and feminism in socialism and post-socialist context bridges body art and conceptual with the underground and punk and rock'n'roll, displaying the passage which I will define as *from sexually queer to politically queer*.

What I propose is a genealogy from feminism to queer in the east of Europe, which therefore has further implications concerning the understanding of queer, moving my thesis from the sexual to the political. One of the possible ways of thinking is that the socialist and post-socialist contexts produced a strong political impact on queer (sexual) politics; the result being a transfer from sexual to political, accompanied by a strong desire, almost a political agenda, to think about the conditions of producing and activating the new political subject. The political subject I am concerned with is not the fashionable new subjectivity that is produced and enforced as a paradigm precisely to hide the question of where the political subject is to be found, and who it is.

Today every *situated* (that is, implicated, contaminated) performance and performative production and cultural initiative within the global world opens a space of collabouration, dedicated to resistance. All that was historically achieved in the process of establishing resistance is not something that is a result of the process of sharing, but the outcome of a constant struggle. All that was achieved through history is a process of establishing a set of strategies to subvert mechanisms of exploitation.

The crucial point is to name this process and the new political subject. Furthermore, it is necessary to identify the ways in which this new political subject functions and what are the strategies implied in order to produce paradigms of resistance toward the "Capital" machine. Capital functions as the evacuation of spaces; it is a constant production of non-spaces. Other Worlds and other spaces (that are not part of the First Capitalist World) and their histories and theories, practices and activities are evacuated, abstracted and erased.

Marina Gržinić

This is why to talk about the new political subject of performance via (post-) feminism and queer today means to link it to different new spaces of battle and engagements.

I would like to proceed not with a simple illustration but with a conceptualisation of the proposed three levels of dramatisation with the aim politically to rethink performance art and (post-) feminism.

The dramatisation of heterosexual femininity
Sanja Iveković, Zagreb

Sanja Iveković from Zagreb (Croatia) in her works asked for the re-politicisation of the heterosexual most intimate inner space. In 1979, she developed a performance piece to be staged on the day when the ex-Yugoslav president Tito (who died in 1980) arrived in Zagreb for an official visit. The piece was named *Triangle*, as in a triangle between the symbolic, the real and the imaginary. Iveković appeared on the balcony of her flat in the centre of Zagreb at the same time as Tito's car was passing and a crowd of onlookers stood cheering below on the street. While Tito passed, Iveković read a book while pretending to masturbate. Her action caught the attention of a secret service officer on a nearby rooftop.

Soon after the gaze that watches our lives, a policeman or the neighbour, rang on her door, asking that "persons and objects should be removed from the balcony".

Sanja Iveković in *Triangle* transgressed the masculine public / political space while dramatising heterosexual femininity; with this act of auto-erotisation of a woman "playing the woman", she masked, and softened her performative entrance into the public space which in socialism, and not only there, historically belonged to men. The result of this performance agency is twofold: firstly, it is about the cultural interpretation of the formation of femininity; and secondly, it is a reflection on the division between the private and public spaces. What Sanja Iveković performed is what is today interpreted as a "masquerade", as a distinction between genuine womanliness and the public space out there. According to Beatriz Preciado the prematurely developed postmodern notion of the masquerade was very influential in twentieth century analyses of the dramatisation of heterosexual femininity.

Vlasta Delimar, Zagreb

Vlasta Delimar from Zagreb (Croatia) is one of the most important women performers in the territory known as ex-Yugoslavia. The beginning of her career can be traced back to the phenomenon of the so-called new artistic practice, a complex artistic movement in the 1970s in Croatia. Her artistic work includes, among other things, repainted photos and photomontages which all focus on a single heroine: Vlasta Delimar herself. With her narcissistic gestures, so utterly self-centred that she functions as a sign and icon at the same time, Delimar stages the now already internalised awareness of a constant self-control, or better yet, the notion that we live as if we were about to be constantly photographed. Or in these still post-socialist transitional times, when pure blood and tribal affiliation are existential paradigms in the transitional period of the former Eastern European space, I can talk about Vlasta Delimar as a bastard.

Sexuality just clings to the female body, says Monique Wittig, so why should we try to get rid of it? In her attempt to articulate the desires of the Other, she may be in fact presenting herself as housewife and whore at the same time, yet far away from conventional roles. What is in question here is the process of creating new discursive practices from the deconstruction of corporate systems of representation. Thus she presents herself as a daring acrobat whose inversions and transgressions between the public and the private, the existential and the artistic, lead to a kind of "negative space" (Stallybrass & White). As such, at the same time defiant and submissive in her simulated psychological and excessive sensuality, Delimar stages a displacement of herself (and of the Other); she is an "image" registering, projecting and subverting the desires and metaphors of contemporary society. The interesting thing about her works is not so much gender, but sex and sexuality in performance terms, allowing us to make a connection with the works of the performance porn actress Annie Sprinkle.

According to Judy Chicago the dramatisations of heterosexual femininity – were always aiming at a transformation of the borders between private space and public space, at what was in the USA referred to as a process of consciousness-raising (Chicago in Preciado). In this context we can also recontextualise the 1970s body art performances of Marina Abramović, Belgrade (Serbia).

The dramatisation of femininity in gay culture
I would like to propose a statement that feminist theoretical and critical works and practices in the 1970s and 1980s in art and culture in Belgrade and Zagreb laid the foundations for the avant-garde and critical productions in ex-Yugoslavia, in a manner similar to the way Lacanian psychoanalytic discourse re-articulated the theoretical and art framework of the late seventies and eighties in Slovenia (and vice versa in the manner the underground with Laibach and NSK struck back and modified the social and theoretical discourse). As opposed to the strong feminist movement in the West – which in the 1970s in the entire East European territory politically spoken came to life really powerfully only in Belgrade and Zagreb – Slovenia had to wait for its feminist coming out until the 1980s, in a time of strong subcultural and rock'n'roll movements in Ljubljana, and this happened through performative actions that can be termed as gay, lesbian, (post-) punk sexual and queer. Within and beyond the gay community in relation to punk and post-punk as well as in relation to the visual culture within the underground with alternative music and video from the 1980s, the art scene staged a specific coming out of the political (subject) in relation to the social, history and sexuality. Gay, lesbian and transvestite positions were performed and replayed in front of the video camera or on the stage in the works of groups such as The border of control no. 4 and Borghesia, both from Ljubljana, and others. Performances connected with pornography, sadomasochism and the social presented a clear political investment in the space of performance and new media (film, video) field.

This was a move from the feminist to a queer categorisation of performances. What we got here was firstly the hyperbolic dramatisation of femininity in gay culture. As early as

Marina Gržinić

in the 1980s, some of the projects were as well emphasising what Preciado today calls the dramatisation of masculinity, or questioning of the ownership of masculinity in art, culture and society. Ultimately, these works ask for the politicisation of performance art and feminism as well. The idea was not grounded in the simple game of identity politics, whereby women search for their rights to colonise a public space; it was rather, a militant response to this constant process of fragmentation and particularisation of power.

Drag performances, as pointed out by Beatrice Preciado, appropriated the strategy of linguistic re-signing, which Judith Butler later referred to as "performing inversion of insult", and were appropriated as one of the axes of continuity between radical feminism and queer politics. Judith Butler and Eve K. Sedgwick therefore in the 1990s delivered their definition of gender in terms of performance art. But I would like to push a thesis that in the East (of Europe) the result of this process of performance agency was the production and re-invention of the political subject in art. In the East, the queer body eminently and thoroughly was the political body that moves toward the political subject. Or to put it differently, it was a move from the sexual toward the political queer.

127   The dramatisation of masculinity in the queer context

The dramatisation of masculinity in the post-socialist context opened a different attitude toward feminism and performance. What does it mean to question the ownership of masculinity? It means – through a performance instance which performs the sexual and libidinal context of the institution of contemporary art and culture – to question the new proprietary relations in society, meaning new forms of private property of art and culture, the social and the political, as the most inner motor of the contemporary global capitalist societies; it means to explicate the private property relations with history, intellectual property, copyright as ownership of the institution of masculinity in our contemporaneity.

Are we not today witnessing art projects that have several fathers or owners who establish the brands? New proprietary relations are established that can be seen as the protection of capitalist property rights, which leads to the increasingly privatised ownership of different public projects, exhibitions, etc.. All these new paternal figures make visible that they are behaving as dictators, imposing the absolute right of decisions. So questioning the ownership of masculinity means precisely to question these ownerships.

Tanja Ostojić, Belgrade

A photograph was taken in the 1990s with the title *Black Square on White*, on which the black pubic hair of the performer Tanja Ostojić is styled in the form of a "Malevich" square (a black square centred in the middle of a white plane), and organised in a composition with her white skin, the Mound of Venus. In between Ostojić's legs the real / impossible kernel of the art power machine received the only possible representation in flesh and blood. The so-called touchy nodal point of contention in art today, is the cannibalistic attitude of the art capitalist power edifice that displaces and abstracts, evacuates everything and everybody only for the sake of its survival. Works of art are completely abstracted from their historical roots by the capitalist art market. Malevich stands at the beginning of an art history edifice that completely evacuated its conditions of possibility; meaning that this history is presented as evacuated from any social, political and economical contexts. What we see is the complete disembodiment that perfectly suits the disembodied neo-liberal capitalist democracy. And if we are to re-articulate the way that this real / impossible kernel is to emerge today in the field of (performance) art then it is possible only as tropological / topological incarnation(s). In Tanja Ostojić's work it is precisely the pubic Malevich under the stylish gowns: that is the black square embodied on the topological place, and not some kind of "wallpaper, poster Malevich". What else is Ostojić's *Black Square on White* than a tropological incarnation on a topological place! This is a fleshy (in-carne) embodiment of the total evacuation of the condition of possibility from the capitalistic edifice of modern art.

What was going on in the 1990s between Tanja Ostojić's legs was almost announced in 1984 with a poster done in graffiti style by IRWIN/Dušan Mandić on which was depicted a text by Kathy Acker: "1968 is over, 1983 is over, and the future is between your legs".

It is about challenging the de-sexualised and therefore depoliticised subject and the disembodied notion of citizenship, rights of the neo-liberal capitalist democratic community. Diane Torr (in Preciado's text) argues that with such projects we get the possibility of creating, through theatrical / performance re-appropriation of the ownership of masculinity, a new territory for experiencing / contextualising and politicising the body, which has been, according to Torr, denied to women by a politically correct distribution of gender. A drag king theatrical personification of masculinity generates, says Torr, a redefinition of the borders between private and public, transforming the space of political and sexual action of the body into a political statement that tackles the core of the capitalist machine: private property and ownership of bodies, art works, spaces, patents, knowledge and political rights . In the context of the East (of Europe), I would say transforming the sexually queer into a politically queer.

I can reconfirm Preciado's thesis that camp and queer practices, be they Queen or King, with recycling and parodying models of femininity and masculinity from the dominant popular culture, create a space of visibility, a politics of representation, that enlarge the engendered representation toward a specific dike and trans-gender, politically queer attitude. This is precisely the moment that allowed going beyond the false equation between gender and femininity to be found in many feminist discourses of the 1970s and 1980s.

Eclipse, Ljubljana

Eclipse is a female duo that first exhibited publicly in 1999. One "she" of the duo always performs in front of the camera, as the kitschy porno-functional body, while the other "she" is behind it. The body in Eclipse is constantly being produced through performative actions. In Eclipse's photograph with the title *Blood is Sweeter Than Honey* from the series Pornorama from 2001 some (avant-garde) artists such as Koons, Almodóvar, Abramović, Sprinkle, Madonna, etc., already claimed through the capitalist art market that regulates

Marina Gržinić

and distributes the selling and consumption of images of certain parts of the body. The photograph bears the names of such artists imprinted onto those parts of the body that is owned or branded by them through the Institution (Market of) Art. The result of Eclipse's work is to show that the master artist, each with her or his cannibalistic attitude toward one part of the body, loses part of his or her priority and originality precisely by being dismantled by such recycling and parodying of models of femininity and masculinity from the high arts field, and is displayed as a popular trashy post-socialist double.

Queer performance and performative politics dismantle binary oppositions (being of sexual or political character) by questioning institutions of power and its proprietary relations, thus producing a space for political battles and an agency that can be seen as the political subject that is capable of developing alternatives for not only art and culture, but the social and political fields as well.

[1] Cf. Beatriz Preciado, "Gender and Performance Art. Three Episodes from a Feminist Queer Trans Cybermanga …" in: *Zehar* no. 54, San Sebastian: Arteleku, 2004. All references to B. Preciado's arguments and thoughts are from this text.

"We are not selling Hollywood"
The potentiality of the meeting

Bojana Kunst

For the introduction of my text I would like to borrow the title from the collection of contemporary Nordic artists writing *We Are All Normal (And We Want Our Freedom)*.[1] With the all-encompassing affective economy and global commodification, we are today more and more confronted with the normalness of the artistic subjectivity. This is the time when, as Susan Buck-Morrs said, "the artistic freedom exists in proportion with the artistic irrelevance".[2] Artistic and creative powers are by their normalisation isolated from the social effect, and self-realisation, non-conformism, jouissance of the private and arbitrariness of everyday life seem to be in the centre of post-capitalist production. The real question at stake is therefore not how to find the way out anymore, but how to tackle the overall normalisation with procedures of disobedience and how to persist inside vividly walking around all the time. Namely, the normalisation of artistic subjectivity is not only connected to the exhaustion of subversive and transgressive modes, which became an intrinsic part of contemporary commodification. Neither is it a consequence of the commodified jouissance of the private, which unfortunately lost its potential for revolution in the commodified jouissance of global happiness. The normalness of artistic subjectivity is tightly connected with the contemporary understanding of life, which is progressively appropriated and regulated by capital and economy. Therefore, it is no coincidence that Allan Kaprow, an artist "specialised in life", when writing *Afterthought* in 2002 as a comment on his famous *Notes on the Creating of A Total Art* from 1958, concludes his text with the following paragraph:

131

"But what is then everyday life? Life of any kind? Biological? Personal? Cultural? Political? I don't have an answer, certainly not for anyone else. But it is clear that this is a central question remaining from the Environments and Happening of 1958."[3] We can say that somehow the last potentiality for the constant revolt – life itself – has been appropriated by the spectacle of contemporary economy.

Exactly such continuous revolt stood in the centre of the artistic practices of the sixties and seventies. No matter whether they were coming from the east or the west of Europe, artists were walking, jumping, sitting, lying down, reforming the plain landscape of everyday life with their bodies, arbitrary decisions and desires. The transformation happened in the way it was described in the famous Fluxus score written by Dick Higgins (Gangsang for Ben Patterson): "One foot forward. Transfer weight to this foot. Bring other foot forward. Transfer weight to this foot. Repeat as often as desired." On one side, there was an arbitrary decision, which on the other side was transformed into the form. But there was another, parallel operation going on, too: on one side there was an agency of desire, which gave every form the arbitrariness of the walk. The revolt of life can be found precisely in the constant tension between the plain landscape of the outside and private desire. I would say that – with all the awareness of the problematic non-visibility of eastern modernistic practices – the walkers from the east or west of Europe were walking in common, both were disclosing the common potential for revolt and at the same time exposing themselves to life.

II.

How this strong moment of community was quickly transferred into quite a different kind of common meeting of East and West, can be very well illustrated with one of the Yugoslavian documentaries from 1973. The title of the movie was *We Are Not Selling Hollywood*, it was made by Dejan Karakljajić and Jovan Aćin in 1973 and was later included and quoted in the work of the Serbian visual artist Marko Lulić. The meeting in this documentary clearly reveals the transformation of the common moment of revolt into the common production of pleasure. We can say that the future post-capitalist welfare economy was already mapped in this documentary: the bizarre moment of appropriation of life is clearly visible in this movie.

The communist authorities in Yugoslavia very early realised that the permanent resistance of the sixties and its understanding of life changed radically and quickly to the commodified jouissance of the private. The country, which always has been schizophrenically oscillating between two different ideological kinds of hedonism, therefore opened its socialist borders to foreign tourists as early as in the seventies. In the late seventies, the beginning of high tourism was marked by the opening of a hotel – a masterpiece of modernist architecture (made by Boris Magoš and named Haludovo) in the town of Malinska on the Croatian island of Krk. The architectural masterpiece itself did not suffice for a solemn enough marking of the turning point when Western pleasure finally became part of socialist income. There was also an opening celebration with a guest speaker invited – the editor-in-chief of the American magazine *Penthouse*, together with his yacht and ten pin-up girls. A documentary on this event provides an informative lesson on how symptomatic the normalising meeting of the two hedonistic interests can turn out to be. After a show of Yugoslav folk dances and a communist speaker marked by an awkwardly styled suit and an unmistakable air of obsolescence, there appeared the *Penthouse* editor-in-chief in person, a total opposite of the previous speaker, sporting an elegant white suit, a cigar and the pin-ups, whom he solemnly introduced as peace forces of the West. After the opening ceremony, the sexy peace forces took a stroll around the town to fondle the red stars and ample revolutionary slogans on the stone walls, observed by the locals – old women in traditional black dresses and toothless old men.

The documentary does not only show another bizarre case of the unsuccessful aesthetic meeting between the rigid body of communism and the hedonist body of the West. What it opens is the unusual connection of ideological rigidity and the economy of welfare, commodified hedonism and politics, freedom and pleasure, co-operation and tourism, communist congress and capitalist penthouse. There is no conflict and tension anymore, no revealing, everything is there and on view: it is impossible to exit, the celebrating event wants so much to be total in its common happiness. Even the most bizarre meetings can now become part of the global organisation of happiness. But at the same time the meeting is completely fictional – as the capital which still was not there. The documentary can also be read as the meeting on a territory where capitalism was still not efficient with all its

Bojana Kunst

over-inventive production, but at the same time already globally existing as the main appropriation of life.

III.

It would be then very interesting to establish a cultural agency, which can today reveal exactly the structure of this fiction, the ways how such fiction is reinterpreting the totalitarian imaginary to produce its own phantasm. Maybe that's why we have to stress the illusions of our very meetings together, and ask ourselves into whose futures we are breaking through and what it is that we are leaving behind? How to exert this present in which we are all increasingly dispersed and more and more confronted with the commercial desire to keep ourselves going as an efficient future totality? Is this the future of the inventive and global capitalism, when even our past will not be understood as a deeply intimate and social past anymore, but as the fragmented history of the still non-efficient capital? The common of our meetings cannot be exposed because the meeting of East and West is very rarely used to re-question their propinquity, as a possible alternative to the common future, in this case defined by the cultural market and industry. What is very important here is not really the future, which has been already appropriated by the more powerful discourse of the global capital. It is much more important to open up the questions of the present and past, which demonstrate different temporalities and parallel possibilities to us, also disclosing the ways of appropriation and the most impossible alliances.

Here we can think of *déjà vu* (already seen) and show that this is not only a hegemonic feeling of supremacy over the other, but has other consequences, too. In the case of *déjà vu*, the moment will come to a traumatic halt because of its surprisingness, and fill us with strong unease. In a single moment, our coherent chronology, along with the related territories and borders, will be shattered. In the case of a true *déjà vu*, the traumatic confrontation with the "already seen" deeply interferes with our perception of reality, which suddenly proves to be artificial, and ourselves dislocated in its scope. It deeply shatters our perception of identity and location, and encroaches upon our privilege of the present. So what we really do get with *déjà vu* is not a very powerful position, not a position of the powerful present but exactly the opposite: *déjà vu* reveals our weak side, it dislocates us and takes away our privileges.

This awareness is even more important today, when with the European enlargement the present time of joining countries maybe becomes more visible; but on the other hand, there are now even more invisible parts of Europe which stay outside and have no visible future at all. In our present situation, after both sides were revealed to each other through the already seen, we are confronted with the severe problems of contemporary representative democracy, with borders which are becoming more and more transparent and controlled, with a redistribution of power which is increasingly linked to the economical and globalised procedures. With the global cultural market, there is a feeling at work that we can participate in the cultural spectacle much more, but what is really at stake is that there is an even narrower territory in which to act disobediently and not be normalised. Disobedience has to be understood as described by Paolo Virno: "Civil disobedience represents, perhaps, the fundamental form of political action of the multitude, provided that the multitude is emancipated from the liberal tradition within which it is encapsulated. It is not a matter of ignoring a specific law because it appears incoherent or contradictory to other fundamental norms, for example to the constitutional charter. In such case, in fact reluctance would signal only deeper loyalty to state control. Conversely, the radical disobedience which concerns us here casts doubts on the State's actual ability to control."[4] We have to cast doubts on the life actual ability to be normalised.

Maybe we can be open for different possibilities of such disobedience exactly by experiencing an uneasy affection, the gap of difference, where our present time also reveals itself as constructed and artificial. There are many attempts to overcome the anxiety of closeness, and the most successful ones are always those who never took the common future for granted but always examined the very moment of the meeting – what kind of present political exclusivity really brings two sides together? Is this the future of the globalised cultural market (as was the case in many initiatives in the last decade)? Is this art as "the last space for freedom" which goes perfectly well with the contemporary market and the complex status of commodity, where self-reflexive and critical relation is even welcomed with open hands? Or could this perhaps be cooperation in the field of culture as the only remaining refuge where political alternatives can also be formulated?

I would like to conclude with my conviction that the most important meetings always were brought about through initiatives which were not progressively oriented towards a common future, but were deeply aware of the different potentialities of past moments and the tricky agency of the present. With such an awareness we can become aware of the problematic ways of how we are collabourating on the contemporary cultural and spectacular market towards common normality, so that finally we will be "all normal together". Such an awareness has serious consequences for the state of theory, too. If it doesn't want to become an ideal worker for the weak but nevertheless self-realisable subjectivity of contemporary society, it has to reflect continuously on its own production. It has to do something similar as radical art in Benjamin's sense, which needs to do more than make politics its subject matter; it must change the way it is made, distributed and seen. It has to negotiate between different kinds of knowledge and make them visible, it has to be critical of alliances, mediate but at the same time never turn mediation into procedure. Similar to Irrit Rogoff's notion of criticality, it has to take risks with the inhabitation. When exposing something, it should not only make it present, but also allow something to exit. It has to be a little like a strategic critic in the Von Clausewitz sense, where an important point is to position itself exactly in the position of the actor's point of view. But this positioning is also marked by a constant presence of failure. Most strategic critique would disappear completely or would be reduced to minor differences of understanding if the writers could or would position themselves in all the circumstances in which actors find themselves.

....

Bojana Kunst

This is not the gap between knowledge and art, but the negotiation between different kinds of knowledge about art and different kinds of agencies at the same time. This is strategic mediation, where the relations between "production and ethicality, structure and super-structure, technologies and emotional tonalities, material development and culture, a revolutionising of the work progress and sentiments" is visible and also can be put to work.[5]

[1] Katja Sander and Simon Sheikh, *We Are All Normal and We Want our Freedom: A Collection of Contemporary Nordic Artists Writing*, Black Dog Publishing, London 2001.

[2] Susan Buck-Morss, *Thinking Past Terror*, Verso, 2003, p. 69.

[3] Allan Kaprow: »Afterthought«, in: *Critical Mass, Happenings, Fluxus, Performance, Intermedia and Rutgers University 1958–1972*, ed. Geoffrey Hendricks, Mason Gross Art Galleries, Rutgers University, MIT Art Museum, Amherst College, 2003, p.7.

[4] Paolo Virno, *A Grammar of the Multitude*, New York, 2004, p. 69.

[5] Paolo Virno, *A Grammar of the Multitude*, New York, 2004, p. 84.

135

In and out of control, or significant differences between suffering in theatre, S/M practices and politics as usual

Nataša Govedić

In contemporary theatre studies, it is not uncommon to find that masochism shares its definition with tragedy: *taking pleasure from pain*, being socially "in control" of pain, disciplining suffering by performing it, is exactly how Terry Eagleton (2003) describes the role of tragedy in human epistemology. Timothy Murray, another contemporary philosopher, in his introduction to the book *Mimesis, Masochism and Mime* (2000: 14) also claims that "what lies at the heart of theatricality (…) is the ambivalent pathos evoked by the divisions of mimesis and their profound turn of subject and socius against themselves". Put simply, Murray says, "mimesis is the theatricalisation of masochism". But what kind of a masochism? With Murray, masochism in drama stands for something as "perverse" as people finding pleasure while observing blood and tears involved in scenes of painful family divisions.

I have a problem with this approach. Is it possible for us to be more precise when talking about masochism *and* the drama history? One example: Medea perhaps does take pleasure in Jason's pain at the end of the play, but her main goal throughout the play is to make Jason notice how dreadful it is for her to "calmly" accept the broken contract of their marriage. She, for one, is not taking *pleasure* in her husband's *betrayal*. She is outraged.

137 Although she kills her own children, Medea's performance could hardly be called "sadistic" or "masochistic", and the same is true of her audience: we are, to say the least, perplexed by the unfolding of political violence as presented by the play. Medea does use *her children's bodies* as political manifestos, as tools of revolt, as signs, maybe even as complex art objects or a particular bodily and deadly contract with her community, a contract signed with corpses of children, but her tragedy has almost nothing to do with reaching the point of enacting or participating in a revenge as "pleasure". As for the audience, our need for "social order" is neither satisfied nor "pleasured" by the finale of the drama. Pain remains unsoothed.

My point is that drama, especially Greek drama, cannot be reduced to masochism that easily, especially to a simplistic understanding of masochism as *taking pleasure in pain*. Roman gladiator games are another issue completely, obviously different from either Greek drama, contemporary tragedy or today's performance art. What is even more interesting, is that historical definitions of sadism, masochism and S/M are conflicting in themselves: Freudian psychoanalysis considers sadism and masochism as complementary behaviours, while Gilles Deleuze presents them persuasively as quite *separate* phantasmatic and behavioural practices. All their definitions involve exchange of power and theatralisation of power, but not necessarily pain. The sociologists Thomas S. Weinberg and G.W. Kamel[1] wrote in 1995:

> Much S&M involves very little pain. Rather, many sadomasochists prefer acts
> such as verbal humiliation or abuse, cross-dressing, being tied up (bondage),
> mild spankings where no severe discomfort is involved, and the like. Often, it
> is the notion of being helpless and subject to the will of another that is sexually
> titillating … At the very core of sadomasochism is not pain but the idea of
> control – dominance and submission.

It is important to stress how pleasure and pain entered into their long and, to my mind, unhappy marriage. With the advent of ascetic Christian iconography and the Christian allegoric matrix, pleasure (condemned as it was by the Church) began sharing *the same* territory as pain. We needed Christianity to stage masochists and martyrs joining hands. In his work *Masochism in Sex and Society* (1962: 351-358), Theodore Reik explores the importance of interrelation between visibility and ideality for the Christian concept of moral suffering. For Reik, *the visibility of tortured flesh*, Christ as "body-in-pain", remains central to the conception of moral formation in Christian thought. Christianity shapes moral formation as an economy of visibility by which the visual exhibition or performance of one's own self-annihilation guarantees participation in Christ's ideal, displayed as paradigmatic suffering. Ever since the Middle Ages, for a good servant of the Church the only pleasure left, encouraged, allowed and idealised is the conflicting, self-annihilating *pleasure of pain*. That is why a generic piece about the sexualisation of pleasures taken in suffering, such as Leopold von Sacher-Masoch's *Venus in Furs* (1870), so persistently insists on its own erotic return to the Greeks: only in the pre-Christian era does Sacher-Masoch find license not to feel guilty about approaching the fantasy world of his own sexuality. In the words of Leopold von Sacher-Masoch himself (1991: 49): "I admire the serene sensuality of the Greeks: pleasure without pain; it is the ideal I strive to realise. I do not believe in the love preached by Christianity and our modern knights of the spirit. Take a look at me: I am worse than a heretic, I am pagan … "

But at the same time Sacher-Masoch is not entirely free from pursuing such powerful Catholic desire machines as idealisation or sacralisation of the other, with a full risk of gradually turning a pedestalised female partner into a demonised enemy. *Venus in Furs* ends with Severin dreaming of hurting his former perfect torturess: Venus' idealisation culminates with her demonisation. I quote from the novel (Sacher-Masoch, 1991: 271): "The moral is that woman, as Nature created her and as man up to now has found her attractive, is man's enemy; she can be his slave or his mistress but never his companion. This she can only be when she has the same rights as he and is his equal in education and work. For the time being there is only one alternative: to be the hammer of the anvil."

It seems that the need to stage both idealisation and desidealisation has a high operative value in masochistic performances. Let's hear Gilles Deleuze (1991: 55): "Although masochism always has a theatrical quality that is not to be found in sadism, the sufferings it depicts are not, for all that, simulated or slight, neither is the ambient of cruelty less great (the stories of Masoch record excruciating tortures). What characterises masochism and its theatricality is a peculiar form of cruelty in the woman torturer: the cruelty of the Ideal, the specific freezing point, the point at which idealism is realised". Masochism necessarily includes the economy of an idealised Other, even if s/he is only imagined or internalised, in addition to striking a performative deal with the person who *agrees to act* as a "superior power". But the very methodology of masochist idealisation has many ironic twists: when the idealised Other does accept to perform cruelty, she or he ceases to be "untouchable":

....

Nataša Govedić

the celestial idol turns into a common torturer, which opens the idol to a very real possibility of being criticised. Leopold von Sacher-Masoch constantly stages asymmetrical relationships of power manipulations, made possible through another ironic device: *contracts* signed between participants. These contracts articulate the power relations, giving control over the staged suffering to one or another party, in a limited time-frame and with various fetishist details. Because of the contractual relationship between Sacher-Masoch's actors, Gilles Deleuze (1991) suggests that the typical masochist is not a victim, but a conscious manipulator. He manipulates fantasy, not necessarily bodies. Deleuze (1991: 66): "Through the contract, that is through the most rational and temporarily determinate act, the masochist reaches toward the most mythical and most timeless realms ..."

This manipulation with voluntary participation in pain, the interest in making a display of one's pain, is true of contemporary performance as well. In more recent theatre and performance history, we also find another idealisation (and mythologisation) of pain – I am referring here to Artaud's "theatre of cruelty". Artaud considers theatre based on text as a "perversion of passivity" (cf. Derrida, 1978: 237), of which we can be freed only through the theatre of cruelty as theatre of sensuality, theatre created *from body to body*. "The desire for Eros", says Artaud (cf. Green, 2000: 146), "is cruel since it consumes contingencies. Death is cruelty, resurrection is cruelty, since in all direction within a circular enclosed world there is no room for the true death, since ascension is a rending, finite space feeds on lives, and every stronger form of life passes the others, and so eats them in a massacre that is a transfiguration and a good". Artaud is obsessed with "derepresentation", with the myth of absolute and live presence, presence created through and only through the suffering body (which is why the Christ figure is never too far from this vocabulary). I will not enter here into the wider discussion of why breaking the representation veils or inaugurating "the real presence" by means of performance or the total equation of *life* and *art work*, is impossible in the order of art, and why every body on stage constantly reproduces different cultural references, because those ideas are well developed in the work of Arthur Danto. When something or someone becomes an artwork, it ceases to be a *real thing*, claims Danto. Art necessarily transforms the body into a specific referential order. There are, however, certain phenomena caught *between* art and reality, which Danto calls "disturbational art". Here the artist uses objects that *really are* that which they represent. Danto suggests that disturbational art reflects the cultural desire to regress toward a much earlier symbolic realm, when a god (or a saint) was materially and *magically* present in the ritual symbolically staged around him, in order to present and represent him at the same time. In disturbational art, we are therefore dealing with works or events that are, in Danto's opinion, incantatory and striving to recreate this sense of magical equality between life and art. But that is not all. Furthermore, the disturbational artist aims to transform his or her audience into something pre-theatrical, a body of participants which relate to the artist in a more magical and transformational relationship than the usual conventions of theatre viewing allow. It is often the case in contemporary art that being postdramatic is in fact the same as going back to become pre-theatrical, while the mixture of *violence and the sacred* (especially as they are conceptualised in the works of Rene Girard) aims to create a magical, even liturgical reality, not "merely" art.

One of the paradoxes of performance art or of body art, from its flowering in the 1970s up to the present day, is precisely the aforementioned and extremely conscious "blurring of the line between art and life". That is also why, as Kathy O'Dell claims, performance art has, since its beginnings, created special zones of masochistic representation. Here is O'Dell (1998: 11):

> Masochistic artists responded to this social and political confusion [of art and reality] in two ways. On the one hand, they duplicated the painful effects of such a separation, and, on the other, they showed the paradoxical necessity of splitting the signifier and referent to clarify their difference and to make sense of the representations that shape our lives. Using masochism as a metaphor, performance artists (…) articulated this split and its inherent pain.

It is precisely this anxiety of alienation, the anxiety of separation between art and life, that gets staged in many performance pieces. Or we can quote Anita Philips, who says that every "artist is a professional masochist" (1998: 45), because he or she is supersensitive to suffering; unable to ignore it or keep quiet about it. With Anita Philips we move on to another interesting question: how are we, as civilisation, socially equipped to share pain? Besides the participation in tragedy or in Christ's passion and other *grande* religious tales, are there any accepted secular models of discussing or sharing pain and death? If we follow Freud, maybe we can regard sexuality as the most common erotisation of painful experiences. But contrary to what Freud says, masochism seems to cover much wider range of phenomena than sexual choice, from courtly love and ecstasies of the saints to romantic idealisations and professional self-sabotage, which proves that masochism is not just some kind of secluded and marginal "sexual pathology".

Today, masochism is broadly understood to be a strategic and instrumental behaviour: it aims to accomplish something *through* suffering, which nevertheless goes *beyond* suffering, *by means of* its inscenation. Masochism is indeed most provocatively theatrical, since it demands strict role-taking, which functions as a negotiating tool. The favourite role of masochism is the role of the obedient servant. In masochism, one "pays the price of pain" in order to dare to violate either moral or ideological norms. Especially targeted are oppressive social norms; various costumes that divide society into masters and slaves. Whenever we *stage* oppression as a reversible "costume rehearsal" – and Jean Genet has demonstrated this point brilliantly – we undermine the official rigidity of power representations; we make fun of it; we are opening the stage for the potential ironisation of power structures. The masochist therefore pursues the forbidden pleasures of mocking the superego; the masochist reformulates the violence of the superego, refusing to accept it simply as a norm.

Hence masochism seems to be a powerful transgressive tool.

....

Nataša Govedić

The masochist contract stipulates that pain is mutually listened to, articulated and per-formed. In other words, the pain is shared. Contrary to sadism, masochism tends to personalise cruelty, turning it into a scripted exchange of intimate knowledge and intimate drama-therapy about personal humiliations. Although sadism equally explores power relations, the favorite "drama" the sadist wants to play is the break of trust and the role of "avenger", someone who theatrically identifies with and thereby glorifies the violence of the superego. Sadists and masochists, as the research of Anita Philips shows, do not go well together, because the pain they feel and perform is very different. Still, they do have several things in common: concern with discipline, servitude and trust.

Let us now turn to Felix Ruckert's performance, called *Secret Service*. The "manipulation" of individual anxiety in Ruckert's theatre is literally staged and *shared*: by individually entering the show, each audience member verbally consents to its conditions. The audience is warned in advance that performers will be manipulating (moving, leading, touching) their bodies. If we agree to this, we are blindfolded, asked to be completely silent, to remove our shoes, and then led by the hand through a series of circular movements in order to be disoriented. The entire transaction requires *trust*, not only trust in the theatre as a shield that institutionally protects us from actual violence, but trust in a specific human being, completely unknown to us, unseen by us, who acts as our "guide". What proceeds to unfold gradually is unpredictable, sensual, tactile communication between an audience member and a performer, sometimes a group of performers. The cooperative contract is established exclusively by the languages of two (or more) bodies. I would like to stress that in Western societies, touch-to-touch communication between strangers is extremely rarely exercised in public: it is reserved for the most private of encounters. That is why many people refused to enter the chambers of *Secret Service*: given what they learned from the press and theatre materials, the prospect of being touched by unfamiliar persons sounded far too intrusive. But Ruckert's performers displayed much more sophisticated understating of masochism. His dancers are trained to respond to the bodily reactions of the participants; they can play it rough or gentle, they can choose to move as professional dancers or walk around the stage slowly, as pedestrians. What happens between the participant from the audience and the dancer is constantly open to negotiation. The dancer is not just a passive "mirror" of the participant's choreography. The performer we are joined with also "suggests" to us different movements and gestures, leans over our body or starts to run suddenly, drags our whole body down or in an unexpected direction, chooses to sit down or massage our neck. For our part, we can join in and further develop these performative suggestions, remain passive (which is also a form of acceptance), offer something else or put a stop to everything. Whatever we choose to do, our trained guide (we get a chance to communicate with both male and female dancers) remains "at our service", never imposing himself or herself upon us too insistently, but we are just as much *at his or her service*, because the physical bond, the bond of mutual touch, continues to happen without even the slightest pause. For me, it was very interesting to observe the gendered codes of bodily communication during the performance. I was much more relaxed, playful and experimental when touched by female performers, and more reticent in the firmer grip of male dancers. This is not only a result of my own gender or sexual prejudices and preferences, but also of the different behaviour which my male and female partners chose to exhibit. It was a male dancer who repeatedly tried to tickle my neck by blowing on it softly and scratching it with his stubble, which I found funny and physically pleasant, but at the same time transgressive and indicating a movement toward erotic behaviour. It seemed to me that both dancers and audience were perfectly able to recognise the fragile boundary between "being personally in touch" and "being involved in an eroticised touch". Sometimes the dancers could point or step to that boundary, without ever transgressing it seriously. Nevertheless, the boundary was established. With female dancers I noticed a pronounced concern not to disturb my side of the contract, based on the communication of sheer playfulness, without erotic connotations or provocations leading to an exchange of violence. When I lost my earrings during dancing, a female hand slowly approached my palm and returned them to me. On a few occasions female hands also adjusted my clothes, for instance, when my skirt was crumpled, which also made me feel "secure". I really trusted the female dancers. I felt lonelier with male dancers, because they used a vocabulary of sometimes aggressive, deliberately challenging sudden twists, throwing me off balance or pressing their bodies firmly against mine. I refused to return or repeat any aggressive gesture that was suggested to me; I tried to respond to them in the same way that I would to a hand of a child pushing me: by stopping it and then caressing it in a nonsexual manner. You could say that my efforts throughout the performance were focused on translating the staged asymmetries of power into a much more inclusive choreography. To my surprise, all the partners I met in the performance eventually accepted the combination of bodily curiosity and expressive kindness as a code of our physical communication. We could touch freely, roll on the floor, run or enact most elementary figures of contact improvisation and different playful gravitation exercises, audibly laugh or feel the other gesturing discomfort or even fear, but through it all I persistently refused to perform the conventional roles of master or slave. The *secret service* I needed and enjoyed during the performance of Ruckert's company was closest to a mutual offering of friendship, painful only in the sense that it would not outlive the moment of the performance; it would stay encapsulated in the time of its realisation, in its mute anonymity, the silence of the dance. In a sense, it was therefore a pure "rite of passage": a living, ritualised connectedness that changed not only our levels of consciousness, but also our emotional map of responsiveness. I learned that I can make a connection without language, that I can freely explore different bodies, their gestures, textures and smells, as well as the complex tactile fantasies of the performers themselves. The performance also changed my "social" memory, because after the show I remembered body-to-body exchanges, like the touch of female straight, silky, long hair on my hands; very steady and dry male hands massaging my forehead; a man's back and shoulders in a tight T-shirt, dripping with sweat; the fatigue or firmness of different performers' bodies holding my weight. Some of the other audience members also confessed to me that *Secret Service* or being "at the mercy" of Ruckert's performers changed their traditional "computation" of

Nataša Govedić

bodily information, making them feel pampered, not threatened. Body-to-body communication caused many people to feel and later express the healing power of the event, similar to undergoing physical therapy (especially cherished in the society where so many transactions are virtual).

However, the masochistic dimension of the performance was present in my (or the audience's) consent to be only partially in control of this *more than theatrical* event, while at the same time supersensitive to different levels of performance anxiety. Personally, during the performance I also thought about Yoko Ono's *Cut Piece*, performed in Kyoto (1964) and New York (1965), where Ono offered audience members a pair of scissors with which they could snip the clothing from her body, thereby touching her and leaving her naked. This mixture of the audience starting the bodily dialogue with the artist's voyeuristic pleasures and at the same time ending ironically "caught" with scissors in their hands, reminded me again of the S / M context of performance art in general. Some of Ruckert's previous pieces, for instance, *Hautnah* (1995), similarly play on the sadomasochistic economy of the audience/dancer relationship. This is Andre Lepecki's description of *Hautnah* (cf. *The Drama Review* 43.4, 1999, p. 135):

143   We enter a room. We expect dance but all we get is a body; a body so close we can smell it, spot its imperfections, feel its warmth, even its sweat streaming down our own skin. We are so close we can touch it, or be touched by it. Time goes by and what subsides after that choreographed encounter is the shock of being forced to be present. Ruckert forces encountering down our throats. Closeness replaces nakedness' shock-value. He slaps our expectations of what bodies are supposed to be and do in certain contexts: the dancer's, our own.

As a theatre piece, *Secret Service* seems to be more complex and less cynical, since it profits from the interweaving of ironisations and intimacies, and opens up a possibility of personal encounters between the performer and the audience member. The jouissance of irony is, nevertheless, profoundly and constantly mixed with the jouissance of connectedness. To tackle irony first, to me it seems threefold: directed towards superego laws, then theatre practices (especially the idea of the "passive viewer") and finally towards the conventional understanding of S / M practices as something pathological. In superego laws, we are not allowed to explore each other bodily if we are not in some kind of erotic relationship. But Ruckert's performers become our "slaves" in order to bridge their own and perhaps our own social and emotional alienation. This is both shocking and inspiring. Theatre practice is ironised because the classical boundary or the ancient opposition of actor *versus* spectator is deeply disturbed by turning both parties into "participants", responsive performers[2]. This shift enables the understanding of manipulation as something mutual and creative. Masochism is experienced as a kind of active *corpography*, not as a clinical deviance that proves the human potential for luxuriating in pain.

The valid masochistic contract within the theatre frame is furthermore importantly staged as a stark contrast to *invalid* political and social contracts. In social contracts, from Rousseau and Parsons to John Rawls and Carol Pateman, taking care of other citizens (and their pain) is a prerequisite for any sense of community. But when citizens choose to remain "apparently" passive when confronted with the suffering of their fellow-creatures, they are not simply "breaking" the social contract; they also demonstrate that passivity, just like active participation in communal affairs, powerfully dictates the political priorities and agenda.

Lack of involvement with politics turns out to be *the most* political personal choice. Why? Because it is this paradoxical, false "passivity" of the civil body that enables, verifies and allows state atrocities, wars, injustice, corruption and torture around the world. While masochism as instrumental behaviour acknowledges the personal experience of suffering and often repeats gestures and methods of socially unjust institutions in order to relive it with a newly attained sense of personal power, political contracts – as *public service*, contrasted to Rucker's "secret service" – are only declaratively interested in human beings and their losses, while in reality they constantly affirm the praxis of social indifference, alienation and further bureaucratisation.

In one of the biggest war scandals of the year 2004, photographs of tortured Iraqi prisoners in Abu Ghraib prison shocked the world, traveling around the globe only to end up as exhibits at The International Centre of Photography in New York and the Andy Warhol Museum in Pittsburgh, Pennsylvania. These two art institutions co-operated to present an exhibition called *Inconvenient Evidence: Iraqi Prison Photographs from Abu Ghraib*. Interestingly enough, the prison photos document the choreography of sadistic, predominantly sexual "inscenations" of the prisoners' humiliation (for instance, a US soldier ordering a naked detainee covered with "brown matter" to walk a straight line with his ankles handcuffed, or a smiling US officer torturing a detainee with wires attached to his genitals), which means that political and military violence is, at the first glance, heavily visualised and sexualised. But just like in the case of rape, violence here only mimics sexuality, while actually mirroring destructive and much less visible power structures. It is sad to observe such a speedy reframing of explosive political content of abusive acts by military institutions into something as elusive as art, without any legal action on the part of the international community or large scale civil demonstrations that could force governments to investigate and limit American military power, especially its occupation of Iraq.

I believe civil passivity stems from the citizens' broken trust in official institutions, which indicates that the official social contract – as we know it – has, in fact, expired. The state is performatively inefficient to stop atrocities, regardless of whether they happen on a national or an international level. On the other hand, society bonds that are established only when we make skin-to-skin contact with strangers seem tragically limited. But is there an alternative? Where can we find an operative, nonviolent community? I choose to believe that Felix Ruckert's performances are reformational because they make a huge *personal effort* to approach the audience one body at a time, transforming each participant into a social actor, concerned with body politics. The lesson of *Secret Service* is similar to many lessons learned from green or feminist activism: community is established by the

Nataša Govedić

most ancient methods of personal contact, personal care, bodily presence, and "being-in-touch" physically, not just virtually. If we want to change the system, we must do it with our bodies, not *only* representational thea / tricks.

[1]   cf. Thomas S. Weinberg and G.W. Kamel, "S&M: An Introduction to the Study of Sadomasochism," in *S&M: Studies in Dominance and Submission*, Prometheus Books, 1995, pg. 19.

[2]   Ruckert's metodology is the exact opposite of what John E. McGrath in his book *Loving Big Brother: Performance, Privacy and Surveillance Space* (2004: 170-221) calls "spectators as an event", where the spectators endlessly and passively watch-themselves-watching-the-theatre-or-TV-show, therefore submitting themselves to a global order of visual suveillance (as described by Foucault). Ruckert's performance forbids and breaks the order of the gaze and stages the contact between human skins.

Politics of performing

147

CODEXXI (Manifesto)

Mala Kline

We / AGON feel something is changing, though we curiously wonder as we strive to detect and define the territory of this change. A transformation is in progress; soon we will track down its features.

We look at the arts and sciences, the spaces where new or alternative knowledge is produced, and wonder where and how something will happen. How, with the sensibility, technology and history of this moment, a shift towards a new perspective will emerge. How it will subvert the dominant consciousness and our way of experiencing the world.

Let us, in our search for a possible new opening, re-examine the essential features of performance art, namely – subversion, emancipation, transgression and form. Thus we will speak of the nature and agency of performance art, and try to detect where its political potentiality and actuality lie.

Subversion:

At the beginning of the 21st century it again seems necessary to radically review the political contextualisation of performance art. What becomes important is whether performance art can properly (re-?)act to the demands of the new enslavement and expropriation trendily lightly incorporated into global space and time –

We are all insiders. There is no way out, but there is a way through. Subversion is thus no longer "a reaction against" or "a resistance to", it is rather a passage. The logic of today is rather to "know your enemy and fight without resistance". The potential strategies have to do with finding how to use the power of the enemy through one's own centre. To be there before: avant-garde.

Subversion does not happen as a rebellion against existing structures and patterns of thought and behaviour. It rather happens as an act, an act of creation – genesis – of another order, a different order.

We believe that it is still possible to create a body, an organism, a structure which works like a mirror one can pass through and come out of. We believe that with an awareness of one's own position in the present matrix of space and time, and with the creative use of one's own knowledge of the (web-) structures into which one is integrated; a re-articulation and re-framing of the existing order, and so, a creation of a body of a new form and logic becomes possible. Such a body is a reflection of arising thought, a possible bridge to it, a shift towards it. It is, again, a manifestation of something real and alive, a break through the surfaces, through fixations. A new look.

Emancipation:

Emancipation is a never-ending process of actually taking distance from constructions, from the too obvious. It is a continuous creative transformation of obstructions. It is a constant search for "an action" which creates a rupture. It is a way of opening space, a way of creating conditions, where "anything can happen", where an invention or a discovery is always possible.

149

The awareness of obstructions is calling one to let go of the love-embrace with one's phantoms. To let go continuously is the first condition for coming closer to the real, for participation in a real event, a real encounter.

Emancipation is a necessary condition for negotiating a rupture. Rupture emerges through the creation of a new order. Thus, rupture is always a subject of negotiation – of the present with the past, of the one with the other.

The emancipation of the negotiator brings a higher responsibility – of one towards oneself, of one towards the other that is taking part – in becoming –

Transgression:
Every action, every choice, every decision one makes is a potential act of creation.

It no longer suffices to define transgression as a denial of past doctrines, as the breaking of rules, principles, conventions, taboos, or as an insult, or as the erasing of physical or conceptual borders.

Transgression is an act of creation. An act of creation is an opening of a new territory. Through an act of creation a rupture is negotiated in the present space and time. An act of creation is negotiation between the past, the forgotten and the forbidden within the present and the potential of the present itself.

Transgression as an act of creation is a trace, a presence that resonates both in a cultural context and within the experience of a single human being, and generates new ways of seeing and being.

Political agency:
Every work of art is an uncommitted crime.

For us the political potential of art lies in its form.

Form:
Today it is necessary to re-affirm Art.

Re-affirm the power for resistance and invention through Art.

Art is a process of transformation of the sensual accomplished in the emergence of an idea.

Art can make the invisible visible, it is able to present something before the fact, before the evidence.

Through invention art makes real what was hitherto unknown, surprisingly emerging in the form of a new sensual abstraction that carries and insists with something definite, axiomatic and deeply engaging.

Let us be taken by some truth (or beauty – it is the same thing) instead of carefully focusing ourselves on less important modes of expression. (Badiou)

....

Mala Kline

<u>Response:</u>
The only way we / AGON start to answer these questions is by recognising our need for Labouratory, by creating our vision of Labouratory and by beginning to realise it.

Labouratory is a space where work is continuously evolving through conceptually framed research and exploration.

It is a space where working methods are developed.

It is a place where experimentation is possible and also a mistake, rather in the sense of mutation, stimulating further the evolution of work.

Labouratory affirms the necessity of artistic research, a process that is vitally connected and responsive to the processes of creation.

Labouratory aims towards uncovering a territory where the creation of new forms is possible. Research as well as creation are processes committed to re-questioning the real of the present moment, its aspects, potential and agency, as well as to the interrogation of the past.

It strives for an exchange with the methods of other art-media and for dialogue with theory.

Its strategy is negotiation with different kinds of knowledge and different kinds of agency, and a constant awareness of possible alliances with them and among them.

It feeds on interaction with the real outside in order to be able to give further.

151   In the base of its establishment lies a common agreement: Through the inter-connectedness and co-operation of different, but equally responsible individual artists, the work is the only subject that can happen.

A visit to the museum of Gothenburg N.B. Presenting performative research on the politics of visualisations

Ralo Mayer / Philipp Haupt

Hello, just a second: I am re-arranging the following text as an adaptation of a lecture that tried to present what we might call performative research, i.e. process-oriented investigations employing scripts and settings – not as restrictive rules, but encouraging knowledge production and exchange beyond the methodological frameworks of academia or journalism.

In 2002 we started to research on the effects of the anticapitalist protests at the EU Summit in Gothenburg in June 2001, heading for a film on the transformation of urban space. Besides the protests our second starting point was *New Babylon*, a revolutionary urban utopia by the Dutch artist Constant. Coming from situationist ideas, Constant worked from the late 1950s to the early 1970s on a layout for a nomadic and modular city structure, a revolutionary urban matrix spreading around the globe.

After collecting numerous interviews with activists, our interest shifted more and more towards a general look on visualisation processes and their role in power structures: What is it that makes diagrammatic depictions so fascinating, how can they help to layout both revolutionary situationist ideas and the sophisticated repression of post-Fordist liberal democracy? In Gothenburg the regime of order and control had violently materialised when police shot at protesters: a power vector right through the body. It is through such an escalation that some trajectories of the overall power diagram become visible for short moments.

Excuse me, just one more thing before we go on: The pictures are missing here, but then the argumentation is based so much on images. And the sound of different voices is missing, and how does the multitude sound in printed matter?

So there are two distinct crystallisation points from which we departed: Gothenburg and the protests against the EU Summit are a paradigm for the broader social, economical and political developments of the last years and the new resistance movements. New Babylon, the protosituationist city, on the other hand is an example for the cluster of aesthetic and political radical movements of the 1960s.

"The following presentation will be an illustrated trip across some areas of the politics of information visualisation." Like a guided tour, it will connect scattered places at different times, trying to render an overview of our research of the last years.

"'Our research' means that the material was gathered by many persons, not only the two of us."

As a matter of fact, this will of course produce fragmentary impressions of fiction and reality – but such a multi-faceted image is the one we are working with ourselves. Maybe the tour starts in February 2002 in Den Haag:

"I was part of a student group visiting the *New Babylon* archive in the Gemeente Museum. The guide explained how the artist Constant quit painting in the 1950s and started to deal with architecture, influenced by the nomadic life of the gypsies. He became part of the Situationist International and joined their struggle against the hegemonic capitalist life in the west and the modernist and functionalist planning of life. In line with what later would be coined the 68'-movement, their revolt was against post-war society, trying to break up all the disciplinary divisions between private and public, work and leisure time …"

Constant set out to design plans for a revolutionary urban matrix. For almost twenty years he produced models, drawings, diagrams, maps, texts, etc., to illustrate the structure of *New Babylon*.

New Babylon ends nowhere, since the earth is round. It spreads on top of existing cities, a meta-level of permanent browsing and nomadic life. Although the models and drawings look like building designs, they are more diagrams of the actual flux of social life in a city.

It was not by chance that some art students visited the archive in 2002: Since the mid-90s, *New Babylon* had been rediscovered as an early utopian depiction of ongoing transformations in the context of Information Technologies: *New Babylon* is the Network Society with all its technological and social implications *avant la lettre*.

(*L'Année dernière à Gothenburg*)

"One month later, in March 2002, I visited Gothenburg for the first time: Everything I knew about the city was connected to the protests against the EU Summit one year earlier –"

"– when we first heard that the police had shot at demonstrators, the differing rumours on the net, no one knew if someone had died, the news with pictures of the riots."

(*The well-known picture of the burning EU flag on top of a barricade is shown, in a shopping street in Gothenburg, thick black smoke rising*)

"With these images still in mind, some local people from Gothenburg gave us a guided tour, showing places that we had only seen on indie media and the corporate news. Some months later, people involved in the protests were telling me in interviews that they could not manage to bring together the different images and realities during and after the protests. They could not believe that the same familiar street had been the site of riots where they would now sit and drink coffee again. The only trace left was where one of the police bullets had scratched a light pole …"

But some of the activists said that no real change had happened – that just hidden faces of everyday violence and repression had come to the surface during the protest. The riots and the police violence had destroyed the image of the "good" Sweden, thus performing a visualisation of ongoing struggles in society.

"The following winter we visited the Museum of Natural History in Vienna. We were out for the world-famous mineralogical collection."

About a century ago, the German art historian Worringer distinguished two aesthetic regimes – the organic and the crystalline: *The crystalline represents a will to abstraction. When a culture feels that it is in conflict with the world, that events are chaotic and hostile, it tends to produce pure geometric forms as an attempt to pattern and transcend this chaos.*

Gilles Deleuze adapts this notion in his second book on cinema, *The Time Image*, to theorise on the notion of the "Time Crystal":

Whereas an organic image shows the object directly, a crystalline description is more provisional and contingent. It replaces the object, continually "erasing" it and creating it anew, giving way to other equally adequate descriptions, which may also modify or contradict the ones preceding it. In the crystalline it is now the description itself which constitutes

the decomposed and multiplied object. Crystalline images presuppose a special relationship
between perception and memory. For each actual description of a physical object, there
corresponds a virtual memory-image of the mind and memory. This virtual image is recol-
lected from chains of associations and memories of past experiences. Each time a virtual
image is called up in relation to an actual description, the object depicted is de-formed and
created anew, widening and deepening the mental picture it inspires.

To put it very simple, one can paraphrase this with a line from the song *Life is Life* from
the Slovenian band Laibach:

Jeder Augenblick der Zukunft ist ein Gedanke an vorher.

or:

Every minute of the future is a memory of the past.

What we found in Deleuze's "Time Crystal" was a model of bringing together our two poles
of research: the old network utopia of *New Babylon* with its revolutionary promises, and the
current rather dystopian realities of the postfordist liberal democracies, exemplified for
instance by structural violence, surveillance and control, repression and the instant re-
integration of all resistance practices.

When looking for a way to spatialise our research, we came across another model of
mixing the past, the present and different places between fiction and reality:

"In 2000, I visited the Salon de Fleurs, a permanent installation situated in an apartment
in Manhattan. The doorman, introducing himself as Goran Djordjević, explained the space:
it was an exact copy of Gertrude Stein's Salon in Paris in the early 20th century. Copies of
essential modernist paintings are hanging on the walls. The whole apartment has an
overwhelming atmosphere of irreality, underlined by the doorman telling stories about the
construction of the history of modern art. When our group was about to go, he handed
over an envelope containing materials of several art pieces."

One of the art works was a small model of a museum-like space. Photos show the model
from above, there are thumbnail-like copies of famous modernist paintings on the mini-
ature walls. There's also a diagram in the envelope, about the history of modern art, by
Alfred Barr, director of the MOMA in New York in the 1930s. The model piece is called
Alfred Barr's Museum of Modern Art. It's a 3D-spatialisation of the diagram. Both the Salon
de Fleurus and the MOMA model remind us of the 1990s conception of "virtual reality".
They are not "real spaces", but rather try to depict structures and connections, links
between the real and the virtual.

For our installation, the *Museum of Gothenburg N.B.*, we tried to build such a space,
a cheap "real" Virtual Reality room, where copies and print-outs would be on the wall, like
results from different web researches. The whole space as rendered Google; for navigation
one could use an audio guide, like in a museum.

The audio guide brings together some background texts and fragments of interviews with
activists:

(During the interview excerpt and the following paragraphs we see several pictures of an art
installation: a small room made of wood and cardboard – mirrors, prints and photocopies

inside: situationist graphics, Debord, Jorn, The Naked City, surveillance diagrams, torn city maps seized by the police.)

"They made it with this computer program to look like … it was so simple, it was just a list about where the apartment was and who they had phoned. But they made these lines all over – like this is one phone and it leads to that phone and that phone leads to that phone and that other phone leads to the other phone and … So it looks really complicated and professional, because it's all these lines and telephone numbers so it looks like it's codes. They tried to map all the sms phones. If you just were in contact with the phone, then you were in this whole net by mobile phones and lines through different phones.

Yeah – in the court – I think that's really when it differs. – Can you say differs? My experience to be in streets and this organised map of the situation was so separated. Like it's something totally different from each other … like in the society … The court, the order, wants it to be organised and that you can have a look at it, like 'here we have the situation and let's look upon it' – when for me it's really impossible to have this overview of the true story."

(The pictures' perspective has shifted from inside the small room to a position above, where we also see a real time 3D rendering of the same space on a monitor.)

"Our idea was that the visitor can both be part of the space and see it from above, starting to see the links between the different data, building info-clusters on her own out of dispersed fragments."

The whole space is actually filled up with invisible lines, connecting all the presented material, reconstructing and opening up hidden paths. While we prepared the installation, we saw in a documentary how police and forensic experts were reconstructing shooting incidents: in order to visualise the lines of shots in space, they would use canes and pipes to trace those invisible trajectories.

We decided to do another field trip, this time to the Vienna police department. They were quite suspicious … Why would artists want to know this? We told them: "Well, we are doing a work about the aesthetics of lines in space". After showing us the old cane and pipe concept, they would then explain that ballistic experts nowadays use a bi-directional laser to follow shooting trajectories.

"– Like an inversion of a laser target finder on a gun."
"It was quite a strange feeling to go to the police to find out more about visualisation models … and it brought to the front once more a feeling we had had for some time: The strange fascination that we felt with all those structures."

We cannot deny that we are quite fascinated with lines and diagrams. This awful impact is a central part of such an aesthetic function in a power structure. A bit like how Walter Benjamin describes fascism as the aesthetisation of politics … Stating this ambiguity of our research, we should come back to another important aspect of Deleuze's "Time Crystal":

One of the key features of the mix of actual and virtual, real and memory is indiscernibility. This term, indiscernibility, refers to the state of being indistinguishable: the real and the

Ralo Mayer / Philipp Haupt

imaginary become indistinguishable in a crystalline description – the crystal rewrites the relations between the forms of the True and the powers of the False, it fractures them into many facets and interweaves their emissions.

This indistinguishable remix of the real and the virtual is the key to understand what Deleuze means by a crystalline image. Like an image produced in a mirror, it always has two poles: actual and virtual. However, it is often difficult to decide what is an "actual" image and what is a "reflection". What this indiscernibility makes visible is the ceaseless fracturing or splitting of nonchronological time.

In the movies, there's often one classic scene connected to museum sites: "In the dark of the night, the thief enters the secured exhibition halls. He or she sneaks in and in order to make the laser beams of the alarm system visible – blows some powder in the air. All of a sudden the space is filled with an enormous structure of red lines ... and now it's possible to navigate in the imposed order of overwhelming structures."

And this certainly brings us back to what some of the activists in Gothenburg said: it only needs some smoke and all of a sudden you see the hidden faces of capitalist liberal democracies, a hidden face that is the everyday reality for marginalised groups in society.

(Once again we see the low-resolution picture of the burning EU flag from the streets of Gothenburg. The image fades to black and suddenly re-appears. A final comment is read from the script:

157   "Until recently we agreed with such a political statement for 100%, but right now we feel that this image – and the specific activist strategy connected to it – turn into what might be called a 'memory of the political' – and that is not the political as such any longer. So the struggle for the means of visualisation and representation continues.

Based on statements by Gilles Deleuze, Goran Djordjević, Tomas Haglund, Alex Hall, Gustaf Hansson, Kajsa Johansson, Laibach, Linus Lundin, Kevin Lynch, Constant Nieuwenhuis, Christophe Nilsson, Jennie Oberg, D.N. Rodowick, Oskar Sjödin, Jonas Söderqvist, Nina Sörensen, Leila Vianden and others.

Short remarks on the politics of collabouration

Claudia Bosse / Christine Standfest

a bang.

… the light falls onto a bare-shaven skull in which a bomb just has exploded. the spot widens, and the light reaches the tightly packed podium on which one place is empty. in the auditorium, a man wearing a coat detaches himself from a conspiratory conversation with a group of men. he jumps onto the podium, effectively taking the empty place. ever so often, he gives strange signs to the group which he has just left. the man with the bomb on his head now tries to regain the attention he has lost, alternating between complaint and humour of the suppressed. because of successively entering vips and ips, he has to repeat himself continuously, while the man in the coat ignores him suavely, waving now and again to the group of men left behind, which now begins to disperse evenly throughout the whole dimly lit auditorium …

thus – or similarly – might begin a piece about the scenario of the panel *politics of collabouration* in vienna, during which we had presented our theses on the politics of collabouration. the theses are contextually linked with our practice. a practice which among other things takes place under the label *firma raumforschung*.[1]

to begin with, there's the problem of totalitarian measures and the authorisation of the spectator, the problem of theatre itself:

in order to disrupt certain habits of watching and certainties of receptions, totalitarian acts are necessary which set free the production of meaning, and in the best case create positions in the audience. a position is provoked, challenged by artistic strategies – to be more exact, several positions, confronting themselves with theatre, the reception of theatre, and the production of text and bodies.

most theatrical assignments presuppose acquiescence – something is shown, presented, one agrees. however, the main thing is not shown in the showing but provoked in the space between showing, production, and the recipient. theatre can provoke communication and political positions through the usage and materiality of its medium, not only through that which is staged and presented. the act of taking up and deciding oneself about actions and positions is the possibility of the theatre – for the actor as well as the recipient, the co-producer of the theatrical situation. all are present, spending a common time together which is exceptional, structured by artificial means. this makes it possible to reflect everyday matters in the situation of another logic and sensitivity of time and signs. a reception and communication capable of attacking everyday experiences and questioning their logic.

only the wilful disruption of habitual perception can enable the process of authorisation of the spectator. questioning the ruling aesthetic and political and communicative strategies through a theatrical concept, in the materialisation of another: of another language, other bodies in other situations, etc. – that is the subversion of the theatre. the theatre is capable of being a labouratory of societal as well as aesthetic and representative practices at the same time. that is its potential. the one strategy can be juxtaposed to the other, but only in open spaces in which everyone shares the situation and becomes an actor. actor of himself / herself within a negotiable situative contract, and spectator of the other societal actors, their mien of acceptance or denial. thus not only is the actor an actor or the dancer a dancer who observes, but all on this societal stage observe each other simultaneously, acting in the representation of their kinship in following the observation of all bodies, in reading their economies of attention. here, though, this is a collective act of production in the sharing of concentration, in following formulation.

and secondly, there are the economies, spaces, temporal economies and other frames which form the conditions of collabouration: the spatial, temporal, economical and hierarchical structures of the working process define the potentiality of each artistic work and have to be understood as a creative, political and aesthetic definition and act. the frame of every artistic work has to be (re)defined because these are the possible structures of collabouration – internal, meaning within the artistic process, and external, meaning the public part of the artistic process. the frame of every institution has to be questioned and redefined for each artistic process; otherwise, the institution would predefine the artistic potentiality.

spatial settings and space implications are part of the social structure as well as part of the artistic possibilities and potential, and they shape the relations concerning public collabouration. a way to create something like collective knowledge has to ask for its spatial, social, and economic situations and conditions.

the institutional space settings are self-reproductive. they are part of saving the institutional hierarchies of working structures as well as communication structures with the public. the ghost of collabouration often means the possibility for curators to manage better the symbolic capital. how does the deal of values in the artistic field work?
we (still) believe that there is political – not to say radical – power in the modes of cooperation, which become if not visible, then sensible – and sensitive – for the actors as well as the audience in production, who at their very start have something like an agreement (*Einverständnis*) with rules beyond the rules of the market (economy, hierarchy, structures – the frames).

let us add another highly questionable word: commitment. here, the question is how far this commitment is, let's say, personal, mimicking family structures in its modes of dependence, trust, libido, considering the often shameful payment – or whether it is the commitment of entrepreneurs, linked via economics – or the narcissistic force nourished by the image of the artist-"genius". all this should be reflected more, and we would very much wish that theory and the theorists could be interested in these questions, stating that these frames shape every production of "meaning", every performance and every collabouration with the spectator / the audience / the public.

we claim that there is as yet no language for that. again this could be linked to the very way in which neoliberal capitalism shapes the surface of behaviour and de-regulates every communication. structurally, we would wish to discuss the frames of production, developing not results but further questions.

....

Claudia Bosse / Christine Standfest

¹ firma raumforschung is a project started in june 2004. it was, and is the attempt of theatercombinat to create a public place of discourse in order to investigate the relations of political, artistic, art historic, city planning, culture critical, sociological, as well as architectural and administrative positions, methods and usage of language.

setting out from henri lefevbre's conception of space, the investigatory issues of the first series were required to perceive space not as given or as a *vis-à-vis* to be observed, but as something which is produced continuously. consequently, the title of the series was *produktion des raums* (documentation at www.theatercombinat.com / raum.htm).

161

Reflecting journals

163

Why do we produce ourselves, promote ourselves, distribute ourselves, explain ourselves and why are we "as well" around?

Goran Sergej Pristaš

Starting from the experience of being the editor-in-chief of performing arts magazine *Frakcija* for already ten years now, I'd like to emphasise the fact that most of Eastern European performing arts journals (*Maska*, *TkH*, *Frakcija*) came out not only because of some scholars' interest in performance reflection and theory specifically, but also because of the clash of the laws of the art-market and the "law of energies and interest". Reflecting this experience I realise that each issue of the magazine we published was an event for us; and it never engaged theorists only, but mainly the artists who are always in the situation or the need of producing themselves, promoting themselves, distributing themselves and explaining themselves. At the same time I realise that we've been seriously considered in the performing arts circuit mainly because of our writing on brand-jokers, which was not the case in circles not related to the performing arts. *Frakcija* achieved international interest after we started writing on artists who were already in the focus of interest. Why are the pages on Eastern European artists still blank pages in our magazines? Why are those texts not referential at all? Is it because the overall interest and existing energies do not produce a pregnant moment? And, are we simply too *egoEastic*?

It seems to me that Eastern European artists spent a long time striving to make a transfer from being regionally, contextually defined into being whatever they *want*.

But the basic transfer was made from the so-called transitional identity (transition meaning that we are becoming the same, just more redistributed and actualised) into a dis-orientalised exemplarity. Most of the Eastern European artists present on the "scene of redefinition" in performing arts figure as exemplary; those who are paradigmatic, shown alongside, purely linguistic beings, those who take part in the language, who are there as well, their own neighbours, over-identified with themselves. They are being-called, they communicate in the empty space of the example, without being tied by any common property. As Agamben would describe examples, they "appropriate belonging itself, tricksters or fakes, assistants or 'toons, but exemplars of coming community". (*The Coming Community*)

So, what is wrong there? I would say: nothing.

Taking the place of their own presentation, "but also" the neighbours' place, or the place of "as well", those artists are taking the place of existence, but also they have the power of not being and the power of not-not-being at their own disposal. Or to be subject to their own will. Taking the place of an artist on the market, "as well" as the places of producers, promoters, distributors, publishers and critics, they do take part in the game, they are a part of the problem, but they also invest their own will in multiple common space, being by their own will, being actually non-representable.

That might be the reason why we will find one of the most interesting artistic strategies in the work of artists who operate in the volatile field of dramaturgy: who knows the difference between Bojana [Bojana Kunst] and Bojana [Bojana Cvejić], are they pronounced as Bozhana or Bodžana, Tsveik or Kviich, are they philosophers, performers, editors, cultural politicians, do they deal with music or body art? But everybody knows who is Kunst. I don't want to enter now the enumeration of "they are not this" or "they are not that" which would serve me to express something ineffable, because those "not's" are deprived of all representative functions, in order to point to something which is beyond representation, which would then be some new Eastern European mysticism. It would be too *egoEastic*.

I would keep here on the line of Boris Groys who says that in the time of drying up of affirmative, legitimizing discourse, the chance of Eastern European artists lies in the production of discursive value. Or as Badiou would say, to fight the easy language, the language of journalism, the expression of hatred, of any inventive and delivered naming. Instead of repeating the question, "Did I choose the wrong language?", we have to understand that the production of discourse value brings up a new paradox: The confrontation of discourse and capital manifests itself in the fact that capital is also a legitimising force – that's the way how capitalism regulates discourse.

The paradox of the contemporary artist is that he / she is in a mimetic relation to capital, he is like a capitalist, especially the conceptual artist – he is the appropriator, he selects, combines, transports, resituates.

The paradoxical situation of Eastern European artists is that they are most often the capitalists with a positive *ressentiment* especially towards the commercialisation of life style and the commodification of discourse. But they still requalify, they are mobile, regularly change jobs and combine differing fields of work. If there is the thesis that East = West, then the theorem of exchangeability would say that East = East – which is not the case because the East is always old-fashioned, and West always equals West. And does West = East hold true? Even in such a discourse of equivalence, we still find at least a field of possible but non-representable differences. One of them is the difference of where something takes the place, the basic difference that Groys makes between Eastern European and Western art – Eastern European art comes from Eastern Europe, it's always seen as information on the state of society of its origin.

The best example of the artistic project with *ressentiment,* which would be seen totally different if it was done by Western artists, might be the *East Art Map*.

But what happens to Eastern European artists being on the blank pages of our magazines? They are examples, they are purely linguistic beings. How come? If we try to think what Eastern European Art is, we will look for its taking-place. But the paradox is that its taking-place, its act of will, its property is defined only linguistically in the word East, because Eastern Europe exists only as being-called. The class of Eastern European art is therefore defined only as a variable, in its "illegitimate totality", as Bertrand Russel would say. Therefore the name=being is amorphous and offers the lifestyle of constant inactuality – which is one of the properties very often annotated to Eastern European art. So, the blank pages are the point of contact, in Agamben's words, with an external space that must remain empty, they belong to an illegitimate class. Our contributors' practices of being whatever, being editors by their own will, artists, producers, curators of their own performances at their own festivals, cultural politicians, is always the event of an outside coming out into the open, "as well" with western artists. But the blank pages, being on the outside, are the face of European arts just as Eastern Europe is the face, the threshold, the passage of Europe, the exteriority that gives it access. The experience of the two Bojanas, of

Goran Sergej Pristaš

the editors of magazines who also are editors in at least two other magazines, of Emil Hrvatin who is from Croatia or Slovenia, or is he Jan Fabre or Janus (or is it only Maska?), directors who are dramaturges actually but perform, they are transformers, the collectives which are their own tactical networks, cultural capitals which are *das Kapital*, all of that is an experience of the limit itself, being on the outside. Their political engagement is to spread their fullness of exteriority that communicates only itself into a badly mediated representation of Eastern Europe. The act of discursive self-legitimisation is not an act of solution in order to overcome limits, but to legitimate the *outside* as strategy both of appearance and disappearance. The act of going and the act of staying.

Dancing sitting down:
Ten years of *Performance Research*

Ric Allsopp

Performance Research:

Performance Research[1] has been publishing critical writing, curating artist's pages and producing collabourative digital publications for almost ten years since 1996 during which time we have produced thirty book-length thematic issues in the field of contemporary performance arts. From the beginning our aim "to promote a dynamic interchange between scholarship and practice in the expanding field of performance" has been paralleled by an interest in the relationship between publication and performance arts. Publication does not in our view simply mean providing a location for publishing or an academic service – though we are classified as an "academic journal" – but questioning and developing the possibilities of publication, its forms and media, as a means of promoting and making visible the breadth and range of contemporary performance arts practice and its shifting and fluid relationship to contemporary culture.

Addressing issues of curating, producing and publishing as crucial aspects of the contemporary, suggests opening up the relationships between social structures and practices, and institutional and scholarly philosophies (about what it is that constitutes arts practice, writing and research) and allows us to make connections between literary, performance and visual cultures. Publishing, curating and producing are not invisible servicing and support practices but active agents of cultural production. The question of visibility / invisibility – how far the activity of producing a journal is recognised or recognisable as a form of cultural intervention, and how we can practically engage with that – is one that has concerned us since our first issue. We see our work as curating a textual and visual object – a material object and familiar book-object that tries to provide a thematic, typographical and editorial framework within which to understand (or at least engage with) its contents. We have tried not to be simply a site or container of discrete objects – a listing of the latest research which is of course the primary role of the conventional academic research journal. The academic journal as typically a neutral framework which can contain a multiplicity of work and discourse announces its own invisibility, hides the apparatus of its own production and becomes an assumed and therefore unproblematic and normative frame from which problematic questions of publication (especially in its relationship to the performance event) disappear. Forms of publication become like the ubiquitous construction and service workers in yellow reflective clothing whose very visibility renders them invisible. Our sense then as a publication has been (in Benjamin's terms of the radical artwork) not to make performance our subject but to attempt to change (in small ways) how contemporary practice performance and the discourses that participates in is published, distributed and made visible – attempting to deal with the problematics of publication through acts of publication.

My approach here will be to provide an inventory of sorts – a stock-taking or listing of our approaches to publication with a recognition of all the exclusions that are implicated by

169

any form of inventory or taking stock. Editing and publishing are conventionally precise zones of exclusion and exclusivity – with systems of peer-review and so forth and we are aware of course of the spoken and unspoken exclusions that *Performance Research* inevitably participates in.

Origins:

The first issue of a journal – or perhaps any equivalent cultural production – is always a form of taking stock and is at the same time projective (a wish-list perhaps)– projecting a sense of possible frameworks for thinking into an uncertain future. It also marks in some way a moment of fracture or rupture from what has gone before.

In the first issue of *PR* (March 1996) called *The Temper of the Times* we invited Forced Entertainment, Mike Pearson (Brith Gof), Heiner Goebbels, Nick Kaye, André Lepecki and others to comment on the temper of those times and imagined the journal as a site of active conversations between artists, writers, and academics.

In our 1996 editorial Claire MacDonald and myself wrote:

> In starting a new journal at a time when concepts of 'the performative' have been widely absorbed into other disciplines, and especially into literary studies, and when the constellation of practices which make up theatre, performance art, dance and music is increasingly broad and cross disciplinary, it seems appropriate to begin with a kind of cultural temperature taking, a placing of way markers which will indicate the direction in which artists and critics may be moving. (…)

In this issue we have placed things together to see if and how they fit, and what they might (not) fit into, to see if the voices and conversations between artists and scholars, curators and editors, that will be heard by the reader, add up to some sense of "temper". It would seem that they do; but the first tentative conclusion that might be drawn is that we cannot any longer imagine ourselves living in "tempered" times. The performance culture of the late twentieth century no longer makes sense within accepted classical or modernist notions of aesthetics, of temperament. The voices that speak through the first issue of PR seem to bear this out. They are not only "out of tune" and "distempered" but have already shifted into building from other starting points, other ideologies, other identities which begin to make their own instruments with which to encounter, celebrate and confront the temper of these times. Performance now seems more a means of tampering with the times, trying to shift the fixities of identity, culture, ideology, formal concerns. We hope that the voices that emerge will add to a new and dynamic sense of tuning for our times.

So almost ten years later, despite significant cultural, political and ideological shifts, we would still see these as central questions, positions and approaches to the problems of publishing in the field of performance, that is, in relation to live, event-based, sited work. Looking back over time we can now see the ruptures, fault-lines and shifts that we could not have predicted, and that have inexorably altered the conditions in which performance, dance, theatre, publication, can be made or can be read, or experienced.

....

Ric Allsopp

We founded the journal in 1996 negotiating with the London-based academic publishers Routledge so that we could take a long view on performance as a set of cultural practices and not be beholden to the fluctuations and trends of arts policies and funding. We saw the conventional journal format as a challenge – negotiating a print-media publication that could contain as much visual / graphic material as we wanted – that could use its format to find ways of approaching the problematics of performance: its event-based nature, its ephemerality, its disappearance. So from the beginning our aim has been to make an enquiry into publication as means extending performance.

In our first issue André Lepecki wrote that "by promoting a new logic of moving, dance can establish new time, new choreographies of giving, new routes away from home", and our work over the last ten years suggests that publication too, as an act of making public, of making visible the complex cultural connectivities of the art work, can establish new time, new ways of giving, new ways from home. We are certainly not unique in this endeavour, but we would like to think that we are distinctive.

Approaches:

How does *Performance Research* operate as a "cultural production"? *Performance Research* does not see itself primarily as a site for the systematic elabouration of theoretical discourse or practical research, or for the advocacy of particular methodological approaches or groups of artist / practitioners – which is often the perceived role of the academic journal or the cultural magazine. This isn't to say that *PR* is not produced for a rather specific readership – which it clearly is. *PR* is heterogeneous and heterglossic. It is held together by its thematic approach both within each single issue and within the framework of the four-issue volume. It reflects in the distribution and array of its contents (a balance of scholarly, critical and artist's work) a linkage to the academic world (particularly over the last twenty years in the UK) as a supportive, and generative site for contemporary artists / practitioner research – but also makes links to locations and networks of practice and research outside the academy – for example: TQW / Mousontum / independent journals / artists' groups and artist-run institutions, galleries etc. / regional and international networks in performance.

A number of approaches have made the journal distinctive as a site or forum for research set within a framework of "conventional" academic journal publishing. I will mention a couple:

Critical Page:

It is interesting to note that the format / metaphor of the critical page typically conforms to a normative disposition of the human body: the head(er), the gloss or tongue; the spine, the body, the figure, the appendix, the foot(er) – and reading of course to the verticality of the body and the presentation of the visual (and by extension textual) world. The contingencies of publishing mean that texts that attend (as a part of the construction of meaning) to the visual page, to typography and to space as part of a critical work, are seen as either unpublishable or merely "creative". It is assumed that they cannot cross into critical space, which is highly conventionalised textually. *PR* has consistently tried to question the conventions of critical space and actively work with artists and writers to find suitable forms for critical work (for example Nick Kaye's 1997 work with Need Company).

Artist's Pages:

This has constituted curatorial work with artist's and the page as site for performance resulting in the publication of around 110 artists' page-based work to date. Artist's pages, page-works and prepared pages are some of the terms we have and continue to use since the inception of the journal in 1996 when we conceived of the page in terms long appropriated by composers, language poets and visual artists – as a bounded piece of space time which has to engage the reader / viewer within a range of conventions which can be ignored or creatively disrupted. Inviting artists to consider the page as a material, visual and textual space, as a site of performance and or its traces, or as a key to, of foundry of performance, has enabled *PR* to reflect the de-stabilisation and dislocation of text in its relation to performance events, and use the printed page (the literary site) in ways that move beyond the customary format and design constraints of the journal as print-medium and format.

Collabouration:

Publication (if not simply thought of as a conduit or print-media service) is always collabourative and PR has in various ways been a collabourative project: with artists, with academics and with art institutions. To take two brief examples:

Our collabouration with the Institute for Digital Arts and Technology (at the University of Plymouth) is an ongoing project (or series of projects since 2000) focusing on the publication of performance-based, event-based and other types of live and otherwise difficult and unstable materials for a wide audience of researchers and practitioners. We are currently developing a suite of digital tools called Liquid Reader that enable a reader / user to explore content and material that can flow through diverse media forms. The *On the Page* DVD commissioned a collabourative project with five event-based artists (or groups of artists) which explored the possibilities of work that flowed between the fixities of the printed page and the ephemeral performance event, between screen-media and page-based print media. The recently published *On Civility* DVD represents the third project that has enabled PR to engage with publication as itself a research practice centrally engaged with issues of documentation, dissemination, curation, editing and the cultural contexts that surround critical arts practice.

Our current collabourative project with the Slovenian journal *Maska* and the Croatian journal *Frakcija*[2] is partly based on the complementarity of approaches that can be identified between the three journals and based on a collabourative impetus to provide profiles of the work and focus of each of the journals, and the current contexts (political, ideological, theoretical) of contemporary performance work within the orbit (local and

....

Ric Allsopp

international) that each journal publishes within. The collabouration also wants to address and describe the differences of conceptual and practical approach to performance (and its publication) that are always in danger of being erased where traditions of eastern and western european work and thinking meet and in the contexts of wider political and ideological shifts. The questions of language, of translation, of forms of discourse and how they shift and transform within the current European context are also a part of this collabouration.

[1] For further information see http://www.performance-research.net.
[2] The joint issue is published as *Performance Research* Vol.10, No.2 "On Form" (Summer 2005), London: Routledge / Taylor & Francis.

Executing multiplications, issuing publications

Attila Tordai-S.

1 In Bucharest right at the beginning of the nineties, Lia Perjovschi created in her own art studio the Contemporary Art Archive that collected publications, art magazines, catalogues, reproductions taken or photocopied at different exhibitions. By the end of the nineties, CAA had started to function as a database for all those independent alternative artistic initiatives that were created without any support by the state or the local government. She published black and white publications from her archive several times a year. These on the one hand informed and on the other hand put side by side different tendencies. Her newspaper displayed the many independent art initiatives as belonging to the same art scene. She excluded some, included others in her collection, the objectivity of the newspaper was rooted in Perjovshi's subjectivity.

2 Ioan Godeanu's publicational project is strongly interconnected with the virtual institution (The Institute of Construction and Deconstruction) founded and run by him. He reports about the quasi-functioning of the Institution in the Official Bulletin in a regular manner. Godeanu expropriated the bureaucratic language characteristic of institutions and he talks about pseudo-problems of the different pseudo-sectors (The Cultural Reconstruction Program, The One-way Ticket Worldwide Travels, Post News Net, The Black Worker, The Art Departments, Weather Report, The Class Struggle, The .Com Department etc.). The dominance of corporal identity over the personal in everyday life as well as in professional circles indicates the tendency that encloses our daily life in the labyrinth of an institutionalised language game.

3 The *Version* magazine created and edited by the artists Mircea Cantor, Ciprian Muresan and Gabriela Vanga identified itself as a platform for professionals, artists, curators and theoreticians coming from various fields. Actually it functions as an institution – with the only difference that the editors themselves are the artists, curators, managers, etc. of the *place* that is not a building with a serious budget, but a magazine. The *Version* can be an issue with a certain theme; it can be edited by guest curators; at the same time, it can take the form of an art project. The *Version* appears as an art group in different projects as well.

At the end of the nineties, when the Soros Foundation left Romania, a few Romanian artists had already joined the international art circles. The void left by the absence of contemporary art institutions and the dysfunctionality of the existing ones had not been filled with apathy and resignation but with energies that mostly determined the art developments of the following years. To this the recognition has been added that there are new possibilities for art production and cultural distribution at the beginning of the new millennium.[1] While before 1989 in Romania only public institutions and state-owned foundations got the necessary equipment and staff for publishing, in the new century it has become possible to do independent publishing as well as recruiting professionals for the work. Moreover, it has become possible to publish and manage year-long materials that have a low budget and are done either by one person or by a small group of people. Artists have quickly learned the technique of making a publication, so as a consequence publications made by artists have proliferated, and the relation between publishing, artist and art work has changed as well.[2] Discursive artworks have also proliferated. It has become easier to work with documents, to refer to different materials due to the new techniques of multiplication, data acquisition and archiving.[3] Of course, the status of newspapers and art magazines has been changed by the large quantities of photocopied material, the vast number of images that can be digitised, the possibility to download written and visual information from the net – their editing, cutting and subjective selection.[4]

At the same time a view has also become popular claiming that individual art discourse in itself has much less impact than one that belongs to an institution, or quasi-institution, or a certain cultural platform.

In Romania at the end of the nineties, a self-organising process has started that resulted in the appearance of art magazines, newspapers with low budget, all kinds of multiplications and institutions and quasi-institutions founded by artists. This self-organisation has resulted in the simultaneous functioning and weaving of circles of interest that under normal circumstances would have formed different programs, tasks. Overnight, the artist has become a publishing house, leader of an institution, editor without giving up his / her artistic career. This practice has not only increased the visibility and social involvement of the artist but helped to create collabourative projects.[5]

The above mentioned publication projects use the possibility of publishing in different ways, and they show how a publication is created, what is its relation with artistic production. The magazine *IDEA art+society* is not an art publication, but due to its certain methodological solutions it can be easily considered as an institution interested in the production of art. Its columns answer the requirements of the traditional model that a magazine publishes articles that were called upon, or were written earlier and asked to be translated. These articles belong to different columns, they represent archives, answer the art scene, debate socio-political questions or question the intercrossing of society and art.

However, the magazine has two columns (*gallery* and *insert*) that combine publishing and artistic production similar to *art publications* rather than the strategies of publishing a traditional magazine. In this way they connect the magazine to art production. These two columns do not present existing, exhibited artworks, but help to create a work that has not been displayed before. They relate to these works as the workshop that collabourates with the artist relates to the artwork it supports.[6]

Since this, *IDEA art+society* magazine does not claim to be a neutral academic organ either politically or culturally. It considers publishing as an engaged civic practice, a work that challenges people to choose, by presenting before the community questions that are a matter of general concern.[7]

When everyone writes, edits, makes archives the most relevant thing (which connects the different publications) seems to be to create different but authentic cultural platforms.

....

Attila Tordai-S.

Insofar as they describe real contents, hopefully smaller or bigger communities can team up and exist as *places* people like to *visit*.

1 The development of computer sciences has made the moving of data and access to cultural events and texts much easier than it has ever been before. But we need to mention that the prognostic that magazines and other publications made by traditional printing techniques will disappear has not proved to be true. We experience that the old and the new medium are having a simultaneous effect. Artists who edit pages proliferate, magazines printed with traditional technique have the same legitimacy.

[2] A few artists have not only created works with an inkjet printer, but have thought of a format that was the vehicle as well as the publishing/display of the work. These works included cards, posters, notebooks, books and objects that can be multiplicated and distributed.

[3] We had to acknowledge the spreading of conceptual art; however, we need to differentiate between discursive art practice that discusses the ontological questions of art (first of all meaning the art that practices institutional criticism) and art practice that applies formal solutions and mediums just for creating art.

[4] Similar tendencies appeared when photography started to be used for documentation, its influence upon concept art, minimal art, happening, land art or performance art. See Laszló Beke:, *Media/Theory*, Balassi Publishing House, 1997.

[5] But apparently in Romania publications, magazines edited by artists did not work as manifestoes as it would have been expected. Artists considered magazines as the possibility of creating an institution rather than an independent project. (While in Western Europe some artists had started to question more and more the adequate functioning of the institution. This is why in Romania institution criticism was understood pretty late. In most cases institutional models worked out by artists encouraged responsibility for public affairs rather than the incursion of the underground. Moreover, if an art platform that had a low budget could work together with a mainstream institution from abroad or with an artist who displayed in such institutions, this was considered a very important achievement. These artistic initiatives tried to fill the void created by the absence of institutions and legitimacy.

[6] The *gallery* has about twenty pages where an artist taking advantage of the characteristics of the magazine can present a project. The *insert* in most cases is two pages and between them an object is included that can be taken out of the magazine.

[7] The magazine is interested in promoting its own views, has got the identity of a forum that "participates in the process of things". Thereby it is invited as an art platform or partner in many projects. (As it happens with Lia and Dan Perjovschi, Ioan Godeanu or the Version.)

Working on dance schools

179

Choreography school: Criticism, curiosity, creativity

Robert Steijn

Working at a choreography department in Amsterdam I am struggling with an interesting dilemma: do we consolidate the format of a dance school or an art academy? On the one hand, you could consider making choreography as a highly skilled craftsmanship of people whose education is strongly embedded in didactic traditions and established modern dance styles. On the other hand, you could transform a choreography department into a labouratory, a research centre where new strategies and concepts about making dance are developed, questioned and tested. The latter has the format of a progressive art academy where a future generation of choreographers are challenged to think independently, where they can develop and formulate their own ideas about art, dance and society.

Working as a theory teacher I position myself at the research side of making choreographies. Also because I know others already fill in the more practical side of dancing and making. So, in Amsterdam the education of choreographers is not only to teach starting choreographers how to make choreographies, but also how to reflect on what you make, how to contextualise your work in a broader field than only the dance tradition. A team of very supportive didactic highly skilled teachers mostly represents the craftsmanship side of a dance school. Most of them have chosen to become teachers because their first interest is not to make works themselves; they turn their gaze mostly into the realm of didactic discourse, with fixed sets of assignments, established by the years they teach. Theory teachers, dramaturges and visiting up-coming choreographers, who also work in the dance field, most of the time only give workshops at the school and support more the labouratory side of the school. Their gaze is outward; they want to enter into dialogue with the current discourse in the dance field outside the school.

These two sides have to be in a constant struggle with each other. They can feed each other, although they often do not speak the same language. They even speak about the students in a different way. The defenders of the modern dance approach talk about students as pupils who have to follow a specific curriculum. The research teachers consider the students as colleagues, as the new generation of artists. They speak about the potential of the work of the students. This tension between traditional craftsmanship and immediately reflecting and questioning the ideologies behind this craftsmanship gives a perfect base to the student to develop his / her own artistic identity.

Sometimes this tension becomes clearly visible in the student. It shows the dilemma between the drive to dance and the wish to think first, to first conceptualize what in fact you are doing. Most of the times, in the middle of the education period there is a moment where the student becomes almost paralysed, loses any desire to move, and starts to reflect too much, even to the point where the reflection stops every impulse to move freely. The result is highly conceptual work, with a lot of standing in stillness. It easily seems the fault of too much theory and discussions in a dance school. But I discovered it could also be the influence of the critical environment, of what a dance school is by tradition in defending its aesthetics and standards. In dance education the student is constantly criticised, he is never good enough, his physical capacities can always be better; teachers always emphasise what the student still can develop. The students become overly self-critical and loses trust in their instinct to move. The teachers consider this critical approach as their main function. It looks as if they were afraid that if they were too positive with the students they would not learn anything anymore. Some of these teachers still talk about the students in terms of kids, persons who still have to learn a lot of things.

Let's investigate this teacher–kid relation somewhat deeper. How do we see these kids? Do we really see them as the generation which at a certain moment will dictate new content and aesthetics in our discourse of dance making? Traditionally a lot of dance schools are quite protective in their aesthetics of dance making, and the teachers want to see their ideology mirrored in their students; otherwise, they'd be afraid that the students did not understand what they gave to them. They demand a confirmation of what they represent, and take the students in a strong boning of taking for absolute what they represent in their teachings. The only possibility for the student to become an independent creator and thinker is to fight himself or herself out of the system, and reject the things which are offered to him. Often the only way is to provoke strong anti-reactions in explicitly breaking the taboos of the dominating style on school. This kind of work easily loses every contact with the outside of the school and does not communicate more than an internal reaction towards the teachers.

But let's go even further and talk a little bit more about education in such metaphoric terms as kids and adults, children and parents, students versus teachers. To focus on parenthood, I myself had a very problematic relationship with my parents. They never understood, or did not want to understand my decisions in career, lifestyle and relationships. They only saw it as a denial of their values, dreams etc.. They wanted to see their choices in lifestyle mirrored in my life. It is amazing to see how parents force their children to affirm the rightness of their decisions in life. And the danger is that the children will be more concerned with how their parents can be happy and comfortable instead of looking for what they want from life. Suddenly the impossible situation between my father and me changed totally when I took care of my father, who was in hospital for the last three weeks of his life. He even died in my arms. The last three weeks I met my father in an inspiring, fascinating and harmonic space. He was not afraid to die and he could say farewell to everyone he loved, he was in a space where all social structures were not important anymore, where he felt free to express what he had to say. And only in this moment he could say to me the things every father has to say to his children, I guess. He said – and till then I never had experienced what he now said – he said: My whole life I stood behind all the things you did, all the choices you made, and in the future I will also stand behind all the things you do. Although perhaps this was not really true, by just saying it he gave me an enormous feeling of freedom about what I did, I felt a lot of love and respect for what I tried to do, the failures included.

This moment, which perhaps was a turning point in my life, made me think a lot about how we really can meet the other, in freedom, when all the masks are gone, in this situation the mask of being a father, or a child.

....

Robert Steijn

And I ask myself how to translate this free space to the field of education. How to meet a student without any mask, any false ambition? At the school I always try to be in a space with the students where we can see each other as creative minds. I see the art school as one of the few places in our society where creative minds can meet without the eye of the public. One of those creative minds, the teacher, is a little bit more experienced in making, the others (the students) are just developing this channel to create. In being more experienced the teacher can show himself in the vulnerable process of not knowing, of giving up control, in having doubts and allowing the creativity to come. But he has to understand that his approach to creativity is not the creativity of the students. They have to find their own channels and, more important, their own horizon to direct to. He can only support the students by encouraging them to find their own passion. He has to learn not to be disappointed or even insulted when they do not mirror back to what he creates himself. He has to stand behind them, and he has to encourage them to look into the unknown, and not to look back to what their teachers did. The teacher has to be curious about the difference, about what the students can teach him. Not a bad thought for a teacher that students also can teach him a lot. You can give to the students the things you believe in, and at the same time you have to be open and supportive towards the things the students start to believe in even when you don't immediately understand them. And as a teacher you have to feel free enough to allow different approaches. So, there's still a lot of work to do.

The Bologna process: An opportunity to bring higher education in dance closer to the contemporary professional field?

Gil Mendo

For some years now, higher education in Europe has been undergoing a process of reorganization aiming to enable the mutual recognition of courses and degrees and to facilitate the mobility of students, teachers and professionals inside the European Union. This process was triggered by the Declaration of Bologna and has since been the object of several agreements in European Councils of Ministers of Education (Prague, Berlin) in an attempt to harmonize the higher education systems of the several countries, namely: as regards the number of cycles in higher education and their duration – there will be three cycles extending over a period of not more than eight years (BA – 3 to 4 years; MA – 1 to 2 years; PhD – 3 years); as regards the definition of clear professional profiles and skills at the end of the first cycle, as regards the implementation of a universal system of credits based on the amount of time that a student spends per year in the study of each matter (ECTS – European Credit Transfer System) which will enable the award of credits to studies followed by a student in another school, and as regards the implementation of a supplement to the diploma which will provide each graduate with an official document in two languages describing the contents of his / her course and detailing its contents, etc..

Part of this is already in function, students and teachers exchange has been going on in Europe for a good number of years now, and some people argue that all the effort being made aims mainly to cut public expenditure in higher education (a real issue in those countries where only the first cycle (BA) is financed by public funds and where universities are under pressure to reduce courses from 4 and sometimes 5 years to 3 years).

Personally, I think that this might prove an opportunity for a revision and updating of courses and curricula, which are otherwise quite difficult to change owing to the weight of routine, and that in a field like that of dance this might prove an opportunity for new courses to be started on a different and more contemporary basis.

My main concern is whether this effort being made in favour of harmonization will also favour diversity. Diversity is, in my opinion, the best motivation for mobility. What better reason for a student to go and take a part of his / her course elsewhere than the enriching experience of difference? Diversity is also at the core of the contemporary arts, and it is both cause and consequence of transdisciplinarity. Cross-discipline processes produce many "nameless" objects that we might hesitate to attach to one discipline or other, but not necessarily new disciplines. If you think of examples like photography, film, video and multi-media, digital arts, actual new disciplines, they are all linked to technological developments appropriated by artists. What I think is relevant is the understanding that the creativity an artist develops working in one discipline can also be applied to another, and that the system should facilitate mobility in between courses and disciplines so that if you are working in a cross-disciplinary manner you can go as deeply as you need in matters pertaining to different disciplines. And the same goes for different approaches and different curricular organizations in the same discipline. In the case of higher education in Dance, and considering that a Higher School of Dance will normally exist within an Institute, a Faculty or a Campus containing many other courses, it is to be expected that Dance Courses that are included in Faculties of Performing Arts, or of Visual Arts or of Physical

Education, to name just a few examples, will have different approaches as a result of their environment. And this is not a bad thing. A diversity of approaches will enable students to choose at the beginning the course that suits them better, to correct their choice along the way without loss of time already invested if a proper system of credits is established, or to take part of their course in another of the schools if they can replace one matter of their original course by another that suits their purposes better, and which they can find in another school. Mobility does not necessarily have to do with travelling a big distance. It just has to do with being able to move forward, with not being stuck with your choices or your chances.

My own experience as teacher in a Higher School of Dance tells me that mobility and diversity will be far greater in the second cycle (MA) than in the first cycle (BA). Owing to the amount of time that a student has to spend in the school in the first cycle, and the amount of group work involved, it is not very realistic – although it should not be completely overruled – to think that the student will easily be able to go and do lumps of his/her course elsewhere. (It will be easier to do successive parts of the course in different schools). But the courses should nevertheless be designed to give the student progressively bigger autonomy, to encourage choices and definition of aims as the course progresses.

If I may outline just a few of the skills that I think should be developed in the first cycle, at a BA level, these are: creativity, ability to improvise, the necessary technical skills, ability to work in a collabourative way, understanding of dance as a part of culture in a broader social context, ability to express concepts, ability to analyse and appreciate dance, basic understanding of dance production, ability to realize a concrete project. I think that the first cycle in a Higher School of Dance should concentrate a lot on actual artistic practice and experience. I also think that the school should promote the closest possible relationship with the field, specifically with those artists and professionals that are closest and more relevant to the student's generation. I would also include pedagogy in the curriculum and pedagogic projects in the student's field practice. For two main reasons: the first is that a pedagogic approach, in its broadest sense, will broaden the artists view and approach to society and his ability to convey ideas and concepts with positive reflexes on his/her future integration in the community; the second is that those who will later on opt for a teacher's training course should first go through a strong artistic practice and research.

It is not always easy to maintain the liveliness of an arts course within the framework of formal higher education. It is easier, I am sure, in less bureaucratic countries – like the Netherlands, the United Kingdom, the Scandinavian countries. Where I come from I must tell you that it is quite difficult. Routine is a killer and the procedures of higher education demand a lot of routine. We need to have artists in the field coming to the school on an intense basis, but it is difficult to have money in the budget to pay temporary collabourations. Nevertheless, I would venture to recommend that in our field higher education courses should be organised in the manner that the contemporary dance field works, i.e., that most of the training should be organised as a succession of workshops including technique, improvisation and composition/choreography rather than a regular set of

....

Gil Mendo

disciplines per week, on and on. It is impossible to conceive a higher school of dance that is devoted to contemporary dance and performance but has to function in the manner of an oldfashioned repertory company. To those of you who are considering to start a higher school in this field I would also give an advice: try to have a small permanent faculty and to be able to invite the maximum number of guest teachers every year, thus maintaining a permanent relation with the field and moving along with it.

The second cycle (MA) should be more flexible although of course more exigent in academic as well as artistic terms, and this is where one can foresee the more clear application of the principles of mobility and diversity and the biggest autonomy of the student. An MA can be organised in collabouration with another school or university, but also with the field. Hopefully, the possibility of crediting professional artistic experience for direct access to an MA will, with the Bologna Process, extend to all European countries. It would help solve a lot of difficulties. Likewise, artistic MAs and PhDs where the core matter is the creation process and the thesis can be a creation should be accepted in all the European countries.

One final word to tell you that although I try to be optimistic I feel quite unsatisfied (I might say frustrated) with what I see as a serious gap, in many countries, between formal higher education in dance and the contemporary performance professional field. There are reasons for this, some of which I have pointed out above: the routine, the bureaucracy, the faculties that lose interest and go on as if time had stopped, and also the prejudices from both sides. The fact is that some of the more interesting and more successful professional training projects of today have either opted for being out or not been allowed within the formal system of higher education. I do hope that the current reorganization of higher education in Europe will enable us to overcome some of these gaps. For one reason, which is that dance artists and professionals, like everybody else nowadays, might sooner or later find themselves in a position where they will need academic recognition, a degree, for access to positions to which they are entitled and should not come second to people who in fact are less prepared than them.

But there is a lot of training and research carried by professional organizations in the field that can never be replaced by formal education. It is important to recognize this, so that we can concentrate on what must be incorporated in formal education, and on what although not fully incorporated can be the object of collabouration between academic institutions and professional organizations and individual artists, and then also value what is beyond formal education, that which no longer has to do with cycles and degrees and institutions, but only with art, artists and their growth, their need to pursue research and their need to share it, which is where things happen that later will be studied, and without which everything else would be pretty irrelevant.

Upbringing – educating – further training – research

Maja Delak

Systematisation of dance education

The renovation of the educational system in Slovenia started in the nineties. The base of this activity was the "transformation" of the secondary school system. The moment when the whole secondary educational system was changing turned out to be the right moment to improve the education of artistic fields as well.

What was the heritage of Slovenian contemporary dance education? Although the first private school of Meta Vidmar had opened already in the thirties, there had been no successful attempt to bring contemporary dance into the governmental school system. The idea of a school for artistic, creative and innovative dance did not fit into the existing political and cultural climate for a long time. In the period of the 1960s and 1970s, the Yugoslavian government tried to reduce all dance art which existed at that time to the level of amateur activity. The state gave to dance the formal status of carrying out its activities in the framework of a cultural association, established for amateur culture – or on the other hand, private initiative. With such forms of dance pedagogy, it was neither possible to get an official diploma nor to distinguish a vocation, nor was it possible to detect the job profile of a dancer, choreographer or dance pedagogue. The professional level was not accessible for dance art and its creators, so all the activities stayed on the level of private initiative and amateur flushing out until the return of Ksenija Hribar.

But let me return to education. The existing arts programmes that had been dispersed in different schools (visual art, music, and ballet) were brought together according to a concept similar to that of an Arts Gymnasium. What does the newly established concept of gymnasium imply?

The gymnasium program prepares students for continuing their studies at the university. Newly established was a branch called professional gymnasium. To the existing music, visual arts and ballet, contemporary dance and theatre departments were added. These are secondary level schools that enable students to finish with a baccalaureate in five subjects (mathematics, Slovene and English language, as compulsory subjects, and two more subjects of choice, one of which is contemporary dance). The subject of contemporary dance is evaluated externally in several practical performing tasks, a written paper, and a test. The achievement in the subject contemporary dance is added to the sums of other subjects, and this determines the level of achievement on the baccalaureate. With this, the students finish their secondary level education. They do not have a vocation, but they have the possibility to continue studies at a university. They are then at the age of 18 or 19 years.

What does such a programme give to the students? The students who enrolled with these programmes can accede to baccalaureate and upon successful completion they can enrol into almost any university or academic studies programme.

What I can conclude at this point of my presentation of education in the field of contemporary dance in Slovenia is that the implementation of the module for contemporary dance was in fact the first integration of contemporary dance in an institutionalised form in Slovenia. In the next years followed the primary school programme, which has been active for a few years now. But it still remains without vocation, and it lacks the possibility to continue on a higher level.

Upbringing and educating

One of the specifics in the development of an educational system is that it took a very long time to make it happen. Another issue which seems interesting to me personally is the idea and differentiation between upbringing and educating which I detected in these 10 years since I have been working in the field of dance education.

In our educational system, upbringing and educating have different goals, and interestingly they are somehow distributed among the subjects.

If I start to observe the beginnings of education in kindergarten, children acquire all the education through activities such as drawing, singing, sculpturing, dancing and other physical activities. It is more an "upbringing" focus if we define "upbringing" as: *spiritual and character developing and forming of a person, especially a child* (*Slovar slovenskega knjižnega jezika* – Slovene dictionary). As they move to the primary and then to secondary educational levels, the amount of subjects that are about art or are creative activities in arts gets more and more reduced.

The child in the beginning grows, develops and builds its capacities on an expressive level of creation and expression through movement, drawing, playing. Then the child grows, goes to primary school and enters different school and non-school programmes that are more and more educative, with subjects that have more educative purposes. Here by education I mean to *by the plan develop capacities and informing about new achievements from different fields of human activities* = giving information, following precise yearly plans and goals of subjects, learning by processes of repeating, reproducing, inventing …(*Slovar slovenskega knjižnega jezika* – Slovene dictionary). And there are less and less arts subjects – and those that do exist have upbringing as their purpose. In our system those subjects were also called: music upbringing (direct translation).

The amount of hours allocated to arts subjects, whether they are practical or theoretical, or history of arts, from primary school to the end of secondary school drastically declines. So the student who does not choose the arts programme, at fourteen or fifteen years of age almost totally loses contact with arts and even more, with developing skills in any art form. If students are not active outside their school in such a way, they will, at the end of secondary school, be very ignorant concerning arts and especially contemporary art. Quite interestingly, art gets a marginalised position in comparison to all the other subjects or other possibilities of spending time, money and interest in a city. The arts are no longer part of general education, except literature and drama which are part of another subject – Slovene language.

Is it that this subtle upbringing which we defined at the kindergarten stage, forming of character, spiritual nourishing, and ethical value development are somehow not important at a later age? Or do other subjects not "up-bring"? And what happens with educating in art?

....

Maja Delak

Research on the influence of dance training on the students

In 2000 I ran a small research with questionnaires in our gymnasium. I was interested to know whether practising dance had positive or negative effects on adolescent self-esteem, especially on their physical (body) self and their perception of their physical competence. I took two classes from different departments: the dance department and the general studies department. They filled in two questionnaires: A questionnaire of self-esteem (samopodobe) for adolescents (SDQIII) and one for the scale of physical competence (PSE). Results showed that the students of the dance department had statistically important higher body self-esteem, higher general self-esteem, and they saw their physical competence higher then their peers in the general school.

The reasons could be numerous, but one conclusion might be that dance as an art form brings into education some of the so-called upbringing, which gives the students something valuable and priceless. My main question here is how to create such a programme and realise it in such a way that it would provide the right amount of upbringing and the right amount of educating that would improve the pedagogical situation and what it produces.

I believe that teaching is not about what is to be taught in the first place, but how, in which situations, with what kind of positions of the people included (meaning, is the situation of "a person who knows" on one side and "a person who does not know" on the other side just artificially created and does it engender a power position which prohibits an unprotected person from developing very far?).

I believe that dance has old models of educating. Dance pedagogy concepts were established according to the wishes of one author who had found his / her own language of presentation and wished to pass it on further. So dance remained without reflection on its pedagogy and did not apply the newest concepts of pedagogy and upcoming work, so it always stayed very much with an eye on the past. Knowledge was passed on to the students by authorities who created a canon. Does this pattern of wishing to do education and to change the existing educating system come from a need to create the next prescribed style and methods of working, or does it imply ideas and knowledge of a wider educational process?

Development of creativity and institutionalisation of stages of creativity

Earlier on, I spoke about the importance and emphasis that the expressive stage of creativity has. But on that level its aim is not appreciation of artistic value and high technical skills, but more the wonder of spontaneity and freedom. This is also the level that satisfies the need for flushing out ideas, energy … Similar to the description of activities on an amateur level, or activities we have when bringing up children. With this – let us call it psychological predisposition, the first expressive stage is the most basic one, but to reach the next stage it is necessary to achieve the tasks the first one presents. We do this at an early age. The next one would be a productive stage in which we achieve the knowledge and skills to express ourselves in more exact, precise, controlled … ways, where students cultivate knowledge, conquer the techniques … These two stages are very common in educational situations. It is to try out and to learn. To keep only these two stages in education seems boring, and maybe it smells a bit of the subtle mechanism of control. The next stages – innovation, invention and emergent stages – would include creative processes, changes and different positions, and relations between teacher, master and pupil. In educational systems, these stages are rare. But they would greatly enrich the whole educational and training processes. The educational situation could become a creative situation, with more risk involved, with more collabourating processes explored, with more research on the methodology implied and with real shifting of the responsibility from shoulders of the teachers to those of the students. I believe that thus the educational process could keep in step with new contemporary forms and not cling to the past or even create generation gaps.

The dynamics of progress through these stages are different for different people. Some might stay at a certain stage. The emergent stage is rare. The characteristics of the invention stage = operating with known elements in new relations is, in my opinion, one of the most common stages of creation in contemporary dance at the moment. It is about little discoveries, inventions, well-done products which do not go beyond works already seen. Can this be overcome within education? If such a level of creation could be systematised as an educational model, then it might be something that is overcome earlier and the graduates might be better equipped for their profession.

<u>Further training as a process of discovering and inventing</u>
I think of education as an ongoing process of development. The individual development of all people is engaged therein. What I have been speaking about until now, education at the secondary school level, seems simpler. It concerns very young students who are not sure about their vocation yet, and their position is: "I would like to learn". They are gaining skills, but at the same time the processes of creativity start to open up to them again. Eventually, they come to a decision about their vocation.

I believe that what they have to achieve up to this point one the one hand are the skills that they can acquire in a specific program, and on the other hand responsibility about what they are doing, interest for what is happening in the arts and in general, discipline for working, capacities of articulation, and communication.

I believe that the higher the creative process goes in an educational system, the more it has to go away from a hierarchical model of teaching. A hierarchical model of teaching implies a teacher with knowledge and students lacking this knowledge. Education in the arts will have to offer possibilities of creative situations that will develop skills of different people with different potentials, knowledge, interests, and profiles. If I may borrow a bit of Vygotsky's idea of the zone of proximal development, which I find inspiring, I'll try to describe creative situations in these terms.

In creative situations with more people involved in problem solving there is a possibility of development – individual and group development and problem solving. I believe that the skills in such situations of non-authority with as few hierarchical positions as possible

Maja Delak

need to be instilled with high self-confidence, communication, curiosity, capacity for divergent thinking, problem solving, high working habits, skills and knowledge of arts, communicating abilities. The interaction that exists there and happens between the people involved, because they are different takes and brings them to the zone of proximal development of the idea, of development … This is the zone which one person cannot yet reach on its own, but with some support, steps into. Such a system of what I call creative situations, could allow a fluidity of ideas and in bringing up tasks for participants create possibilities for invention, mistake and work.

Imagine
The invention of DasArts

Ritsaert ten Cate

Before I begin, I'd like to offer you a bit of wisdom from Eeyore, of Winnie the Pooh fame. Eeyore told us that, "We can't all, and some of us don't. That's all there is to it".

And with that ... Hello, and good morning. I am Ritsaert ten Cate, founder and the first artistic director of the post academic educational system in Amsterdam known as DasArts, or De Amsterdamse School / Advanced Research in Theatre and Dance Studies. DasArts was created in 1994. With the school's creation I also created a set-in-stone policy that no director could stay longer than seven years.

I wanted to tell you about the invention of DasArts, about how it was created, and what made it such an exceptional institute for learning. But the more I dug into material to present in this session, the more I realised that with the creation of DasArts, we accomplished the impossible. I am delighted to report that this utterly impossible institution thrives to this day.

Behind me you can see a visual presentation created by one of the former students of DasArts, Catherine Hennegan. Catherine is a video artist from Johannesburg, and she created this piece as an introduction of my work as a visual artist, work I dived into after leaving DasArts.

Catherine's presentation gives you something a little more interesting to look at than me as I work my way through this text. But it can also be seen as a kind of illustration of the DasArts programme which combines elements in an unusual way, while speaking of the world we're all travelling through, living in, and working with.

For you, the question might seem to be, *what* was DasArts, or, for that matter *what* is DasArts now? You know of it as the only Dutch-based post-academic studies program for theatre, now in its eleventh year.

But if I follow that line of thought I'd be seduced into discussing what DasArts looks like from the outside ... which isn't really going to tell you very much. Instead, I want to address the *how* of DasArts, the way it came into being, and how it became what it is. And that story gives us the first peculiarity of DasArts – *how* it was commissioned, and who it was commissioned from.

When the political Powers-That-Be decided to commission someone to create a proposal for a post-academic arts training, it would have been logical – even assumed – that they would have chosen someone with a heavy-weight academic background, someone who had some experience in how schools are supposed to work.

They didn't do that. They asked a successful producer of the international avant-garde. They asked someone who, for a quarter of a century, presented, co-produced and created some 800 productions from more than 25 countries that were spread over 5 continents. They asked someone who didn't even have a university degree to his name, someone that was invited to depart from the only university he attended (because he spent more time in the theatre than he did in classes).

The Powers-That-Be may have had multiple hidden agenda in the way they commissioned a plan for making a post-graduate study program. At the time I frequently wondered if they were setting it, and me, up for complete failure from the start. You know the drill – "We looked into it, but nobody could give us a workable plan …" And it was easy to guess that whatever plan was produced would have to be unacceptable to the various political bureaus of Higher Education. They certainly guaranteed that much when they asked me – someone who knows less than nothing about education – to develop a proposal for a school.

But … I was given a year to come up with a workable plan. I asked Marijke Hoogenboom to work with me and keep me on course. Which she did, and it cannot always have been easy for her to do this, given the fact that we started our research as a theatrical gambit, a travelling show complete with a set and props.

We began at the place where most theatre ends, at the Netherlands Theatre Institute, which also houses a museum and an archive of all things theatrical in Holland.

We arrived with two antique industrial desks, and a set of Dutch Art Deco copper candelabras that were three meters high and a meter and a half wide. The two of them held eighty fist-thick candles.

I must explain about the candelabras – I was walking through the Amsterdam street that has most of the antique shops in it a few months after I got the commission to design a school. I saw the candelabras on that walk, and was soon completely obsessed by them, for they were beautiful. Magnificent. An example of unparalleled virtuosity. They provided such a comprehensive answer to the political Powers-That-Be and their endless abstract discussion of professionalism.

So I bought them. My wife thought I was insane, but every time I heard the words "professionalism" and "craftsmanship" – and believe me, they came up over and over and over again – I pointed to the candelabras and said, "You mean like these. Yes, we'll celebrate all that".

And they had to take a window out of the Theatre Institute so that we could get them in, but once they were there – and everywhere else we took them – they served their purpose gloriously.

In the Theatre Institute we were part of an exhibition suitably entitled, *The Theatre of the Future*, and we discussed our task with a steady stream of visitors.

Next stop, the Spring Dance Festival. There we reconstructed our set (desks, candelabras, balloons) in the reception area of the Polmanshuis, a bar / restaurant that also served as the Festival centre. Once again we talked with a multitude of people.

The last stop on our tour was at the Westergasfabriek, an industrial site on the eastern fringe of Amsterdam. The Westergasfabriek would become the operational base of DasArts, and our job at that point was to stage what the head office of a school would look like. And at that point, with endless interruptions, we started to write our report.

Our travelling road show, complete with its mammoth set and props, made it possible for us to knock away any possible assumptions we had about what a school was supposed to be. It did the same thing for anybody who spoke to us about what they thought should happen in a school … and we made damn sure that anyone and everyone had a chance to

Ritsaert ten Cate

tell us what was their idea of what a school should do, and must be. We learned a great deal in this process, and what we learned, we applied.

But there's something I've got to add here. And the importance of what I'm about to tell you cannot be overstated. What we learned fifteen years ago about what was needed in the theatrical culture of that time is most emphatically *not* what is urgently required by the theatrical culture now.

Anyone who sets about learning how to build a school today, using the same sort of wide open and confrontational methods we did then would come up with a completely different set of materials, inspirations, needs, desires and responses. Which would then lead to the creation of a completely different school from what DasArts was under my tenure.

Creating and maintaining a school of the sort that DasArts was, and is today, requires desperation, and passion, an overwhelming sense of curiosity … and an ever-present sense of humour. None of these things will work second-hand.

But … we sent our plans to the political Powers-That-Be, using a lot of words to describe a space that we'd purposely emptied of all obvious educational tools. We left a space – almost a vacuum – that demanded to be filled with creativity, with experienced, hands-on information, with challenges and confrontations, with learning by doing and a growing awareness of who you are and what that means.

It was, essentially, a school for people in this world here and now today.

As the commission ran, DasArts was expected to be a school for people involved in theatre, mime, and dance. Anybody who had a diploma from theatre or dance training was welcome. Equally welcome were those who were kicked out of formal training programs, or those who were already engaged in performance-based work. Very quickly we found ourselves stretching the original definitions to the point that anyone with any form of artistic obsession from whatever discipline could apply and would be considered for the school.

Thus it was clearly established that whatever program DasArts had would be completely multidisciplinary. We were not about teaching skills that could be learned in existing institutions, and we were working with people who already had some vision of their place in the firmament. (Even if we might turn that vision upside down in no time, a strong vision to begin with was necessary.)

The student selection process was fierce; it is not an exaggeration to say that prospective students were, quite literally, grilled by Marijke and me. From first moment any prospective student had any contact with us, we made it clear that it was the responsibility of the participants to determine what the future of the performing arts could be. The question was whether or not they were capable of handling that.

What DasArts did was to organise confrontations between the students and international specialists from the fields of theatre and the arts. We added to this list specialists in marketing, police work, South Africa's Truth and Reconciliation Commission, poets, composers, Hawaiian Dancers, philosophers, specialists in the history and preparation of food, musicians, visual artists … the list was very long, and extremely varied. And the point of much of this list was that it wasn't obvious. That was an extremely important aspect of it all.

Each block of ten weeks was designed and supervised by two mentors. The mentors were internationally recognised specialists from various artistic fields. The students and the mentors had a period of ten weeks to work together – a pressure cooker for talent that demanded a performative response to an avalanche of varied input.

A staff of six people supported and assisted in the execution of all activities, while also exposing the students and their work to a continuous process of minutely detailed evaluation. This staff included myself as the artistic director, Marijke as my assistant and dramaturge, a financial specialist, two production managers, and a liaison for students. We all worked pretty much around the clock in the course of each ten-week block. And, of course, the weeks running up to the opening of any given block were also intensely driven periods … there was never enough time; there was only barely enough energy. But like life in the theatre, working at DasArts was a dedication, not a job.

For the students, a full study program took up to three years and required a minimum participation in three blocks. The fourth required block was known as the individual trajectory, and was executed outside DasArts but with a supervisory mentor appointed by DasArts to work with that student.

The preferred number of students for any given block was twelve to fifteen people, but we had fewer if we found that there weren't enough strong applicants to allow into the program.

To give you a flavour of how this worked in practice, I will tell you about the first DasArts block.

I was approached by the drama department of the University of Giessen, in Germany, to be a guest professor in their programme. I told them while I was honoured by their request, I could only do it if we could combine the first DasArts students with Giessen students, and work from there. And with astonishing rapidity, puzzle pieces started falling into place.

On the outskirts of Giessen there was a huge military camp with barracks and bunkers built for the German army, and later used by American occupation forces. In 1994 most of these spaces were unused, and in the middle of the camp was a big empty barrack that still had the word "Theater" on it.

We made the theatre our working place, built a new large stage in the middle of it, and installed on the original one a monstrous bronze sculpture by Wessel Couzijn, on loan from the Kroller Muller Museum near Arnhem. The sculpture's title was *Auschwitz*.

We were operating in a place jammed with elements of the past and from the present, a chaos of ideas and intentions out of which we would define a future for theatre.

....

Ritsaert ten Cate

The Dutch contingent slept in campers parked around the theatre. In the theatre building was a canteen in which we placed our specially designed transportable kitchen, and the two "Amsterdamse School" Candelabra.

Tom Stromberg was the artistic director of Theater Am Turm at that point, and I arranged with him that we could use their Probebühne for two weeks. The Norwegian group Baktruppen was invited to perform at TAT, back to back with whatever we could show as a result of our six weeks in Giessen.

Then the whole circus moved to Amsterdam. In the remaining week, individual members of Baktruppen became teachers and created yet another event with the students.

In the beginning this plan was nothing more than a monstrous balloon filled with hot air. But we had faith in that balloon, and – it all came together. Momentum built on itself – and finally we had it: the impossible lived.

And we all survived. We left Amsterdam in a trail of nervously driven campers, with an idea of a school that was comfortably and clearly defined. Then we installed ourselves on the Giessen military base and – with no hesitation whatever – tore up all plans, understandings, assumptions, and definitions. After six weeks we ended up with a seven hour presentation of performative response to our stay there which left a visiting audience from the Giessen University breathless … whether they liked what they saw, or not, the result was breathtaking.

In Frankfurt we appropriated the Probebühne and fought and ruthlessly cut our way through to a one-hour compilation out of the seven-hours' worth of material. We performed this for sold-out TAT audiences back to back with Baktruppen.

We ended our stay in Frankfurt with a historic football match of our gang against the technical, artistic and administrative forces of TAT that people are still talking about. (TAT won, but they had corrupted the arbiter). We finalised the block in Amsterdam one week later with an event that left our audiences stunned, embarrassed and generally in disarray. The energy level of the performers, Baktruppen and the students soared to unimaginable heights.

None of us had ever made a school, but now we had one. As time went by the structure became firmer, our handling of situations and the people better. The first block ended June 25th in 1994. It took us six months to evaluate what we had and shape the consequences from that Giessen block. In January of the next year, we began the second block entitled "The Art of Survival". The first diploma ceremony was held seven blocks later, on December 4th, 1997.

And by then the system we had devised was in full swing. "Let's Suppose It Is Today: The Making Of A School", followed "Art of Survival". Then came "Object, Objective", "Orchestra Zero and Family Tree", "Culture and the Other", "Cosmologies" and "A Hunger Artist", "The city as a site for questions", "Structures: How to map the complexity of reality today?", "Reconciliation and storytelling", "What's cooking? Still life / turbulent recipes", "The makeable truth". These were loosely held themes, mostly inspired and prepared by the two invited mentors who were also the line producers of a block. The execution and organisation were handled by the staff, and the students moved in and out, weaving their routes towards completion of a degree within the prescribed three-year period.

Everyone joined in the concentrated fullness and madness of it all. First, second and third time students were mingled, as were ages and disciplines. First timers were supported by those who had been there before, and knowledge about a variety of disciplines was shared. It was fairly rare for students to take on back to back blocks – the requirements and experience of a ten-week block were too intense. Most often a break wasn't just a good thing, it was a requirement.

In my time in DasArts we invited two specialists, people we personally respected, to be block mentors. A mentor was not necessarily from a field relating to stagecraft, and neither did the two mentors always know each other beforehand.

We felt that would get a more challenging curriculum for a block this way. It's also true that this occasionally added up to conflict between mentors, sometimes, but we figured that conflicting opinions offered by working professionals would be of more use to students than any kind of homogenised approach. Mentors and guest teachers alike were made to understand that they had to offer more than the basics of their expertise. In so doing, they, like the students, would very probably be changed, perhaps profoundly so, by what came out of a ten-week block.

Individual mentors for individual trajectories, something like a final master's program before a diploma could be granted, were selected specifically for that particular student.

And when all is said and done this spicy, chaotic stew did work. But it wasn't the easiest route to go.

In my time at DasArts we executed twelve blocks. Ten of those blocks had two mentors and two of them had three. One block took place in Giessen and Frankfurt, one in Gent (Belgium), the rest took place in Amsterdam. We had 198 guest teachers, 55 of which gave workshops for more than one day (one of these guest teachers taught for three weeks, and another for five weeks). On average each block had seventeen teachers and four workshops.

It is now almost five years since I was directly involved with DasArts. I'm proud of what we did, I am proud of what DasArts could give to most of its participants and how they manifested in what looked like a new-found strength, energy and focus, to express their talents. I am proud of the fact that none of them looked alike, that we did not create clones.

But did we really make a school? Now I don't think so. We made something that looked enough like a school to operate more or less unharmed within a system that adhered to strict rules, with a recognisable structure, with a curriculum that could be repeated year after year after year.

....

Ritsaert ten Cate

I think we created a container for ideas, and impulses, inspiration, red herrings, contradictions, experiences; a first-aid kit for talented narcissism and neuroses to deal with the absolute fear and vulnerability of what it means to perform to be a creative entity in its own right. Operating within a socio-cultural environment and not adjust to it, but rather passionately and professionally working on what you might add, what might be given.

Meanwhile I have to believe that even now the structure devised for DasArts can be as flexibly interpreted as before, as an energy resource bank. Or, in the words of M Scott Momaday: We are what we imagine. And for all of you, don't copy DasArts, imagine or invent what might work for you. Then go for it.

Edited by Colleen Scott

Talking about precariousness

Governmentality and self-precarisation:[1]
On the normalisation of culture producers

Isabell Lorey

For some of us, as culture producers[2] the idea of a permanent job in an institution is something that we do not even consider, or at most for a few years. Afterward, we want something different. Hasn't the idea always been about not being forced to commit oneself to one thing, one classical job definition, which ignores so many aspects; about not selling out and consequently being compelled to give up the many activities that one feels strongly about? Wasn't it important to not adapt to the constraints of an institution, to save the time and energy to be able to do the creative and perhaps political projects that one really has an interest in? Wasn't a more or less well-paying job gladly taken for a certain period of time, when the opportunity arose, to then be able to leave again when it no longer fit? Then there would at least be a bit of money there to carry out the next meaningful project, which would probably be poorly paid, but supposedly more satisfying.

Crucial for the attitude suggested here is the belief that one has chosen his or her own living and working situations and that these can be arranged relatively freely and autonomously. Actually, also consciously chosen to a great extent are the uncertainties, the lack of continuities under the given social conditions. Yet in the following, concern is not with the question of "when did I really decide freely?", or "when do I act autonomously?", but instead, with the ways in which ideas of autonomy and freedom are constitutively connected with hegemonic modes of subjectivation in Western, capitalist societies. The focus of this text is accordingly on the extent to which "self chosen" precarisation contributes to producing the conditions for being able to become an active part of neo-liberal political and economic relations.

No general statements about culture producers or all of those currently in a situation that has been made precarious can be derived from this perspective. However, what becomes apparent when problematising this "self chosen" precarisation, are the historical lines of force[3] of modern bourgeois subjectivation, which are imperceptibly hegemonic, normalising, and possibly block resistance.

To demonstrate the genealogy of these lines of force, I will first turn to Michel Foucault's concepts of "governmentality" and "biopolitics". We will not focus on the breaks and rifts in the lines of bourgeois subjectivation, but instead, on their structural and transformative continuities including the entanglement in governmental techniques of modern Western societies until today. What ideas of sovereignty arise in these modern, governmental dispositifs? What lines of force, i.e., what continuities, self-evidences, and normalisations can be drawn to what and how we think and feel as "self chosen" culture producers that have been made precarious in neo liberal conditions, how we are in the world, and specifically also in so-called dissident practices? Do culture producers who are in a precarious state possibly embody a "new" governmental normality through certain self-relations and ideas of sovereignty?

With the genealogy of the force lines of bourgeois subjectivation, in the course of the text I will differentiate between precarisation as deviance, and therefore as a contradiction of *liberal* governmentality, on the one hand, and as a hegemonic function of *neo-liberal* governmentality on the other, to then finally clarify the relationship between the two based on the example of the "free" decision for precarious living and working.

Biopolitical governmentality
With the term "governmentality", Michel Foucault defined the structural entanglement of the government of a State and the techniques of self-government in Western societies. This involvement between State and population as subjects is not a timeless constant. First in the course of the 18th century could that which had been developing since the 16th century take root: a new government technique, more precisely, the force lines of modern government techniques until today. The traditional sovereign, for whom Foucault introduces the character from Machiavelli's *The Prince* from the 16th century as a prototype, and Hobbes's contract-based voluntary community of subordinates from the 17th century, were not yet concerned with ruling "the people" for the sake of their welfare, but instead, they were primarily interested in dominating them for the welfare of the sovereign. It was first in the course of the 18th century, when liberalism and the bourgeoisie became hegemonic, that the population entered the focus of power and along with it, a governing that was oriented on the life of "the people" and making that life better. The power of the State no longer depended solely on the size of a territory or the mercantile, authoritative regulation of subordinates,[4] but instead, on the "happiness" of the population, on their life and a steady improvement of that life.

In the course of the 18th century, governing methods continued to transform toward a political economy of liberalism: self-imposed limitations on government for the benefit of a free market on the one hand, and on the other, a population of subjects that were bound to economic paradigms in their thought and behaviour. These subjects were not subjugated simply by means of obedience, but became governable in that, on the whole, "their life expectancy, their health, and their courses of behaviour were involved in complex and entangled relationships with these economic processes". (Foucault 2004b, p. 42; own translation) Liberal modes of government presented the basic structure for modern governmentality, which has always been biopolitical.[5] Or, in other words: liberalism was the economic and political framework of biopolitics and, equally, "an indispensable element in the development of capitalism". (Foucault 1980, p. 141-42)
The strength and wealth of a state at the end of the 18th century depended ever more greatly on the health of its population. In a bourgeois liberal context, a government policy oriented on this means, until today, establishing and producing normality and then securing it. For that, a great deal of data is necessary; statistics are produced, probabilities of birth rates and death rates are calculated, frequencies of diseases, living conditions, means of nutrition, etc.. Yet that does not suffice. In order to manufacture a population's health standard, and to maximise it, these bio-productive, life-supporting biopolitical government methods also require the active participation of every single individual, which means their self-governing.

....

Isabell Lorey

Foucault writes in *The History of Sexuality:* "Western man was gradually *learning* what it meant to be a living species in a living world, to have a body, conditions of existence, probabilities of life, an individual and collective welfare, forces that could be modified, and a space in which they could be distributed in an optimal manner". (Foucault 1980, p. 142, emphasis I.L.) Here, Foucault describes two things that I consider essential: the modern individual must learn how to have a body that is dependent on certain existential conditions, and, second, he or she must learn to develop a relationship with his or her "self" that is creative and productive, a relationship in which it is possible to fashion his or her "own" body, "own" life, "own" self. Philipp Sarasin shows the emergence in the context of the Western hygiene discourse of the waning 18th century and early 19th century, of "the belief that the individual was largely capable of determining its health, illness, or even the time of death". (Sarasin 2001, p. 19; see also Bublitz et al. 2000) This idea of the ability to shape and fashion one's self never arose independent of governmental dispositifs.

In the context of liberal governmental technologies of the self, the attribute "own" always signifies "possessive individualism". (Macpherson 1962) However, initially, self-relations oriented on the imagination of one's "own", were only applicable to the bourgeois, then gradually towards the end of the 19th century, the entire population. At issue here is not the legal status of a subject, but structural conditions of normalising societies: one must be capable of managing oneself, recognising oneself as subject to a sexuality, and learn to have a body that remains healthy through attentiveness (nutrition, hygiene, living) and can become sick through inattentiveness. In this sense, the entire population must become biopolitical subjects (see Lorey 2005).

With reference to wage workers, such imaginary self-relations[6] mean that one's own body, constituted as the property of the self, becomes an "own" body that one must sell as labour power. Also, in this respect, the modern, "free" individual is compelled to co-produce him or herself through such powerful self-relations, that the individual can sell his or her labour power well, in order to live a life that improves steadily.

Therefore, in modern societies, the "art of governing"– which was another name given by Foucault (1991) to governmentality – does not primarily consist of being repressive, but instead, "inwardly held" self-discipline and self-control.[7] It is the analysis of an order that is not only forced upon people, bodies, and things, but in which they are simultaneously an active part. At the center of the problem of government ruling techniques is not the question of regulating autonomous, free subjects, but instead, regulating the relations through which so-called autonomous and free subjects are first constituted as such.

Already in the second half of the 17th century, John Locke, who according to Karl Marx, "demonstrated ... that the bourgeois way of thinking is the normal human way of thinking" (Marx 1999), wrote in *The Two Treatises of Government*, that man is "master of himself, and proprietor of his own person, and the actions or labour of it" (Locke 1823). At the beginning of the modern era, property acquired a supposed "anthropological meaning" (Castel 2005, 24) for both the bourgeois man as a prerequisite for his formal freedom as a citizen, as well as for the worker, who owns his own labour power and must sell it, freely, as wage labour. It seemed to be the prerequisite with which the individual could become independent and free from the traditional system of subordination and security. With a biopolitical governmentality perspective, the meaning of property, however, surpasses the limited levels of citizenship, capital, and wage labour and is, in fact, to be understood as something entirely general. For in a biopolitical dispositif, relations of bodily ownership apply to the entire population as governmental self-governing, not only to citizens or workers.[8] The modern person is, accordingly, constituted through possessive individualistic self-relations, which are fundamental for historically specific ideas of autonomy and freedom. Structurally, modern self-relations are based – also beyond an economic interpellation – on a relation to one's own body as a means of production.

In this broad sense of economy and biopolitics, the lines of the labour entrepreneur, "the entrepreneur of one's self" (Pühl 2003) as a mode of subjectivation, reach back to the beginnings of modern liberal societies and are not an entirely neo-liberal phenomena.[9] This type of genealogy of course skips over the era of the social, the welfare state since the end of the 19th century, and ties together, the for the most part compulsively constituting self-entrepreneurs in the current reconstruction and deconstruction of the social / welfare state with fundamental liberal governmental methods of subjectivation since the end of the 18th century. With the interpellation to be responsible for one's self, something that had already failed in the 19th century seems to be repeating itself now, namely, the primacy of property and the construction of security associated with it. Property was introduced in the early stages of bourgeois rule as protection against the incalculability of social existence, as security against vulnerability in a secularised society and the domination of the princes and kings. Ultimately this applied to only a limited few, and at the end of the 19th century the nation state had to guarantee social security for many. However, it does not automatically follow that today the State must once again take on a more comprehensive social function of protection and security (e.g., Castel 2005). For this would quickly reproduce the utterly flexible, Western nation state nexus of freedom and security with similar structural inclusions and exclusions, rather than break through it.

Normalised free subjects
In biopolitical governmental societies, the constitution of the "normal" is always also woven in with the hegemonic.[10] With the demand to orient on the normal – which could be bourgeois, heterosexual, Christian, white male, white female, national – in the course of the modern era, it was necessary to develop the perspective of controlling one's own body, one's own life, by regulating and thus managing the self. The normal is not identical with the norm, but it can take on its function. Normality is, however, never anything external, for we are the ones who guarantee it, and reproduce it through alterations. Accordingly, we govern ourselves in the dispositif of governmentality, biopolitics, and capitalism in that we normalize ourselves. If this is successful – and it usually is – power and certain domination relations are barely perceptible, and extremely difficult to reflect on, because we act in their

production, as it were, in the ways we relate to ourselves, and own our bodies. The normalising society and the subjectivation taking place within it are a historical effect of a power technology directed at life. The normalised subject itself is, once again, a historical construct in an ensemble of knowledge forms, technologies, and institutions. This ensemble is aimed at the individual body as well as at the life of the population as a whole. Normalisation is lived through everyday practices that are perceived as self-evident and natural.

Additionally, the normal is naturalised with the effect of actuality, of authenticity. We thus believe, for example, that the effect of power relations is the essence of our self, our truth, our own, actual core, the origin of our being. This normalising self-governing is based on an imagined coherence, uniformity and wholeness, which can be traced back to the construction of a white, male subject.[11] Coherence is, once again, one of the prerequisites for modern sovereignty. The subject must believe that it is "master in its own house" (Freud). If this fundamental imagination fails, then usually not only others perceive the person in question as "abnormal", but the person, too, has this opinion of him or herself.

Let's remain with the learned way of self-relation, which is so existential for the biopolitical governmental modern era, and which applies to the entire population in very different ways. This relationship with one's self is based on the idea of having an inner nature, an inner essence that ultimately makes up one's unique individuality. These kinds of imagined "inner, natural truths", these constructions of actuality, are usually understood as unalterable, merely able to be suppressed or liberated. Until today, they nourish the ideas of being able to, or having to fashion and design one's self and one's life freely, autonomously, and according to one's own decisions. These kinds of power relations are therefore not easy to perceive as they commonly come along as one's own free decision, as a personal view, and until today produce the desire to ask: "Who am I?" or, "How can I realize my potential?" "How can I find myself and most greatly develop the essence of my being?". As mentioned, the concept of responsibility of one's own, so commonly used in the course of neo-liberal restructuring, lies within this liberal force line of possessive individualism and actuality and only functions additionally as a neo-liberal interpellation for self-governing.

209 Basically, governmental self-government takes place in an apparent paradox. Governing, controlling, disciplining, and regulating one's self means, at the same time, fashioning and forming one's self, empowering one's self, which, in this sense, means to be free. Only through this paradox can sovereign subjects be governed. Precisely because techniques of governing one's self arise from the simultaneity of subjugation and empowerment, the simultaneity of compulsion and freedom, in this paradoxical movement, the individual not only becomes a subject, but a certain, modern "free" subject. Subjectivated in this way, this subject continually participates in (re)producing the conditions for governmentality, as it is first in this scenario that agency emerges. According to Foucault, power is practiced only on "free subjects" and only to the extent that they are "free" (see Foucault 1983).

In the context of governmentality, subjects are, thus, subjugated and simultaneously agents, and in a certain sense, free. This freedom is, at the same time, a condition and effect of liberal power relations, i.e. of biopolitical governmentality. Despite all of the changes that have occurred until today, since the end of the eighteenth century, this is one of the lines of force through which individuals in modern societies can be governed. This normalised freedom of biopolitical governmental societies never exists without security mechanisms or constructions of the abnormal and deviant, which likewise have subjectivating functions. The modern era seems unthinkable without a "culture of danger", without a permanent threat to the normal, without imaginary invasions of constant, common threats such as diseases, dirt, sexuality, or the "fear of degeneration". (Foucault 2004b, 101f.)[12] The interplay of freedom and security, self empowerment and compulsion, also with the help of this culture of danger, drives on the problems of the political economy of liberal power.

Against this backdrop, all of those who did not comply with this norm and normalising of a free, sovereign, bourgeois, white subject including its property relations were made precarious. Furthermore, in the context of the social state, which was meant to guarantee the security of modern insecurity, not only were women made structurally precarious as wives, through the normal labour conditions oriented on the man. Also those who were excluded as abnormal and foreign from the nation state compromise between capital and labour were likewise made precarious.[13] Precarisation was, accordingly, until now always an inherent contradiction in liberal governmentality and, as abnormal, disturbed the stabilizing dynamic between freedom and security. In this sense, it was often the trigger for struggles and resistance.

Presently, normal labour conditions oriented on a male breadwinner, a situation largely accessible only for the majority society, is losing its hegemony. Precarisation is increasingly a part of governmental normalisation techniques and as a result, in neo-liberalism it transforms from an inherent contradiction to a hegemonic function.

Economising of life and the absence of resistance
The talk of "economising of life," a discussion often struck up in the past several years, provides only very limited explanations of neo-liberal transformation processes: not only due to its totalizing rhetoric, but also because of the associated proclamation of what is supposedly a new phenomenon. "Economising of life" usually refers to certain simplified theses: no longer only work, but also life has fallen prey to economic exploitation interests; a separation between work and life is no longer possible and in the course of this, an implosion of the distinction between production and reproduction has also taken place. Such totalising implosion theses speak of a collective victim status and distort the view of modes of subjectivation, agency and ultimately of resistance.

However, the thesis of the "economising of life" makes sense from a biopolitical governmentality perspective. It points to the power and domination relations of a bourgeois liberal society, which for more than two hundred years now has been constituted around the productivity of life. In this perspective, life was never the other side of work. In Western modernity, reproduction was always part of the political and the economic. Not only reproduction, but also life in general was never beyond power relations. Instead, life, precisely in its productivity, which means its design potential, was always the effect of such

Isabell Lorey

relations. And it is precisely this design potential that is constitutive for the supposed paradox of modern subjectivation between subordination and empowerment, between regulation and freedom. A liberal process of constituting precarisation as an inherent contradiction, did not take place beyond this subjectivation, it is an entirely plausible resulting bundle of social, economic and political positions.

In this sense, the currently lamented "economisation of life" is not an entirely neo-liberal phenomenon, but instead, a force line of biopolitical societies, which today perhaps becomes intelligible in a new way. The associated subjectivations are not new in the way that they are usually claimed to be. In fact, their biopolitical governmental continuities have hardly been grasped.

Were living and working conditions, which arose in the context of social movements since the 1960s, really in no way governmental?[14] Indeed, the thoroughly dissident practices of alternative ways of living, the desire for different bodies and self-relations (in feminist, ecological, left-radical contexts), persistently aimed to distinguish themselves from normal working conditions and the associated constraints, disciplinary measures, and controls. Keywords here are: deciding for oneself what one does for work and with whom; consciously choosing precarious forms of work and life, because more freedom and autonomy seem possible precisely because of the ability to organise one's own time, and what is most important: self-determination. Often, being paid well hasn't been a concern as the remuneration was enjoying the work. The concern was being able to bring to bear one's many skills. Generally, the conscious, voluntary acceptance of precarious labour conditions was often certainly also an expression of the wish for living the modern, patriarchal dividing of reproduction and wage labour differently than is possible within the normal work situation.However, it is precisely these alternative living and working conditions that have become increasingly more economically utilisable in recent years because they favor the flexibility that the labour market demands. Thus, practices and discourses of social movements in the past thirty, forty years were not only dissident and directed against normalisation, but also at the same time, a part of the transformation toward a neo-liberal form of governmentality.

But to what extent are precarious modes of living and working, formerly perceived as dissident, now obvious in their hegemonic, governmental function? And why do they seem to lose their potential for resistance? The following will offer a few thoughts without any claims of presenting a comprehensive analysis.

Many of the culture producers who have entered into a precarious situation of their own accord, the people of whom we are speaking here as a whole, would refer consciously or unconsciously to a history of previous alternative conditions of existence, usually without having any direct political relationship to them. They are more or less disturbed by their shift to the center of society, i.e. to the place where the normal and hegemonic are reproduced. That does not mean, however, that former alternative living and working techniques will become socially hegemonic. Instead, it works the other way around: the mass precarisation of labour conditions is forced upon all of those who fall out of normal labour conditions along with the promise of the ability to take responsibility for their own creativity and fashion their lives according to their own rules, as a desirable, supposedly normal condition of existence. Our concern here is not with these persons forced into precarisation, but those who say that as culture workers they have freely chosen precarious living and working conditions.[15]

It is amazing that there are no systematic empirical studies of this.[16] The common parameters of culture producers, however, should be that they are well or even very well educated, between twenty-five and forty years-old, without children, and more or less intentionally in a precarious employment situation. They pursue temporary jobs, live from projects and pursue contract work from several clients at the same time, one right after the other, usually without sick pay, paid vacations, or unemployment compensation, and without any job security, thus with no or only minimal social protection. The 40-hour week is an illusion. Working time and free time have no clearly defined borders. Work and leisure can no longer be separated. In the non-paid time, they accumulate a great deal of knowledge, which is not paid for extra, but is naturally called for and used in the context of paid work, etc..

This is not an "economising of life," that comes from the outside, overpowering and totalizing. Instead, these are practices connected with desire as well as adaptation. For these conditions of existence are constantly foreseen and co-produced in anticipatory obedience. "Voluntary," i.e., unpaid or low paying jobs in the culture or academic industries, for example, are all too often accepted as an unchangeable fact, and nothing else is even demanded. The necessity of pursuing other, less creative, precarious jobs in order to finance one's own cultural production is accepted. This forced and, simultaneously chosen, financing of one's own creative output constantly supports and reproduces precisely those relations from which one suffers and of which one wants to be a part.[17] Perhaps those who work creatively, these precarious culture producers by design, are subjects that can be exploited so easily because they seem to bear their living and working conditions eternally due to the belief in their own freedom and autonomy, due to self-realisation fantasies. In a neoliberal context they are exploitable to such an extreme that the State even presents them as role models.[18]

This situation of self-precarisation is connected to experiences of fear and loss of control, feelings of insecurity through the loss of certainties and safeguards, as well as fear and the experience of failure, social decline and poverty. Also for these reasons, "letting go" or forms of dropping out and dropping off of hegemonic paradigms are difficult. Everyone has to remain "on speed" otherwise you might fall out. There are no clear times for relaxation or recuperation. This kind of reproduction has no clear place, which, in turn, results in an unfulfilled yearning and a continuous suffering from this lack. The desire for relaxation to "find oneself" becomes insatiable. These kinds of reproductive practices usually have to be learned anew. They are lacking in any self-evidence and have to be fought for bitterly against oneself and others. In turn, this makes this yearning for reproduction, for regeneration, so extremely marketable.

....

Isabell Lorey

As a result, not only the side of work, of production, has become precarious, but also the so-called other side, which is often defined as "life", the side of reproduction. Do production and reproduction therefore coincide? In these culture producers, in an old, new way, yes. What they reveal is that in a neoliberal form of individualisation, parts of production and reproduction are deposited "in" the subjects. Panagiotidis and Tsianos (2004/05, p. 19) also argue along these lines when they state: "The progressive vanquishing of the division of production and reproduction does not occur at home or at the workplace, but instead, through an embodiment of the work itself: a reflexive way of precarisation"! Though what is materialised in the bodies, beyond the work, is also always the governmental life, as biopolitical governmental power relations function doggedly through the production of hegemonic, normalised bodies and self-relations.

The function of reproduction consequently changes in the present context of precarious immaterial, usually individualized work and "life". It is no longer externalised with others, primarily women. Individual reproduction and sexual reproduction, the production of life, now becomes individualized and is shifted, in part, "into" the subjects themselves. It is about regeneration beyond work, also *through* work, but still, quite often beyond adequately paid wage labour. It is about regeneration, renewal, creating from one's self, re-producing one's self from one's own power: of one's own accord. Self-realisation becomes a reproductive task for the self. Work is meant to guarantee the reproduction of the self.

Presenting "precarised" culture producers (that is, cultural producers who have been made precarious) in their entire heterogeneity in such a uniform fashion, it is possible to say that their subjectivation in neoliberalism has obviously been contradictory: in the simultaneity of, on the one hand, precarisation, which also always means fragmentation and non-linearity, and on the other, the continuity of sovereignty. The continuity of modern sovereignty takes place through the stylizing of self-realisation, autonomy, and freedom, through the fashioning of and responsibility for one's self, and the repetition of the idea of actuality. An example of this is the (still) widespread idea of the modern male artist subject, who draws his creativity from himself, because it supposedly exists within him, there, where Western modernity also positions sex and has made it the nature, the essence of the individual. In general, for the culture producers described here, sovereignty seems to rest mainly in the "free" decision for precarisation, therefore, self-precarisation. Yet this, in turn, could be a central reason for why it is so difficult to recognize structural precarisation as a neo-liberal governmental phenomenon that affects the entire society, and is hardly based on a free decision. Culture producers therefore offer an example of the extent to which "self chosen" ways of living and conditions of working, including their ideas of autonomy and freedom, are compatible with political and economic restructuring. How else can we explain that in a study of the living and working conditions of critical culture producers, when asked what a "good life" is, they had no answer?[19] When work and life increasingly permeate one another, then that means, as one interviewee expressed: "work seeps into your life". But obviously, not enough ideas of a "good life" seep into the work, whereby this could then, in turn, transform into something that could collectively signify a "good life." The resistance with the view to a better life, which has less and less of a governmental function, is missing.

Apparently, the belief in precarisation as a liberal governmental oppositional position can be maintained with the help of contradictory subjectivation, between sovereignty and fragmentation. However, in this way, continuing relations of power and domination are made invisible and normalisation mechanisms become naturalised as the subject's self-evident and autonomous decisions. The totalising talk of "economising of life" only contributes to this by causing hegemony effects to disappear from view and with them, battles and antagonisms. One's own imaginations of autonomy and freedom are not reflected on within governmental force lines of modern subjectivation, other freedoms are no longer imagined, thus blocking the view of a possible behavior contesting the hegemonic function of precarisation in the context of neo-liberal governmentality.

What is the price of this normalisation? In neoliberalism, what functions as the abnormal? As the deviant? What can't be economically exploited in this way? Rather than focusing on the messianic arrival of resistance and new subjectivities, as Deleuze rhetorically formulates with the question: "Do not the changes in capitalism find an unexpected 'encounter' in the slow emergence of a new self as a centre of resistance?" (Deleuze 1988, p. 115)[20], I believe that it is necessary to continue to work further and more precisely on the genealogies of precarisation as a hegemonic function, on the problem of continuities of bourgeois governmental modes of subjectivation, also in the context of notions of autonomy and freedom that look upon themselves as dissident.[21]

Transl. by Lisa Rosenblatt and Dagmar Fink

[1] There is no single English word to describe the ongoing process of becoming precarious; this is an attempt to do so.

[2] Here I refer to the expression "culture producers" according to the definition by the group kpD / kleines postfordistisches Drama (little post-fordist drama) which I belong to along with Brigitta Kuster, Katja Reichard, and Marion von Osten (the abbreviation KPD with all capital letters stood for the Kommunistische Partei Deutschlands, the German communist party; translator's note). "We employ the term 'culture producers'" in a decidedly strategic way. With it, we are not speaking of a certain sector (cultural industry), nor of an ascertainable social category (for example, those insured by artists' social security in Germany, which is a health, pension and accident insurance for artists and writers) or of a professional self-conception. Instead, we are speaking of the practice of traveling across a variety of things: theory production, design, political and cultural self-organisation, forms of collabouration, paid and unpaid jobs, informal and formal economies, temporary alliances, project related working and living." (Kleines postfordistisches Drama 2005b, 24)

[3] By lines of force, I understand formations of actions or practices that have homogenized and normalised in time and place through decades or centuries and ultimately are hegemony effects (see, also Foucault 1980; Deleuze 1988).

Isabell Lorey

[4] Mercantilism was also oriented on the growth of the population, but oriented more in terms of quantitative aspects than quality of life "of the people".

[5] For one of the few places in which Foucault points out the inseparability of modern governmentality and biopolitics, see Foucault 2004b, p. 43. On biopolitical governmentality as a socio-theoretical concept, see Lorey 2005.

[6] Following Louis Althusser's thoughts, these imaginary self-relations cannot be separated from "real living conditions," which are here the governmental techniques for ruling the population which, for example, materialize in the constitution of bodies.

[7] I assume that it was not first under neo-liberalism that self management shifted "inward" and replaced a regulatory principle. Regulation and control are not techniques that were first established under neo-liberalism to oppose discipline (different Deleuze 1992; Hardt/Negri 2000). Particularly when reproduction technologies along with hygiene and health are attributed a central biopolitical productivity of (gendered and raced) bodies, then for the bourgeoisie the introduction of these practices of subjectivation must be positioned at the beginning of the modern era, at the end of the eighteenth century, at the latest.

[8] This biopolitical subjectivation is, conversely, differentiated through gender, race, class affiliation, religion, and hetero-normativity, which I cannot go into in detail here. Generally, the text focuses solely on these force lines of bourgeois subjectivation. It is not aiming at a comprehensive look at the problem of ways of subject constitution.

[9] Foucault (2004b) on the contrary, speaks only in connection to the formation of neo-liberal governmentality in the U.S. of the self employer; as does the research based on his work (a.o. Bröckling 2000; Pieper/Gutiérrez.Rodríguez 2003). Lemke et al. (2000) argue, for example, that first when the liberal regulation of "natural freedom" transformed into that of "artificial freedom". was it possible to detect "entrepreneurial behavior of economically-rational individuals". (15) Yet what is this "natural freedom" other than the effect of governmental techniques and social struggles? And what, in contrast, is "artificial freedom"?

[10] In his genealogy of governmentality, Foucault does not draw any explicit connections between the normal and the hegemonic. In order to understand the dynamic and meaning of governmentality, normalization mechanisms must be viewed explicitly in connection with the production of hegemonic discourses and the related battles. On the connection between Foucault and Gramsci, see Hall 1997; Demirovic 1997.

[11] On the connection of imaginary wholeness and whiteness, see Lorey 2006.

[12] Biopolitical governmentality structures modern societies in a specifically paradoxical way. "It enables" as Cornelia Ott so succinctly states, "people to come to understand themselves as unique 'subjects', and at the same time, brings them together as an amorphous, unified, 'population mass' … Hereby, the flipside is always the 'right to life' rather than the exclusion or annihilation of life". (1997, 110) On the connection between biopolitical sociation and colonialism, see Lorey 2006.

[13] On this broad understanding of precarisation see also: kpD 2005a; 2005b and Mecheril 2003.

[14] Boltanski / Chiapello (2001), in contrast, assume an appropriation. According to their study, the changes in capitalism since the 1960s can be traced back to a specific integration and strategic reformulation of an "artistic critique". a critique that complains of the uniformity of a mass society, a lack of individual autonomy, and the loss of authentic social relations (see also Lemke 2004, pp. 176-78).

[15] On self-precarisation in the context of migration, also beyond "culture producing" practices, see Kuster (in this book) and Panagiotidis 2005.

[16] Initial approaches can be found in Böhmler / Scheiffele 2005; the study by Anne and Marine Rambach (2001) on precarious intellectuals in France; the theses by Angela McRobbie (2004) on the functionality of artists for the new economy; or the study by kpD (see note 1 and 18; kpD 2005 b).

[17] The performer Jochen Roller thematizes precisely this dynamic in his pieces.

[18] See, for example, the Schröder / Blair paper from 1998, or the interpellation of – among others – journalists, academics, and artists in the context of the Hartz-IV reform in Germany to act as "the nation's professionals" (www.bundesregierung.de / artikel-,413.445340 / Bundesregierung-richtet-Steuer.htm; 10 / 21 / 05).

[19] As part of the film project "Kamera Läuft!" ("Action!" Zürich / Berlin 2004, 32'), at the end of 2003, the group kpD (kleines postfordistisches Drama, see note 1) interviewed fifteen Berlin culture producers (including kpD) "with whom we work together for a specific form of political practice in the cultural field or whose work we use as a reference. … Our questions were based on those from Fronte della Gioventù Lavoratrice's and Potere Operaio's questionnaire action carried out in early 1967 in Mirafiori, *Fiat is our University*, which among other things, also asked about the ideas of a "good life", and organisation. … With regards to a potential politicization of culture producers, we were, however, also interested in collective refusal strategies and in the associated wishes for improving one's own life, the life of others, and ultimately, social change. The only thing that was present at a general level in all of the interviews was the suffering from a lack of continuity. … We, too, found almost no alternative life concepts in our horizon of ideas that could counter the existing ones with anything clear or unambiguous." (kpD 2005b, 24f.; s.a. kpD 2005a)

[20] Extreme example of a current messianic idea is naturally the end of the book Empire by Hardt / Negri (2000), but also, although different and in a greatly weakend from, Foucault (1983) with his demand for new subjectivities.

[21] Thanks go to Brigitta Kuster, Katharina Pühl and Gerald Raunig for critical discussions.

....

Isabell Lorey

References

BÖHMLER, Daniela; Scheiffele, Peter (2005): Überlebenskunst in einer Kultur der Selbstverwertung. In: Franz Schultheis; Christina Schulz (eds.): *Gesellschaft mit beschränkter Haftung. Zumutungen und Leiden im deutschen Alltag.* Konstanz, pp. 422-448

BOLTANSKI, Luc; Chiapello, Eve (2005): The Role of Criticism in the Dynamics of Capitalism: Social Critique vs. Artistic Critique. *Worlds of Capitalism. Institutions, Governance, and Economic Change in the Era of Globalization.* (Ed.) Max Miller. London, New York, pp. 237-267

BRÖCKLING, Ulrich; Krasmann, Susanne; Lemke, Thomas (eds.) (2000): *Gouvernementalität der Gegenwart. Studien zur Ökonomisierung des Sozialen.* Frankfurt / M.

BUBLITZ, Hannelore; Christine Hanke; Andrea Seier (2000): *Der Gesellschaftskörper. Zur Neuordnung von Kultur und Geschlecht um 1900.* Frankfurt / M. / New York

CASTEL, Robert (2005): *Die Stärkung des Sozialen. Leben im neuen Wohlfahrtsstaat.* Hamburg (French Original: *L' insécurité sociale - qu'est-ce qu'être protégé?* Paris 2003)

DELEUZE, Gilles (1988): *Foucault.* Trans. and ed. by Seán Hand. London

DELEUZE, Gilles (1992): Postscript on the Societies of Control. In: OCTOBER 59, Winter, pp. 3-7.; also available at http: / /www.nadir.org / nadir / archiv / netzkritik / society-ofcontrol.html (20 / 10 / 05)

DEMIROVIC, Alex (1997): *Demokratie und Herrschaft. Aspekte kritischer Gesellschaftstheorie.* Münster

FOUCAULT, Michel (1980): *The History of Sexuality, Volume I: An Introduction.* Trans. Robert Hurley. New York

FOUCAULT, Michel (1985): *The Use of Pleasure.* Trans. Robert Hurley. New York

FOUCAULT, Michel (1983): "The Subject and Power." In: *Michel Foucault: Beyond Structuralism and Hermeneutics,* ed. by Hubert L. Dreyfus; Paul Rabinow. Chicago, pp. 208–226

FOUCAULT, Michel (1991): "Governmentality." In: *The Foucault Effect: Studies in Governmentality,* ed. by Graham Bruchell et al. Chicago, pp. 87–104

FOUCAULT, Michel (2004a) *Geschichte der Gouvernementalität I. Sicherheit, Territorium, Bevölkerung. Vorlesungen am Collège de France 1977-78.* Frankfurt / M. (French Original: *Sécurité, Territoire et Population,* Paris 2004)

FOUCAULT, Michel (2004b): *Geschichte der Gouvernementalität II. Die Geburt der Biopolitik. Vorlesungen am Collège de France 1978-79.* Frankfurt / M. (French Original: *Naissance de la biopolitique,* Paris 2004)

HALL, Stuart (1997): The Spectacle on the "Other". In: Stuart Hall (ed.): *Representation. Cultural Representations and Signifying Practices.* London, pp. 223-290

HARDT, Michael; Negri, Antonio (2000): *Empire.* Cambridge / Mass., London

KLEINES POSTFORDISTISCHES DRAMA / kpD (2005a): Prekäre Subjektivierung. Interview. In: *Malmoe,* No. 7, p. 20

KLEINES POSTFORDISTISCHES DRAMA / kpD (2005b): Prekarisierung von Kultur-produzentInnen und das ausbleibende "gute Leben." In: *arranca! für eine linke Strömung*. No. 32 (Summer), pp. 23-25

LEMKE, Thomas; Krasmann, Susanne; Bröckling, Ulrich (2000): Gouvernementalität, Neoliberalismus und Selbsttechnologien. In: Ulrich Bröckling; Susanne Krasmann, Thomas Lemke (eds.): *Gouvernementalität der Gegenwart. Studien zur Ökonomisierung des Sozialen*. Frankfurt / M., pp. 7-40

LEMKE, Thomas (2004): Räume der Regierung: Kunst und Kritik der Menschenführung. In: Peter Gente im Auftrag des Zentrums für Kunst und Medientechnologie (ZKM) (ed.): *Foucault und die Künste*. Frankfurt / M., pp. 162-180

LOCKE, John (1823): Two Treatises of Government (Concerning the True Original Extent and End of Civil Government §44). from The Works of John Locke. A New Edition, Corrected. In Ten Volumes. Vol. V. London,. http://socserv2.mcmaster. ca / ~econ / ugcm / 3ll3 / locke / government.pdf; (10 / 19 / 2005)

LOREY, Isabell (2005): Als das Leben in die Politik eintrat. Die biopolitisch gouverne mentale Moderne, Foucault und Agamben. In: Marianne Pieper; Thomas Atzert; Serhat Karakayali; Vassilis Tsianos (eds.): *Empire und die biopolitische Wende*. Frankfurt / M. / New York

LOREY, Isabell (2006): Fetisch Körper und Weißsein. Eine Kritik am Primat der Kategorie Geschlecht. In: Anja Weckwert; Ulla Wischermann (eds.): *Das Jahrhundert des Feminismus. Festschrift für Ute Gerhard*. Frankfurt / M.

MACPHERSON, Crawford Brough (1962): *Political Theory of Possessive Individualism: Hobbes to Locke*. Oxford

MCROBBIE, Angela (2001): "Everyone is Creative": artists as new economy pioneers? http://www.opendemocracy.net / arts / article_652.jsp (10 / 18 / 2005)

MECHERIL, Paul (2003): *Prekäre Verhältnisse. Über natio-ethno-kulturelle Mehrfachzu-gehörigkeit*. Münster / New York / Munich / Berlin

MARX, Karl [1859] (1999): *A Contribution to the Critique of Political Economy*. http://www.marxists.org / archive / marx / works / 1859 / critique-pol-economy / index.htm (10 / 19 / 2005)

OTT, Cornelia (1997): Lust, Geschlecht und Generativität. Zum Zusammenhang von gesellschaftlicher Organisation von Sexualität und Geschlechterhierarchie. In: Irene Dölling; Beate Krais (eds.): *Ein alltägliches Spiel. Geschlechterkonstruktionen in der sozialen Praxis*. Frankfurt / M., pp. 104-124

PANAGIOTIDIS, Efthimia; Tsianos, Vassilis (2004 / 05): Reflexive Prekarisierung. Eine Introspektion aus dem Alltag von Projektlinken. In: *Fantômas. Magazin für linke Debatte und Praxis: "Prekäre Zeiten"*. No. 6 (Winter), pp. 18-19

PANAGIOTIDIS, Efthimia (2005): DenkerInnenzelle X. Prekarisierung, Mobilität, Exodus. In: *arranca! für eine linke Strömung*. No. 32 (Summer), pp. 12-14

PIEPER, Marianne; Gutiérrez Rodríguez, Encarnación (eds.) (2003): *Gouvernementali-tät. Ein sozialwissenschaftliches Konzept im Anschluss an Foucault*. Frankfurt / M. / New

York

PÜHL, Katharina (2003): Der Bericht der Hartz-Kommission und die 'Unternehmerin ihrer selbst': Geschlechterverhältnisse, Gouvernementalität und Neoliberalismus. In: Marianne Pieper; Encarnación Gutiérrez Rodríguez (eds.): *Gouvernementalität. Ein sozialwissenschaftliches Konzept im Anschluss an Foucault.* Frankfurt / M. / New York, pp. 111-135

RAMBACH, Anne; Rambach, Marine (2001): *Les intellos précaires.* Paris

SARASIN, Philipp (2001): *Reizbare Maschinen. Eine Geschichte des Körpers 1765-1914.* Frankfurt / M.

Some thoughts concerning Isabell Lorey's theses

Roger M. Buergel / Alex Demirovic

Alex Demirovic: I don't want to present another concept or another strategy here but discuss some thoughts concerning Isabell Lorey's theses. I think that it's a fruitful approach to focus on the imaginary of artists and art producers, that is, their imaginary relation with themselves, their own life conditions. And moreover to ask oneself what those conscious processes, those intense considerations, those discourse effects of one's own activity mean regarding the sustenance of that activity. I believe that this can be done pretty well with Foucault, and I also find that this leads farther in cultural analysis compared with what Bourdieu does. Also, I'm playing them off against each other a bit, because Bourdieu asks the artists quite soon how far they're aiming at increasing their artistic capital, for which they accept many forms of self-deception about their own activity.

In my opinion, Bourdieu often leaves aside this formation process of subject positions, heavily restricting self-deception to utilitarian issues: How can I, as an artist, survive in the field which I'm working in, which I'm investing in, which I'm producing in, and make, so to speak, a larger profit? Opposed to this is the analysis of regarding this process in connection with government and self-government. And this is where I'm coming back to one of Isabell Lorey's thoughts. She referred very strongly to people's self-relationship, i.e., their imaginary relation with themselves and the activities connected therewith. We could see that very nicely described in the former paper on dance. Dance is conceived as a performative, always searching for a letter but never finds it. When you see how this search fails but in a way moves on over it, and thus creates a relation between theory movement and body movement, then you could also understand this as a possibility to make an issue of the imaginary.

Another viewpoint seems important to me – the question how much this is about governmental engineering which is connected with the development of a modern political education. Art production occurs in the framework of a state government, a self-direction in which certain activities are fulfilled. I think this area can be further expanded, and this is what always has fascinated me about this topic: To what extent do intellectuals – through their activity on the stage, as artists, as writers, as scientists – produce a certain political knowledge even in the form of their active autonomy? The question which arises here is determining the autonomy of that activity. How does this autonomy come about? And after all, it is being cultivated – many of the arguments which Isabell presented aim at culturally active people practising this autonomy, but at the same time deceiving themselves about it, and not reflecting their dependence as part of their activity. Here I'm coming to a first question, a first problem: Should this autonomy which is so questionable be defended? And are art producers really so oblivious in their activity, like this idea of governmentality and a governmental self-relation of the artists insinuates? I believe that a large share of the practice we've been able to observe for decades in the field of art – it could be more than decades, maybe it's the modern self-relation *per se* – shows that many artists enter into a relation of self-questioning and even "self-denial". So the question is whether this self-relation really is so affirmative that they simply subject themselves to this precariousness voluntarily, or if they also question their activity by way of their approach whether this kind of division of labour is principally rational. I won't go into the definition of rationality now, but I believe that it allows for a critical and self-critical practice.

How do I question myself and my own activity with regard to rationality? That is Foucault's question – the question how that which I'm doing comes into existence. What is the rationality of that which I'm doing? My answer is – I've already hinted at it – reproduction of dominant division of labour with its unequal distribution of manual and intellectual work. When I'm putting this question to myself and my activity as an artist, actively and, so to speak, in the endless loops of a performative which I never really can overtake – but want to in order to deny it – then I'm explaining myself hermeneutically and making myself a governmental technology, which I actually wanted to interrupt by my self-questioning. I want to escape the governmental logic, but I go about it by questioning myself and a questioning self-relation with which I'm actually causing this governmental technology to unfold.

Perhaps the apory into which these questions are leading me doesn't get solved on the level of artistic activity itself, or not on it alone. The self-relation can only be made topical, and then it's about the socio-theoretical shift about which, I believe, we have to say more yet. I agree with much of what Isabell has pointed out here. There are significant changes in the situation of art producers which we have to observe closer, for on the whole our knowledge about them is scant. There's very little research about the drastic changes of the situation. The number of artists increases considerably, while at the same time the possibilities of materially reproducing oneself by artistic activities are decreasing. The working situation for many necessarily becomes precarious, and a socio-political change sets in. That's the second issue I want to go into – and that's why I said that I'm playing off Bourdieu and Foucault against each other: We have to see how the cultural field currently restructures and also re-polarises itself. For there is not only precarisation by necessity but also new forms of polarising. The few books I know about this mention that with the new working structures, with the network of discontinuous employment situations will arise where the winners will get everything. To me it seems to be a very important point that economising cultural reproduction goes along with a restructuring of the field, so that single groups and single persons can really count on gaining high profits for their cultural activities, their investments, which considerably contributes to the field's continuing to function. This also applies to the field of all this aestheticising Bohemian self-conception mentioned before.

This means that we have to concentrate much more on which new forms of polarisation there are in the field of precariousness. Statistics show that only one or two percent of cultural producers make enormous – really enormous profits. In a way, they're engendering a new market structure of artistic production – extreme monopoly formations, a hierarchical restructuring of the presentation forms of cultural production.

Roger M. Buergel: Thank you for all those proposals. I, too, agree to the idea of searching for that, or investigating artistic procedures and performance methods with regard to what can be universalised, what could be valid on a social level in them. And I also feel

Roger M. Buergel / Alex Demirovic

indebted for Alex's cue concerning the forms of polarisation, although I would like to look at its form rather than polarisation itself. In this context I was reminded of a performance which Maja Bajević did in a cultural centre in the suburbs of Barcelona. She mirrored the performance space in her setting: The room, modernistic with a concrete ceiling, had a grid which she reproduced by laying barbed wire on the floor, and in this setting she acted. However, she was not alone but with a group of women who themselves run a space in the vicinity. What they did was winding the barbed wire pattern, the grid, the empty spaces with wool. They let the wool hang down or stretched it out between the wires, building another pattern, standardised on the one hand, but singular, too. That was a very meditative activity which also had a religious character, an air of collection. What made sense to me and what basically interests me in dance performances – and that's also the frame in which we're moving here – was the moment where the work becomes detached from the person, where the human figure exposes itself in its precariousness, exhibits itself, gives itself up and thus creates a situation which implies others – maybe not a collective, that would seem too severe and emphatic, too stereotype – involves them in its own compositional activity. At this point one can't really talk about "own" any more because the threshold actually is the disillusionment towards the work, the movement, the cipher in space. I believe that the mediality, the radical mediality of human figures, of subjects is the potential of precariousness, which I'll come back to presently. First of all I'd like to answer Isabell, i.e., take up this thesis and allow an orientation towards that which she terms cultural producer – a perspective which isn't in my line at all since I'm actually trying to get away from figures and subjectivities especially with regard to this mediality, the possibility of mediality which I tried to underline with Maja Bajević's performance. At the same time, however, I think it's great that she talks about herself or about us; for the great weakness in the political discussion of the Left is that it can talk about everything but not about itself. I was co-responsible for a governmentality symposium where the individual speakers, scientists, artists within minutes effortlessly went from Saddam Hussein to Guantánamo – but they couldn't talk about themselves. Meanwhile my opinion is that they are ashamed. But my impression also is that Isabell's focussing of the question on the precariousness of the so-called cultural producers – I'm saying "so-called" because this term insinuates a homogeneity which in my opinion can be held up. You've qualified that yourself already, but one can't say it often enough … And secondly, it engenders a fixation or identification, which I think is part of the problem; you already mentioned that, too. So, my impression is that Isabell's focussing the question of precariousness towards the side of cultural producers swings the pendulum the other way. No more Guantánamo and Saddam Hussein.

Your thesis implies the hope – at least it sounds that way to me – the expectation of mobilisation. One realises a position, a common threat. At the same time, a whole vocational group is becoming transfigured which once again understands itself as the avant-garde of social changes, i.e., an economisation of life. I don't think this is false reasoning any more, but I'm asking myself what value, what surplus value this construction of cultural producers as precarious subjects *per se* has, what its benefits are.

223

....

There's another construction which reacts in the struggle for the scant resources in the field of cultural production: Illusion, which lets us believe in the meaningfulness of our doing. Isabell says that we have to become conscious to the fact that the desire for self-realisation is an effect of the biopolitical distribution of power.

I would reply to this that cultural producers know very well that their work is far from withdrawing from the grip of hegemonic structures. I also believe that the function of the creativity of the individual or the creative worker is obsolete. The politicalisation which Isabell demands, i.e., the implementation of relative acting capacity of cultural producers, to me seems to be paralysed by a compulsion to sell one's own position to oneself as that of a dissident. And indeed your lecture doesn't offer a prospect of forms of politicalisation. Possibly that's not the task you set yourself. But there is no way back to Fordism, which anyway is not what we want. What you call precarisation, what is thematised as precarisation rather is a degradation, a social deterioration in the wake of a proletarianisation of the middle class. I believe that the cultural producers mainly are the fallen children of the bourgeoisie – the classical, national bourgeoisie whose existential desire historically always has been to convert profits into accounts, which doesn't work any more nowadays, Just now I sneered a bit at the incapability of grasping cultural production itself as a governmental action and abandoning the illusion that one is at the fringe or even outside of power; dissidence was the cue. However, I would like to go a step further and say that in my opinion the issue is not just accepting precariousness, i.e., acknowledging it as a fact and working through it, like Isabell demands in the sense of precarisation of cultural production – then, we'd also have to inspect the historical changes within the forms of precarisation. I believe that the actual task is developing a much more basic form of precarisaton, in the sense of referring to each other without identifications like "cultural producers", "filmmakers", etc.. My opinion is that we considerably have to enlarge the whole discussion about the way we are being addressed as people moving in the cultural field, towards forms of relations. I think that in the sense of the mediality I've seen in the dance or performances of Maja Bajević this is a possibility of actually working in the framework of a universal ethic, which would also shed the caste-orientation of our life as cultural producers and offer the chance to co-operate with other vocational groups who are in the same quandary.

Roger M. Buergel / Alex Demirovic

225

Tactile networks in art and performance

To those who watch like poets and listen like thieves

Christine Peters / Iara Boubnova / Lois Keidan / Louise Neri

Introduction

Christine Peters: Welcome everybody to this last panel of the congress. I am very glad that Iara Boubnova, Louise Neri, Lois Keidan and Hubert Machnik are here with me.

Since we are announced as the so called "producer's panel" in the congress folder and since this panel is supposed to be about artistic strategies and methods, I first of all would like to introduce several format aspects and conceptual thoughts to you:

I. Structure

The structure of this panel is an "f-m-classic-REVERSE" – there's four girls ONLY WHO will discuss, AND the boy will STAY MUTE BEHIND his Macintosh G4.

MOREOVER, in case that we would want to change the rules of the game and play (OR MESS AROUND) with Q & A's during the panel, I prepared a paper called *23 questions to curators* which we can always use – So let's see what happens to that …

II. Method

There is a seven-minute film masterpiece by Daniel Huillet and Jean-Marie Straub, *En rachâchant* (Text: Marguerite Duras) which in my opinion gives a great definition of "interdisciplinary research": When Ernesto at the age of five had to go to school, on his first day he briefly checked out the situation and then immediately decided to leave again. When the teacher asked him why Ernesto said "I don't want to learn things I don't know". So the teacher asked: "So, Ernesto, how do you want to learn?" Ernesto replied, "*en rachâchant*", which as a word is a new creation and means something like "ploughing and researching" at the same time. Being asked by the teacher what "*en rachâchant*" meant, Ernesto replied: "It's a new method".

III. Artistic strategy

Let's zoom to the boy behind the Macintosh G4: Concerning an applied panel strategy, I invited the composer Hubert Machnik as the panel's "artist in residence" because there are no curators without artists and no new forms without interdisciplinary research.

Hubert specialises in electronic and computer music and has developed various formats for audiovisual installations and performances. During this audio research project called *Conditional strategical production in real spaces*, he will develop a computer programme with which he will structure and process live the text material whichwill be generated by us during the panel discussion. The panel as production format is therefore itself part of the compositional process. – And, while composing, he will of course remain absolutely silent … being a third man, as Jean Fisher would say:

> Asking how one activates a successful communication, Michel Serres concludes
> that it requires two contradictory conditions: the presence of noise, since
> the meaning of a message emerges only against a background of noise, and the
> total exclusion of what it needs to include, namely, background noise … To hold

229

a dialogue is therefore to presuppose a third man and to seek to exclude him.
(Jean Fisher, *Embodied Subversion*, in: *Live Art and Performance*, Tate 2004)

IV. "If you change the terminal you change the borders" (Guillermo Gómez-Peña): Production Strategy
"Tactile network" as a term came into existence thanks to a complete misunderstanding from my side, when I listened to a lecture by Tomislav Medak in Halle: He explained and screened the opposition he made up between "tactical and classical networks". During his lecture I constantly read and understood "tactile networks" instead of "tactical networks" and felt very inspired, as for me that term provoked crucial questions like: "How do you want to spend your lifetime? How do you want to spend your money? With whom do you want to share things?"

Moreover, "Tactile" clearly refers to friendship and affinity as a concept for artistic production and so – titlewise – I decided to sample it together with yet another crucial aspect: Subversion: "… those who watch like poets and listen like thieves" is smuggled in from Hakim Bey's *Temporary Autonomous Zones* and highlights subversion and piracy as an artistic strategy.

V. Labelling
This title story brings me to the topic of labelling and to one of the reasons for inviting Iara: In 2002, there were two big projects taking place in Frankfurt: The 4th International Summer Academy at Arts Centre Mousonturm (August) and the 4th European Biennial for Contemporary Arts, Manifesta (May–September), organised by the same Arts Centre.

I co-curated this fourth edition of the International Summer Academy together with Mårten Spångberg and Florian Malzacher and, working in a new team constellation, we had some problems finding a title in the beginning: There was even an opposition between "labelling" and "non-labelling", between having a theme or not.

At the same time, Manifesta was prepared in Frankfurt, and the three Manifesta curators, among them Iara Boubnova, must have gone through the same process since they finally decided not to have a title. (Two years before in Ljubljana, the title had been *Borderline*). I thought that it was very courageous to do that – usually there's so many pseudo titles and en vogue titles used which have hardly anything to do with the overall programme content – however, the local journalists totally disliked this decision.

Our decision for the Summer Academy was different: Instead of agreeing to one of our listed suggestions or making a radical cut and not having any title at all, we finally found an artistic solution and asked Tim Etchells to invent a title as an artistic project (*True Truth about the Nearly Real*) AND THUS TO EXPAND THE ARTISTIC PLAYGROUND. – I still think that this curatorial decision process was crucial and important for the productive and successful teamwork experience we finally had.

....

Christine Peters / Iara Boubnova / Lois Keidan / Louise Neri

Q & A – Part I:
Panel Discussion

In the forefield of the congress, Iara, Louise, Lois and me discussed questions like:
What are the criteria for the selection and choice of certain collabouration partners and
artists? – Intuition, friendship, risk and experiment, production of knowledge?
    Critical input? – Tactile or tactical reasons?
    Is labelling a danger?
    Is protection a core task? – How much protection do artists need?

Iara, do you still agree to what you answered to Alexander Kiossev in an interview when
he asked you "Do you think that art today has this function of creating relevant horizons,
of producing visions that have social validity beyond the borders of the Art world?" And
you said: "Yes, I do. For me the relevant horizon is the opening of borders, from political
and ideological borders, to borders between visual languages and structures. The social
validity in this case is predicated on the involvement of large groups of people, on the use
… by the artists of a variety of media and approaches, on the liberating impulses triggered
by contemporary art. Because for me contemporary art is associated with freedom. This
kind of art it is supposed to pinpoint differences, and it tends to attract, seduce, negotiate the general public into getting used to these differences and ultimately into acceptance
and a higher degree of tolerance. Contemporary art has a very strong critical power that is
even more easy to embrace because it tends to be self-ironical as well. However, in its most
interesting examples, artists and approaches in contemporary art, it occupies neither the
position nor the attitude of some higher patronising authority."
    Moreover, Iara, I ask myself: Being parachuted into cities as a curator for different bien-
nials and projects plus continuously working in an institution like the ICA – Is it, is this
"lifestyle" still productive? What is your experience with this power constellation you are
co-responsible for? Where are the problems? And what's your opinion about working in an
institution with an annual programme versus working for biennials / festivals?
    Iara Boubnova: First, let me thank you for the quotation you used. Of course, it looks
like a statement. If I had to do it right now I would use it once more. I still believe in the
things I was saying in this dialogue concerning Manifesta and the idea of doing Biennales,
or biannual events. I can't see why it is something that is "versus" (or contrary to) individual or institutional practice; maybe I don't have such a big experience with institutional
practice myself. Anyhow, what I know is that there are two things about curatorship. And
the "bad" news about curatorship is that it is collabourative and team work. It is bad news
for the curatorial ego, and for wherever and however careers are made. It is not a personal
activity, nor solitary work. From the beginning you are very much dependent and you start
to live up to different expectations. It doesn't matter if you are doing it in a small institution, as in the case of the ICA-Sofia – by the way, that's not to be mixed up with the ICA
London, there is really a big difference. When we established this institution in 1995 we

231

didn't know the word "agency", but maybe now it sounds better in terms of explaining what the ICA-Sofia is.

So, on one side curating is teamwork, and a big problem is how do you start the team work, how do you create this team. One of the best things I know about biennials is starting to do things when the team is not ready yet for the event. You usually start to do things when the team is not yet mature; you usually finish with a great team, consisting of the best artists, producers and curators. Unfortunately this usually is too late, because the event is over, the opening has gone by and you have a great team but nobody ever invites you to do something again with the same team. So, there is a big failure and a big problem. On the other side, it is not such "bad" news because curatorial ego working in a team still leaves space for fun and still has room for individuality. The most important thing is to create this team attitude, without subordinating yourself to anything except the task, or the time frame and the budget.

I have experienced work in many events in locations which were not central or not brave enough to say that they were already producing something of central importance. And in such locations you can see the logic and interest of this particular place to do this particular big event, let's say a Biennale, because it is the most popular format and here is where the teamwork and the political situation come together all the time.

It is not a big secret that political units usually initiate huge events. Of course, we can find an excuse and say that the situation and the context are mature enough, but usually some political units initiate it all and very often they give money, as was the case in Moscow, where I worked recently. So, you are supposed to do something with this political initiative and usually it is not easy – much more because of the logic of expectations than the logic of political will. However, all of this is never explicit. You are supposed to recognise what is expected of you. And in this case I would say that it is the same situation as when you establish a small institution and you are supposed to use this institution as a context producer. Again, that is a political thing. All the people I know in Eastern Europe started to work in the field of contemporary art in a similar way. That was your question, right? Why you started and how? It is difficult to say why; maybe because there wasn't a big choice of work, when I started it was too late to go for Bunny Girl, you know …

But when we did start in the late 1980s, we felt as agents of democracy, a totally different society, a fifth column of development and openness. Then we lost this position and now it is much more problematic. What type of political situation can we express and for what are we really working? It is really difficult, because at the moment we are positioned in different places and locations, we are critical about the development of the situation, its hypocrisy. Practical things are going better than they were, and we still remember that because it is a personal memory. On the other side, one should not to be complaining too much, because it is stupid – outside of art you can do better things with your life and get better money and have good working hours. In between these two situations, in between your own understanding of a political task and in between the demands you have, you are trying to create a small, modest independence of your institution or the unit, and to work with the team and work for the event, which produces artefacts and art works, meaning also artistic careers. Sometimes, very rarely, it even produces money. The other thing is the double weighted word communication. I like the word relations, thanks to the project that is called "relations". Because relations for me still are something a little bit better, more human, but bigger than communication in general. So, this is the logic why I would try to eliminate this "contrary to", or "versus", you know, "institution / institutional curatorship" or biennials. Of course, there is the footnote: Whenever we are talking about biennials, we usually are not talking about the Venice Biennale or São Paulo, because they are too established and they are an exception from the situation I am most familiar with.

Christine Peters: Lois, when I started to collaborate with Tim Etchells and Forced Entertainment some years ago, they recommended you a lot and I thought "she must be the most brilliant producer ever in the world".

However, it seems that their respect for you was not only due to your high quality production but also due to aspects of continuity, reliability and responsibility, and, last but not least: due to your political attitude – your fighting to get the money for those artists, whom you really wanted to support.

However, you left the ICA, Lois, where you worked in the 1990s, and decided to found an agency called *Live Art Development Agency*, which became a very successful tool and with which you gained a very strong political voice within the art community in London and the UK. And I ask myself: Isn't it a paradox to have this agency and at the same time not to have a continuous production and presentation space anymore? What are the advantages and disadvantages? How is it to make your own rules? Do you ever get trapped in your own rules and suddenly have to fulfil them instead of re-inventing them? And isn't it paradox to collabourate with those big machines like Tate Modern or Liverpool Biennial who ask you to stay independent but at the same time make you very dependent on their rules of the game?

So, how would you define the potential of being an "independent dependent"? What is needed, Lois?

Lois Keidan: Well, we have all been producing work for hundreds of years, so I think if we knew what was needed we would bottle it and sell it and we wouldn't have needed these three days of congress. So certainly there aren't any kind of right answers or solutions. But it's a continuous process of trial and error. But what is needed in terms of what we have looked at? Do you mean that?

Peters: Yes, I mean this shift in today's production practice , also according to what you were saying in one of your last essays titled *Thoughts on place, placelessness and live art since the 1980s*: "With live art questions of place come with territory and since the late 1980s this ever expanding and shape shifting field of practice has challenged assumptions and changed rules about who is making art. How they are making it, who they are making it for and where they are making it?"

Keidan: Well, one of the guiding principles behind the Agency is not that we are an agency booking artists, but that we use the word Agency to mean "agent of change". My colleague Catherine Ugwu and I used to run the performance programme at the Institute of Contemporary Arts in London, and the ICA is what it says it is – an Institute of Contemporary Arts that comes with a certain type of formula and all we could do was play with the possibilities of that formula, of it being a multidisciplinary space. Being the Institute of Contemporary Arts gives you a certain kind of permission to do things but also comes with a certain set of expectations about innovative and radical practices.

The eight years we were there we worked with Tim Etchells and Forced Entertainment, and also with some of the "hardcore" artists: Orlan, Franco B., Ron Athey, Guillermo Gómez-Peña, Marina Abramović, etc.. But there was a certain expectation that this was what this Institute was going to present and in fact the most subversive thing we presented at the ICA in the whole of that time was Theatre Group Stan's production of *The importance of Being Earnest*, which was a Flemish company doing an Oscar Wilde play, which raised brows enormously. So there is that kind of expectation that there is going to be a kind of radical work with the ICA. And there is the possibility that these institutions become a kind of ghetto for certain kinds of practices. These were the things we always had to deal with. When we left the ICA it was a fantastic opportunity to kind of look at other ways of doing things, other possible formulas beyond the institution, so it was an incredibly privileged moment to be in a position where we could set up the Live Art Development Agency. But also the funding body for London, the Arts Council of London, wanted to invest in an agency that would be looking at the new and different ways artists are working, and doing that outside of an institutional context. We may say that the agency is the leading organisation for Live Art in the UK, but it is actually the only development organisation for Live Art in the UK. Being an agency of this kind does put us in an interesting position: we are very small and we are very independent and we are basically able to work fluidly, a fluid approach within a fluid landscape. And it offers us the possibility to work strategically across a range of contents, in terms of interventions and in terms of collabourations. And it also raises interesting questions about the relationship to the institution or to institutions. And what we are kind of interested in is choices and possibilities. Of course there is the issue about why an independent organisation would want to collabourate with an organisation like TATE Modern, which is as big and inflexible as you can get. But we wanted to look at the plurality of ways that artists were working at the moment and look at the choices that were out there. And the way that many artists are working in the UK and across the world with interdisciplinary or postdisciplinary practices relates to the quote you read out about the different ways that art can be made and where it can be placed and who it can talk to. So there are artists who are working within cultural centres, within institutional spaces, within galleries and theatre spaces, which are to a certain extent prescribed spaces, almost controlled spaces. I don't mean that in a negative sense, but there is a certain audience-artist dynamic, a certain expectation of that and the way Jérôme (Bel) was talking about it yesterday, in that he makes work for the stage because the stage offers him a particular kind of space for a particular kind of practice. But there are also artists who are kind of choosing to work outside of the constraints of galleries and

Christine Peters / Iara Boubnova / Lois Keidan / Louise Neri

theatres and prescribed cultural spaces. So the Agency was set up to try to find different ways of working that can respond and adopt and change to the way that artists are working and look at the different kinds of contexts and spaces and places that art can be located in. And different types of relationship with the audience and different kinds of critical discourses and cultural strategies. So I think, if there were any solutions, flexibility has to be absolutely at the heart of it, and fluidity has to be at the heart of it.

Peters: Louise, in all our recent discussions I experienced you as a person who constantly asks questions like: Why do they do it? Why is certain work important or happening? Why do most talks deal with ideas and not with experiences or motivations? I prepared a citation for you as well, which will lead to my questions. It belongs to a letter that Peggy Phelan wrote to Marina Abramović: "Contemporary critical writing is severely resistant to the undecided and the shaded. Increasingly criticism is reduced to the thumbs-up or thumbs-down gesture. But I need to find a richer means of response if I am to remain a writer of non-fiction. A task I am less and less sure if it makes much sense. You might think this is my problem, but I am afraid it is yours too. Harold Rosenberg pointed out in a writing from 1952 that in order to form a new school, one needs both a new consciousness and a new consciousness of that consciousness." (Peggy Phelan, *On Seeing the Invisible*, in: *Live Art and Performance*, Tate 2004)

So, Louise, as an editor, curator and critic working today: How would you consider the importance and relevance of critical reflection and the creation of a multi-layered discourse in regards to artistic projects / experiments such as DAS TAT , being both a social vision and multidisciplinary space?

When you worked as curator for DAS TAT, you were trying to translate and define this artistic and social vision, although I personally think that the period of experimentation should have started five years earlier in order to implement its networking potential more substantially.

Nevertheless, would you say that risky projects like this one still have a future, both artistically and politically?

Are there any striking examples existing successfully now?

Louise Neri: For most of my working life up until 2000, I had been institutionally employed. Very early on, after quitting university, I created and directed a non-profit emerging artists' centre in Australia, then I went to New York to work as editor of *Parkett*, a prominent international contemporary art journal. While I worked at *Parkett*, I also co-curated several very large-scale biennial exhibitions, including the Whitney (1997) and São Paulo (1998 and 2000). Yet I always felt myself to be making and experiencing these curatorial projects from my position within another institution. So, five years ago, I decided that I had to leave *Parkett* to explore my interests and test the limits beyond my institutional life.

Independent cultural workers are like immigrant workers. One of the important formative experiences of being an immigrant is what kind of welcome you receive at your destination, how you are inducted into a new and foreign environment, a job, a living situation, a social context. At the Whitney Museum, I was the first non-staff curator ever to work on

235

a Biennial. Much of my time was spent negotiating, outmanoeuvering or altogether avoiding the paralysing political web of a large museum. By the time I completed that enormous project I felt that I knew almost enough to begin.

In Sao Paulo, the situation was richer, more flexible, more clear, more unexpected, more convivial, more chaotic. Having made one edition, I was asked back for the next. I was very excited to be able to move beyond the novelty. But then, due to the dismissal of our artistic director, we were all fired one year later. No security for immigrant workers.

An encounter with Bill Forsythe, the choreographer, became a friendship and a passionate professional dialogue. This often involved our finding equivalents in our respective fields of expertise through which to discuss various concepts and ideas. Along the way, I included in the Whitney Biennial a solo dance film Bill had made. To introduce dance into the visual arts context was not a new concept in the city where Judson Theater had happened twenty years before, but definitely a forgotten one. Bill's film was one of the most remarkable and remarked-on works in the show, although at the time (amazingly) the American art public did really not know who he was. Following that, we spoke for years about doing adjunct projects with the Ballet, which never happened because we could never find enough time outside our respective commitments in order to generate them.

In 2002, together with other colleagues, Bill proposed a radical new concept for the TAT. In response to the city's decision to close the historic experimental theatre the building and its programme would be temporarily recast to ask the questions, "How many ways and by how many different people can a theatre be used, while remaining a space for the presentation and production of the performing arts? Can a theatre double as a truly public facility? How can a space become a place?"

The TAT was divided into two zones. The rear zone remained a controlled professional theatrical facility; the front became, literally, a huge living room or comfort zone, a foyer for the city designed by local architects Nikolaus Hirsch/Michel Müller and Bill, a choregrapher. They covered the floor with woolen felt and furnished it with robust modular felt furniture. Everything could be easily rearranged and transformed at will. This was interesting for me because it coincided with and outstripped many similar attempts in the visual arts at creating social spaces – in museums, in contemporary art spaces, in all kinds of large scale public exhibitions. Most of the artists whom I invited to TAT couldn't believe the level to which this project had been envisaged, physically realised and inhabited.

The space was open every afternoon to the general public with various free activities offered, but none proscribed. For several hours a day, it became an enormous crèche, taken over by hordes of mothers who had nowhere else to take their children. Every day 100–150 very small and ecstatic children rampaged, clothes on, clothes off, with all their attendant paraphernalia: strollers, food, garbage, toys. Most other interest groups and activities perished in their wake. By six o'clock they were herded out in preparation for the evening's performances and events. The artistic community was alternately fascinated and horrified by this experiment in cohabitation. On the documentary video that we shot of the whole season, this Darwinian situation looked like utopia realised.

. . . .

Christine Peters/Iara Boubnova/Lois Keidan/Louise Neri

The year before, Bill had asked me to organise a series of events that would complement the other programmes that were in effect in this place where children could play during the day, student groups carried out ideas for interactive art projects with the community of Frankfort, and professional programming continued. Given that there were several cooks for this broth, the situation was competitive and at times antagonistic. I came up with a simple string of events at short notice, basically by calling up my "tactile network" to see who I could divert from existing itineraries and circuits to come and show their work in Frankfort. It was a hasty sketch, but involved certain artists and practitioners – Raqs Media Collective from New Delhi, the artist Jeremy Deller, Boris Charmatz the choreographer, and Barbara Vanderlinden, the curator of the experimental project Labouratorium – whose wisdom I thought could be instructive to the situation at the TAT.

As a result of that brief and stimulating programme, Bill asked me to direct the next season from the beginning. As an immigrant worker and an interloper from an adjacent cultural field, it was a fantastic opportunity: a legendary space beautifully appointed and equipped, some financial, technical and staff resources, a city with its diverse and disparate communities. I went back to my sketch and, together with my given team, produced a much more ambitious and charged programme. In the spirit of creating an open house, we invited the people of Frankfurt to propose projects. Thus directed community productions were brought alongside experimental artistic projects, ongoing discussions, and challenging theatrical, musical, and choregraphic works.

But beyond the satisfaction and thrill of an experimental situation and new artistic production, the atmosphere was extremely antagonistic. What represented a unique creative opportunity for me was the end of job security for many others, as many of the theatre staff were to be jobless by the end of the season with the closing of the theatre. And the city officials behaved as if the theatre had already closed. For theatre purists, it had.

I was not a performance programmer but I had worked with disciplines and ideas whose content I felt related very strongly to this new hybrid situation. I think that this prior knowledge gave me the confidence to attempt to structure a situation that I probably wouldn't have gone near otherwise. In hindsight, we had an impossible task. To develop a programme as ambitious and complex as the one we attempted should really have taken a few years because it involved articulating and linking many different networks, with artists as the catalysts, as well as fostering interest, curiosity and trust across many fields and communities. New structures require time and space because they require flexibility and willingness to change.

Peters: So, jobwise: "What do you understand as your core tasks?" and reflection-wise: "What are you allergic to?" (in terms of composing a programme, choosing artists, the overkill of production, etc.).

Neri: To be actively curious and open; to be supple; to ask incisive questions; to play the devil's advocate; to be a good listener, a generous host and a stimulating partner; to make strong choices; to be competent, consistent, focused and challenging in my thoughts and practices. To bring artists from different fields together into stimulating and unexpected contexts, both private and public; to manage expectations of artist and audience. To find new ways of mindfully engaging audiences for art and artists.

I am allergic to the syndrome of lack of time and space to which most of us are subject; the total freneticism that has invaded art and its consumption; impostor artists and star curators with concepts that are too easy or too difficult.

Boubnova: What I am allergic to is easy to answer. Geert Lovink, a media activist and theorist in conversation with Luchezar Boyadjiev, an artist, coined one of the things many years ago and that's the so-called "Culture of Complaint". When they used these words they had in mind the early 1990s and Eastern European cultural discourse. But I think that "Culture of Complaint" is a type of trend that I am allergic to, on whatever level this professional form of complaining is, because of the circumstances, situations and realities. And it is easy to say, what is the main satisfaction of the professional activity? Well, when you have conceptual justification of what you are doing, when there are more right things, choices and results than mistakes. And it is a type of system you can follow; for example, artists with whom you work are very often invited and have other people to work together with. And things you try to predict and you are a little bit scared of doing, but they are really happening. And of course it is a very personal regional situation for the people from Eastern Europe because they / we have evidence of changes and developments within cultural situations. Of course, this is very pleasant.

Keidan: I have an allergy to the abuse of the word "innovation". I have an allergy to inflexible systems and unresponsiveness to change. Innovation is a word that is really banded around a lot in the UK, especially by the funding bodies, and I think it is one of those words that is very easy to say but difficult to understand: what it means in real terms in relation to risk. But I think the core task that we try and set out to do is really some kind of brokerage. We are somewhere between the system, whether it is institutional museums, galleries, theatres or the funding systems or critical systems, and the frontline of artistic practice.

We try and use that position as a kind of lever: to lever our money out of the system in the ways the system wants it to be spent and to pass the money on to artists so they can do what they want to do or what they aspire to do in self-determined ways. So our tasks are that kind of brokerage position, but also to contribute to the development of artist practices , whatever they may be. To develop new cultural frameworks, new curatorial contexts and new critical discourses around contemporary practices. With the ultimate aim of trying to develop new audiences and different kinds of relationships with audiences, but also with the parallel aim of trying to sustain artists' practices over the duration of their careers.

Q & A – Part II:
Audience Discussion

Jan Ritsema: I am very much aware of the complication in the task of the programmer, and you have to combine four different, sometimes even controversial things. Maybe they are not controversial and maybe you can enlighten this a little bit. You are event makers, you want to make an event and you also want to develop discussion in the art world. You want a concept and with this concept you want to influence what is going on in the art world. You also have to get enough audience into your theatre or museum and you want good connections and you want to support the artists and take the side of the artists. Those are north, south, west and east. The question is how can you combine this? Can you say something about this? Or am I wrong? Are there six more?

Keidan: There are probably six more but I don't think those things are necessarily mutually exclusive. That is all.

Ritsema: But how do you balance in this field, which in my eyes is often controversial? When you do the one thing, when you make sure to get enough audience, your artists might not be happy, or the theoretical discussion that you want to support or that you want to develop something, some directness in the art world and so on.

Neri: It's about making choices and , more importantly, being able to generate enough space and time to explore those choices. Artists are consummate generators of their own time, space and context, so we can learn from their examples. I think "less is more", I think that as curators or programmers, we feel ourselves under an invisible pressure to process as much information as quickly as possible – and, idiotically, we comply with that pressure, and cooperate with consensus.

I would like to see a more specialised and diverse form of curatorial support for artistic creativity, with a far higher degree of articulation. (Ritsema: What prevents us from doing it?) That this rarely happens is largely due to the conventions within which we work. The organisations that employ curators like us are becoming more and more pragmatic, conservative and product-orientated. They prefer neat concepts to evolutive processes. Telelogical rather than exploratory models.

Of course there are exceptions.

So, as curators, we need to find ways to create exceptional structures by working more closely with artists on the development of structures themselves rather than accepting inherited models.

Boubnova: Biennales are a very clear illustration. I mean they are different and have different contexts, but the case of Biennales allows a very good examination of what is going on and how it is possible to connect all different kinds of interactions with which curators start to work. There are interactions with organisers, with financial supporters and artists, and of course in the end it is the public and the logic of the public, reacting positively or not. And it is important how the reaction is mediated. So, it sounds like you are supposed to balance all of this, but I think that one of the interesting and very difficult things to be clarified is a very specific research; for example, the research of the audience. There is a lot of text produced about it and there are even a lot of instruments and tools for researching the public, but I think audiences are more and more differentiated also because more and more different things attract them. So, the attention of the public is very specific. And how to recognise these audiences as positive or negative is a problematic thing. The previous panel mentioned the regulated and contracted, in advance, relations between perform-ance artists and their public; that impressed me. Those who come to see the performance already know in what situation they appear at this moment. My concern about our public is that we practically can never know its response. And the amount of visitors doesn't help much either. For example, in Moscow the biennale lasted only one month, but it was visited by 200,000 people. Does this mean that it is interesting for the public? Or is this a general curiosity, the first step towards a new development? It is very pleasant, to show off the 200,000 number, we are maybe going for a record number in one month, but nobody knows what this public is and what there is to do for this type of public. But we will start research and try to establish specific relations with those people who were never classified as a public for contemporary art in Russia. And now we already know that at least 200,000 people in a city of 12 million visited a contemporary art event. So, we can already oper-ate with the word public, in this case. While doing things you learn a lot about why you are doing them, this is clear. So, the public is one important thing. But before it appears there is one more important task: you are supposed to produce and educate this public. So, somehow these are different steps for me and they are steps in one process, things which curators or programmers or producers are supposed to do in order to be good.

Keidan: For me, with the agency and ICA, it wasn't a case of "this or that" but "this and that". It depends on the strategic imperative, and sometimes the strategic imperative is to make events and sometimes the strategic imperative is to look at different strategies for supporting artists, in the way they want to work or are aspiring to work. And sometimes the strategic imperative is to look at relationships with an audience and the development of different kinds of audiences. And sometimes the strategic imperative is to contribute to critical discourses; and sometimes those things can happen all in the same frame and sometimes within different frames. But I don't think they are mutually exclusive.

Ritsema: Lois, when you say sometimes it can be this and sometimes it can be that, of course I can imagine that when you organise something there is an accent more on one of the four things I mentioned. But I am interested in this – do you make choices, do you make accents? You answered more or less "Yes, I do all four, it depends on the different projects".

Keidan: No, what I meant was that it depends on the strategic imperative of things and those are things that will influence the choices and the strategic imperatives are usually done in collabouration with artists. And of course, we don't have a house that we need to fill every night, absolutely. At the ICA we did, but now we don't and those kinds of eco-nomic pressures aren't part of the equation now, no.

Peters: Well, concerning an institution with an annual programme versus a festival: I've been a freelance curator only since LAST YEAR, and right now my main job is the curatorial work for the theatre triennial / festival *Theater der Welt* where I am in charge of performance art.

After twelve years of institutional work I am very happy right now to have this luxury opportunity to focus on visual versus performance art and to research and develop new

Christine Peters / Iara Boubnova / Lois Keidan / Louise Neri

formats of production and presentation. When I worked as artistic director of Arts Centre Mousonturm, an interdisciplinary contemporary arts institution in Frankfurt, I had the responsibility for the annual programme with 300 performances (dance, theatre, concerts, symposiums, etc.), plus I dealt with fundraising and management.

Contentwise, I was responsible and thus privileged – it was me who profiled the house – I made every final programme decision, which was fantastic to do. Structurally I was dominated and directed by politics and management and was asked to raise the output every year. So I could either "supersize" the programme with mainstream artists and projects or – which I did – create different kinds of new programme formats in order to attract different and more audiences. The task was – as Jan Ritsema might put it – not only to multiply north, south, west and east but even to create hybrids …

I finally got stuck in a management trap, and now, after having stepped out, I can better see the problems and traps around me, which definitely not only concern institutional work.

Concerning the contents of my work the core questions remained the same: "Why do I do it? How do I do it?" Am I offering a service to a city that can afford my work / institution / festival, or am I an opinion maker and context producer who wants to create a platform for dialogue and express/defend/discuss a specific international profile? How can I develop this specific profile on a long-term basis even if I deal with a biennial or festival? Personally, I have always been interested in developing a clear programme profile which not only entertains an audience but also serves as generator of their artistic knowledge and conscience.

Structurally and politically one could compare *Theater der Welt* to Manifesta – both are organised in the same classical / hierarchical manner: First there is the organisational head with the board – the ITI in Berlin versus Manifesta board in Amsterdam – second there's the hosting structure – the particular city and its participating / organising institutions. Third there's the festival / biennial managing director plus the directors of the organising institutions. Fourth, on the content level there's a difference – Manifesta's general content outline and concept is developed by a curatorial team, whereas Theater der Welt's final decisions are made solely by the artistic director.

Politically spoken, there's another parallel: The job precariousness. The decision makers/directors have mostly parallel / regular / institutional jobs to do which they interrupt only for a certain period (which paradoxically and usually is valued as a "positive quality") whereas the organising and some of the curatorial staff members are mostly freelancers who have to look for new jobs already before the project starts (which paradoxically and usually is valued as "normal").

I think that not only this accumulation of power and privileges is a crucial problem in general – and certainly not only one of touring biennials or festivals – A lot of institutions and locally stable festivals are also structurally going into a totally wrong direction and thus have a precarious impact on artistic production. (The change in law concerning freelancing versus permanently employed is of course co-responsible for that situation in Germany;

however, it is a European / global problem as well – see also the criticism and strike of the *Intermittents* at Festival d'Avignon last year.)

Anyway – My crucial point and main criticism here is: In order to raise the amount of programme plus guarantee the content quality, one would need more content-related staff working on a long-term basis. This staff would for example have the advantage to profit from the results and analysis of previous events. Whereas in reality, employment-wise one usually has to deal with project based freelance curators who are of course not concerned about the overall context but interested in defending their own concepts and artists. – Structurally this is a regular model; however, in my opinion it supports a precarious system, built on exploitation and profit. – This is unfortunately the standard globalised capitalist model, a model which some years ago Richard Sennett brilliantly analysed in his book *The Corrosion of Character. The personal consequences of work in the New Capitalism.*

I think that a lot of institutions and festivals don't dare to resist but instead keep spitting out a maximum programme quantity (financed by a mixture of partly very badly payed and partly overpayed artists – depending on their market value) and thus run behind their core tasks. Which in the arts should not be about giving priority to output and le *dernier cri* (because "attention creates value" as Brian Eno MATTER-OF-FACTLY says …) but about paying attention to quality – to quality work, quality time, quality poduction, quality reflection and quality money according to each concept's needs – and thus gaining quality results.

I see a lot of professional, however hollow high speed production with a worn-out staff, and I don't see that many powerful and inventive counter-positions that create new insights and build networks of agency.

I certainly don't want to contribute to Iara's allergy against a "culture of complaint" with what I am saying, however, I am allergic to these kinds of business and career machines disguised as progressive art institutions and inventive festivals.

Neri: Artangel in London is perhaps the best example of creative agency versus institutional programme. Artangel develops unusual projects with visual and performing artists, and writers. They have an office but they have no permanent space, theatre or gallery. Their schedule is determined by the artists' time and needs. A project might take one year or a few months to realise, or it may unfold over several years in various stages. For example, the composer Jem Finer developed a project *Longplayer*, housed in a lighthouse on the Thames, which will last an entire millennium. Francis Alys made a project of *walks* in London over several years, which culminated in a large documentary project in an old house. Sometimes projects remain open-ended because they have so many potential dimensions.

Artangel invents the structure for the artist each time, raising money, developing the project in all its dimensions (including the eventual public interface, education and so on), and finding and coopting unexpected spaces around London that will add resonance to the event. This necessity makes the curators extremely agile, inventive and resourceful. Their core task – of partnering artists – is not diluted by the drain of heavy institutional

....

Christine Peters / Iara Boubnova / Lois Keidan / Louise Neri

responsibilities that can often lead to jaded attitudes. I think this exploratory rather than teleological model is very fertile.

Boyan Manchev: I would like to ask Iara Boubnova a question about public space. You said that your aim was to address or even to develop different publics. Earlier in your comments you mentioned in the same vein the role of the ICA in the democratic process, and you spoke about the creation of political "meanings" as a very satisfactory outcome of your organisation. My question is: What kind of public space were you aiming to create with this intention, being an agent in the democratic process in Bulgaria? What kind of meanings have you produced, how do you measure them and how did your artists react to that kind of strategy on your part? Didn't they feel as if they were no longer producing art but as if they were forced to produce political meanings? Or was this precisely your aim: to erase the border between "esthetical" and "political" activity?

Boubnova: I will try to connect to several parts of your question. First, when I said something about "agent of democracy", I didn't have in mind an institution. If it would be an institution at such an early stage, it would be much easier and then we'd be talking about something different. I was talking about people, personalities, individuals who recognised in one moment that what they are doing is very oppositional to the whole reality of the society in which they live, more specifically oppositional to the cultural politics of this time. So it was their opinion. I would say that to define the political in this case is much easier, because you can define it as an opposition. Now, it is more complicated to define the political impact and even the political effort. This is a very tricky situation; I am not sure that the artists with whom I am working, that all of them are totally aware of their own political role. I am not sure that my task is to insist and to know absolutely that they are political agents. It is much more mediation, of course it is a mediation of production and interpretation of what is happening with art, and art producers in your own context. In my case this is Bulgaria. And to shape it every time to the situation, when it is a united moment, that it is a group of people, that it is a community, an opinion, and the community and opinion are representative for an even bigger part of the population. What are the exact tools for doing it? It is a little bit difficult to enumerate right now. But in my case I remember very well when we started this initiative in the late 1980s with a small group of people, colleagues, curators, artists (we didn't have the profession of a curator at this time, so mainly we were all educated art historians). The first thing that we decided was that we needed to announce, in whatever professional way, that contemporary art and contemporary thoughts existed in our country although nobody had ever heard about it. And we spent a lot of energy on it. At one moment we realised that this type of parceling out of the product and all the tight communication outside, left our local situation abandoned. So we had to turn around and we started educational programmes and multidisciplinary collaboration, inviting very different people with different languages who already had their different audiences, and to bring those different publics, theirs and ours, together. I am talking about academic people, who have a very interesting and very strong influence on the younger generation, but of course this is a limited situation. People who are connected to commercials and the design of videoclips for television have a much broader public, although they are disconnected from it. So this type of discussions and searching for a common, interesting platform is one of the possibilities. I should not forget to mention the project we are working on now – with many people, it is absolutely not my own individual project. It is entitled *Visual Seminar*. Yesterday, during one of the meetings for the preparation of this panel, we discussed my experience in Moscow. I know more or less the situation there for several years, but when working on this biennale I was really surprised by the public, which was very passionate, because it is still the public that inherited the logic according to which art belongs to the people. So this is producing expectations in the public and in that we must be clear, transparent, understandable, easy and attractive. Provided that contemporary art sometimes isn't so attractive and spectacular and – for sure – very easy, may create a big conflict. Then the public is left unsatisfied, it feels like: Why, before we did understand what art is doing, but now it is a totally ununderstandable and unfamiliar thing. We are very interested, but does it really cost that much money, does it really deserve this attention? So, this is very a different public in Moscow compared to the Sofia public.

Emil Hrvatin: Iara, you said that the audience for the biennale in Moscow identified very much with it and it is quite a big audience. Do you think the public actually still recognises art as a resisting field, because of the memory of communism and so on? And the other question is, when you think about your programme and the public, you think about the public you generate. But do you think about why you generate it?

Boubnova: To the first question from Emil – of course, in some places, Russia and Moscow for example, art associates totally and absolutely with resistance and specifically with anti-ideological activity. It is very interesting to discuss this topic, not in the talk but in the exhibition and next to the works, because what the entire international contemporary art milieu – being a little bit rude – operates with as "Russian art" since the late 1960s and 1970s, still is largely unknown to the Russian public. There are shows here and there, but not as many shows as needed, especially museum shows – well advertised, in big spaces, etc.. So, it is still that people only hear about it, but don't know it so well. They expect very much to see "classical" contemporary art, and part of the Moscow Biennale was dedicated to this; and at least a part of the new conceptual art was shown in the National Gallery, the State Tretyakov Gallery in Moscow, which was considered as a big step ahead. On the other hand, the younger generation, which has no idea about this type of resistance art but has heard of it because of its popularity (again the word of mouth is lost and there are expectations that it is supposed to be published in periodicals and books), they have a different understanding of art; for them it is much more – and I am talking about Moscow now – art as an entertaining element in a difficult life and difficult period, historical period, in which these people are living. So, again it is a different public.

Marina Gržinić: You constantly refer to the public, it sounds like a First-Aid taking care of the public. I think the question of the biennale is the involvement of a lot of money, a lot of power; it is a selection of people that will be involved in such a structure, it is a politi-

Christine Peters / Iara Boubnova / Lois Keidan / Louise Neri

cal decision. Also, if these biennales are exported, the word exported is very important. Exported for example where? To Moscow. For Moscow it is the first biennale, I suppose, so a certain structure that was developed in another space is transported here, which involves important political, economical and social aspects. For me this is misleading, it is nothing about the public. If you look at Russia, who is there thinking of the public? I think other interests are behind it. I would like to expose also other structures: why to install such a big institute like the Biennale in Moscow, from where comes the interest. Money is the first point, and then comes the public as the second and third one. Because of this, it is a totally distorted image. I think the whole logic must be reversed, things are generated on a different level. The public is important, but this is not the primary task. The whole institution of the biennale has first and foremost a lot to do with money and political interests. More specifically there remains the question who is involved from the national and international space. These relations are crucial.

Boubnova: Marina, this is a totally correct analysis of what biennales are: They are about power and money and about the transmission of specific models produced in specific moments, but there isn't such a big difference, because the reasons are still the same. To attract people and to show that our local situation is much better than what you imagined it to be, before you came to see our biennale. In my understanding the only possibility to correct these political manipulations of the biennales is to talk about the public and be orientated towards the public, in terms of what kind of public you would like to produce and expect. It is easy to say: opinionated people who are aware of what is going on, this is the public I would count on. The public that knows, when it is public, it becomes a public situation; that it is not personal, not somebody's decision and an ideologically prearranged situation. It is a choice which you can express yourself and motivate yourself. You are not on your own, so it is tolerance of course, even you can import the system of the biennale. (Hrvatin: Tolerance to what?) Tolerance of the public and audience / visitors who see it, can only be educated; tolerance to the unknown, to those things that are difficult to be recognised as art and culture in general, not aggressively at that. For Moscow it is easy to discuss these things, because, as you maybe know, there are a lot of lawsuits against artists and performers mainly, writers too, because they touch on very specific topics, mainly orthodox religion which is represented by the state itself in Russia. So, it is one of the things where you can talk about tolerance first.

Katherina Zakravsky: I changed my opinion about the occupation of the curator a lot in the last years, because we had this age of the star-curator and there was a lot of criticism and I see this has changed a lot. Now it is considered to be a collabourative job. I want to point out that this occupation of curating is very paradigmatic of a lot of social / political problems that are maybe not made explicit. We can come back to the first day of the congress, because on the one hand it is all about the ambiguity of the flexibility attributed to the artistic practice. But on the other hand it also answers to the pressure of privatisation. So in this sense the independent and instable work of a curator is a stand-in for the institution that is either becoming too stable and conservative, or is simply vanishing away because art practice is under the pressure of privatisation. And that is why I found the story about the mothers who suddenly occupied this open space very allegorical. This space should be even more open and public, but it was simply private and – these are very old fashioned words, as Emil pointed out, but I think that there is a nodal point of problems there. Because at least in Vienna, I think it is a European problem, artists cannot find private agents who simply represent their interests as agents. They cannot book an agent and pay him or her provisions for the gig he or she can find for him or her. This is an American system which doesn't work in Europe. An artist still has to be supported publicly or half publicly. In this sense the curator is the only agent an artist can address. A curator is still a public figure. But I noticed, when I was with artists in Holland, that the relationship between artists and curators is extremely charged psychologically. Because they want to and have to be chosen as persons. As we live in the age beyond and after the work, it is not their particular work they are chosen for, but because the curator trusts this artist to do good work. That is why there is no transparency for them to offer works and be chosen for the quality of their work. They had to offer themselves as persons; and I wanted to point out that the intimacy and friendship concerning the relationship between artist and curator sounds very good, but it can also have this dark side.

Neri: I think that the most beneficial structure for art – like life – is a healthy mix of public commitment and private enterprise. Too much of either one is dangerous. The complete withdrawal of public support or responsibility in the U.S. with regard to artistic culture has strangled certain vital forms of experimental or exploratory work, particularly in the performing arts, which is unbelievably conservative and far behind Europe in terms of any kind of consciousness or critical discourse on new work. The rampant capitalistic energy of the visual arts has eclipsed serious critical discourse.

With regard to your comment about how curators choose artists in Holland, as a curator I find that mystifying. I'm interested in the work first and foremost. The personal relationship may follow but it is not a prerequisite from the outset!

Keidan: In relation to that and Emil, I don't understand why it has to be a black and white situation: institutional versus non-institutional. I don't understand why it can't be a plural cultural framework where there are choices – choices for artists about where they want to locate their work, choices for the public about how they want to engage with work. But certainly in the UK there is an increasing appetite amongst the public to engage with different kinds of experiences, the kinds of work that are looking at the nature of art and what it can do and say and where it can be located. There are audiences that possibly don't want to go to institutions because they possibly don't feel welcome there and often aren't welcome, particularly in museums and galleries. One of the reasons that artists are working outside institutions is that they do want to have a different kind of conversation with the public. At the same time I think, because artists are deciding to work outside of the institutions they are engaging with a different audience, it is a two-way process. For me a lot of the exciting contemporary practices are looking at where and how art can be located, who an audience can be and what they are interested in and the means by which they want to be addressed.

....

Christine Peters / Iara Boubnova / Lois Keidan / Louise Neri

Louise Neri: I think a huge amount of work has been done with and for audiences in recent years, as attested to by rapidly rising attendance in every field of the arts. I don't think all art is for everyone, and I think audiences can be tyrannical, impatient and short-sighted, liking what they know and knowing what they like, and so on. On the other hand, they can also be extremely intelligent. As history tells us, audience response is not always a measure of the intrinsic value of a work of art. I think it's important that we, as curators, continue to defend the space and conditions for the development of prototypical artistic thoughts, works and practices.

Hrvatin: I have one proposal. Maybe it is a little bit idealistic. These are the last minutes of the congress and every congress has to finish with a "message to the world". There won't be more money for culture than there is now. So, forget it. And we should find other ways. I have one very concrete proposal on the European level about what should be done. We should introduce a new tax law in every country and this tax should be applied to the privatisation of public space. So whoever privatises public space has to pay a very high tax, and this tax will be used for covering possible damage, which will be done by public performances and public protests. So if people want to come out and lie down on the street and the traffic is blocked for three hours and nobody is able to come to work, the damage will be covered by the money from this tax. This is not a joke. There won't be any more money for culture, so we have to find other ways, outside culture, to find money for culture. This is my concrete proposal at the end of the congress. To continue the idea and spirit, but so we don't finish with a depressing situation, but we have some grounding for further lobbying.

Keidan: Could I add a subtext to that? I only want to mention it because Mårten (Spångberg) raised it yesterday, by showing the Citroën ad and whatever Gene Kelly is advertising for right now. I think the advertising agencies should be taxed for the number of times they rip off artists' ideas and present them as their own. As we saw yesterday.

Boubnova: But they are already, in both cases.

Keidan: Not in the UK then.

Boubnova: One artist, Ivan Moudov, blocked the traffic in a small German town for three hours with his performance; then he sold the video and the performance project and then he paid his taxes. So, I can imagine that is what they would have in mind.

247 Peters: À propos mind … I hope that we all had enough effects on the left or right sides of our brains for now – Because I would like to end here and thank all of you so much for watching and listening and smuggling and copying and stealing and intervening and liking and disliking – Thanks dear panelists for your energy, curiosity and (mute) participation, thanks a lot to Martina Hochmuth and Georg Schöllhammer for your kind invitation, and above all: thanks so much Tanzquartier Wien AND SIGRID GAREIS for your great hospitality.

Contributors

Ric Allsopp, Ph.D. is a co-founder and joint editor of *Performance Research,* a quarterly international journal of contemporary performance (pub. London & New York: Routledge, Taylor & Francis) http://performance-research.net and is currently Reader in Performance Research at Dartington College of Arts, Devon, UK.

Jérôme Bel, lives in Paris. His productions are *Nom donné par l'auteur* (1994), *Jérôme Bel* (1995), and *Shirtology* (1997). This last piece was commisioned by Victoria (Ghent) and Centro Cultural de Belem (Lisbon). A Japanese version was done in Tokyo and Kyoto. Then, Jérôme Bel produced *The last performance* (1998), *Xavier Le Roy* (1999) and *The show must go on* (2001). This piece belongs also to the repertory of the Deutsches Schauspielhaus in Hamburg. For the Paris Opera Ballet, he signed *Véronique Doisneau* (2004), and for the Teatro Municipal in Rio de Janeiro, *Isabel Torres* (2005). *Pichet Klunchun & myself* (2005) is a piece he did in Bangkok with the traditional Thai dancer Pichet Klunchun.

Claudia Bosse, studied drama in Berlin; choreographies, installations, discourse productions. Founded Theatercombinat in Berlin in 1996, since 1999 Theatercombinat Wien. Last projects: *belagerung bartleby* HAU1 Berlin, *firma raumforschung, palais donaustadt.* Currently working on the 2 year project *tragödienproduzenten 1.* Publications (with others): *anatomie sade/wittgestein – eine choreografische theaterarbeit in 3 architekturen* triton 2004, and *belagerung bartleby* revolver 2006. Lectureships.

Iara Boubnova, curator and art critic, graduated at the Department of Art History and Theory of Moscow State University. Since 1984 she has been living in Sofia, Bulgaria, working at the National Gallery for Foreign Art as a curator of the Department of East European Art. During the last three years, she was the Leader of the Visual Seminar multidisciplinary project dedicated to the urban environment of neo-capitalism. Curatorial projects: *Joy* at Casino Luxembourg and *Dialectics of Hope,* 1st Moscow Biennial of Contemporary Art in 2005, Manifesta 4 in Frankfurt / Main in 2002 – all as co-curator; *Talk with the Man on the Street* part of the 4th Biennial in Cetinje, Montenegro; *Double-Bind* (co-curator) in 2003, *Locally Interested* in 1999 – both in Sofia; and *Ars ex Nacionem. Made in BG* in 1997 and *In Search of the Self-Reflection* in 1994 – both in Plovdiv. She is President of AICA Bulgaria and since 2002 a board member of the International Foundation Manifesta; founding Director of the Institute of Contemporary Art – Sofia.

Andrea B. Braidt, Ph.D. MLitt (Dept. for Theatre-, Film- and Media Studies, Vienna University). University lecturer since 1997; Junior fellow at IFK, Vienna; Visting professor at CEU Budapest (2003–2004); Research and teaching focus on: feminist film theory, film history and genre film (theory), queer cinema. Latest publications: Screenwise. *Film. Fernsehen. Feminismus* (Marburg, Schüren 2004; ed. with Monika Bernold and Claudia Preschl). *Film-Genus. Zu einer theoretischen und methodischen Konzeption von Gender und Genre im narrativen Film* Claudia Liebrand, Ines Steiner (eds.) *Hollywood hybrid. Genre und Gender im zeitgenössischen Mainstream-Film* (Marburg, Schüren 2004).

Gabriele Brandstetter, 1997–2003 Professor of Modern German Literature Studies at the University of Basle, since 2003 Professor of Theatre Studies at the Free University of Berlin. Her research focus is on: performance theories; concepts of body and movement in notation, image and performance; dance, theatricality and gender differences. Selected publications: *Loïe Fuller. Tanz – Licht-Spiel – Art Nouveau* 1989, (with co-Author B. Ochaim); *Tanz-Lektüren. Körperbilder und Raumfiguren der Avantgarde* (1995); *ReMembering the Body. Körperbilder in Bewegung* (2000, with co-editor Sibylle Peters); *Erzählen und Wissen. Paradigmen und Aporien ihrer Inszenierungen in Goethes ‚Wahlverwandschaften'* (Ed., 2003); *Bild-Sprung. TanzTheaterBewegung im Wechsel der Medien*, Theater der Zeit (Recherchen 26) 2005.

Roger M. Buergel, curator and author; two children. Curated *Things we don't understand* (with Ruth Noack, Generali Foundation, Vienna, 2000), *Governmentality. Art in conflict with the international hyper-bourgeoisie and the national petty bourgeoisie* (Alte Kestner Gesellschaft, Hannover, 2000), *The Subject and Power – the lyrical voice* (CHA Moscow, 2001). Currently showing *The Government* (with Ruth Noack, Kunstraum of the University of Lüneburg; MACBA-Museu d'Art Contemporani de Barcelona; Miami Art Central; Secession, Vienna; Witte de With, Rotterdam; 2003–05). Books include *Peter Friedl*, Leipzig and Amsterdam, 1999; *Abstrakter Expressionismus. Konstruktionen ästhetischer Erfahrung*, Leipzig and Amsterdam, 2000. Regular contributions to *Texte zur Kunst* and *springerin – Hefte für Gegenwartskunst*. Artistic director to documenta XII (2007).

Bojana Cvejić practises critical theory in writing, teaching, dramaturgy and performance in the field of performing arts, mainly choreography and contemporary music. She published essays in the performing arts magazines *Etcetera, Teorija koja Hoda, Maska, Frakcija* etc., and books, most recently *Open Work in Music* (SKC, Belgrade, 2004). With Jan Ritsema she has developed a theatre performance practice in a number of performances since 1999. Cvejić has been active in teaching in a number of European educational programmes (e.g. P.A.R.T.S. in Brussels), as well as organising independent platforms for theory and practice in performance: TkH Centar (=*Walking Theory Center* in Belgrade) and PAF (PerformingArtsForum in St. Erme, France). Her main interest lies in the changing role of theory in the performance field since the 1990s.

Maja Delak, choreographer, dancer, pedagogue and driving force behind the first high school for contemporary dance SVŠGL in Slovenia and other educational and research programs of Zavod En-Knap as Dance Lab, Agon. She is a councillor for contemporary dance at the Ministry for Education of Slovenia. She has extensive stage and film experience, performing especially in Iztok Kovač's productions with En-Knap Company, and has created and toured with her own choreographies: *Manifestation of the Introvert, Gina & Miovanni* and *Mezzanino*. In collaboration with Mala Kline, dancer and choreographer, Maja Delak in 2004 created *Properly Blonde, Rondinella* and *HI-RES*, together with Mauricio Ferlin, film director and designer from Croatia.

Alex Demirovic, teaches political science and political sociology at the university in Frankfurt / Main. Working Fields: theory of state and democracy, critical theory of society, analysis of culture / ideology / discourse. Publications (amongst others): *Demokratie und Herrschaft* (Münster 1997), *Der nonkonformistische Intellektuelle* (Frankfurt 1999), (ed.) *Modell kritischer Gesellschaftstheorie* (Stuttgart 2003), (ed.) *Kritische Theorie im gesellschaftlichen Strukturwandel* (Frankfurt 2004).

Nataša Govedić, her interdisciplinary scholarly interests include theatre, literary and film studies, rhetoric and ethics. She received MA in Shakespeare studies and continues to write her Ph.D. thesis about contemporary intermediary framings of Shakespeare's works and a broader epistemology of performative selfhood. Writes and regularly publishes poetry. Teaches at the Centre for Women Studies, Zagreb. She is also the editor of the feminist journal Treca / *THE THIRD* / and member of the editorial board in *Zarez*, biweekly magazine for social and cultural issues. Organises *Theatre for Human Rights* based on the model of Brazilian social activist and theatre scholar Augusto Boal. She has

published several books on theatre, literature and film; among others *Beguiling the Time: Rhetoric of Shakespeare's Performances* (2001) and *Choosing the Role, Changing the Model: Feminist Readings of the Literary, Film and Stage Performances* (2002).

Marina Gržinić, holds a Ph.D. in philosophy and works as a researcher at the Institute of Philosophy at the ZRC SAZU (Scientific and Research Centre of the Slovenian Academy of Science and Art) in Ljubljana. She is Professor at the Academy of Fine Arts in Vienna. She also works as a freelance media theorist, art critic and curator. In collaboration with Aina Šmid, Gržinić has been involved in video art since 1982. She publishes extensively, her last book is *Situated Contemporary Art Practice. Art, Theory and Activism from (the East of) Europe*, Ljubljana: ZRC SAZU and Frankfurt / Main: Revolver, 2004.

Philipp Haupt, studied visual media at the University of Applied Arts in Vienna as well as theatre and cultural studies at the University of Vienna and the Humboldt University in Berlin. Engaged in projects concerning authorship, image-politics and auditory cartographies as well as audio-visual and scenic representation. Since 2003 perennial student at the Manoa Free University, developing (re)staging processes and hybrid narrative / theatrical concepts. Craftsman and concierge of the campus of the Freie Universität Mahagoni.

Emil Hrvatin, studied sociology and theatre directing at the University of Ljubljana, Slovenia and performance theory at the

University of Antwerp, Belgium. He is author and director of theatre performances shown throughout Europe and the USA. His piece *CAMILLO – MEMO 1.0: THE CONSTRUCTION OF THEATRE* has been directed by himself at the Piccolo Teatro in Milan, Italy (May 1998). *DRIVE IN CAMILLO* has opened Manifesta 3, the European biennale of contemporary arts (2000). His latest piece is *WE ARE ALL MARLENE DIETRICH FOR – Performance for soldiers in peace-keeping missions* (together with Erna Omarsdottir). Recently, he has been performing in Meg Stuart's improvisation project *At the Table*. His work also includes visual, multimedia and performance art works and the interdisciplinary artistic and research project *First World Camp*. He has published numerous essays on contemporary theatre and art including a book on the Flemish artist and theatre maker Jan Fabre; is editor-in-chief of the performing arts journal *Maska*. He has edited a reader of contemporary theatre theories (*PRESENCE, REPRESENTATION, THEATRICALITY*, Maska, Ljubljana 1996) and a reader of contemporary dance theories (*THEORIES OF CONTEMPORARY DANCE*, Maska, Ljubljana, 2001). Since 1999 he has been the director of Maska, a non-profit organisation in publishing, production and education, based in Ljubljana, Slovenia.

Lois Keidan, the co founder and Director of the Live Art Development Agency London. Established in 1999, the Live Art Development Agency works in partnership with practitioners and organisations on curatorial initiatives; offers opportunities for research, training, dialogue and debate;

provides practical information and advice; and develops new ways of increasing popular and critical awareness of Live Art. From 1992 to 1998 she was Director of Live Arts at the Institute of Contemporary Arts in London. Prior to that she was responsible for national policy and provision for Performance Art and interdisciplinary practices at the Arts Council of England. For more information about the Live Art Development Agency visit www.thisisliveart.co.uk.

Mala Kline, dancer, pedagogue, choreographer and philosophy student; performed in Iztok Kovač's productions *Sting and String – first touch*, *Codes of Cobra* and his films *Vertigo Bird* and *Dom Svobode*, as well as in the Wim Vandekeybus production *InAsMuchAsLifeIsBorrowed*. Since 2001 she has worked as a collaborator in En-Knap *Dance Laboratory*. In 2002/03 she led creative workshops which resulted in the production *Adventures of Samantha Fox or How I caught a beast* (2003). Since 2001 she has taught Creative Work and Contemporary Dance Technique at the High School for Contemporary Dance in Ljubljana. In collaboration with students she made the performance *Garden of Traversing Fates* (2002). Together with Maja Delak she established the educational and research program *Agon*, which resulted in the performance *Properly Blonde* in 2004. In the same year she presented also her first solo, *Campo de Fiori*, followed by the performances *Rondinella* and *HI-RES*, and in 2005 *Gallery of Dead Women*, all in collaboration with Maja Delak. Together they have also established a series of books with

Prehodi, which publishes books on dance, as related to other arts and theatre practices.

Bojana Kunst, Ph.D., philosopher and performance theoretician. She is currently working as a researcher at the University of Ljubljana, Faculty of Arts – Department for Sociology. In the year 2005 she was a guest professor at the Institute for Applied Theatre Science in Giessen. She is a member of the editorial board of *Maska* Magazine. Her essays have appeared in numerous journals and publications and she has taught and lectured extensively in Europe. She published three books, among them *Impossible Body* (Ljubljana 1999), *Dangerous Connections: Body, Philosophy and Relation to the Artificial* (Ljubljana, 2004). She is also working as a dramaturg (recently with Hooman Sharifi, Paz Rojo and Cristian Duarte). She is leading the international seminar for performing arts in Ljubljana.

Xavier Le Roy, dancer and choreographer since 1991. He has worked with Christian Bourrigault, Detektor, Laurent Goldring, Alain Buffard, Mårten Spångberg, Lindy Annis, Bernhard Lang and Eszter Salamon. His works include Narcisse Flip (1997), Self Unfinished (1998), Product of Circumstances (1999), E.X.T.E.N.S.I.O.N.S. (1999–2000), Xavier Le Roy (2000) by Jérôme Bel, Giszelle (2001) with Eszter Salamon, Project (2003) in collaboration with 20 choreographers, the staging of *Das Theater der Wiederholungen* (2003), an opera by Bernhard Lang, and *Mouvements für Lachenmann* (2005). Xavier Le Roy studied molecular biology and has worked as dancer and choreographer since 1991.

Isabell Lorey, political scientist, lecturer for gender and postcolonial studies at the Universität der Künste Berlin; member of the group *Kleines postfordistisches Drama* (together with Katja Reichard, Marion von Osten and Brigitta Kuster). In 2001 / 02 she conceived and performed, together with the group *AnbauNeueMitte*, the *Falsches-Leben-Shows* at the Prater of Volksbühne Berlin during the first season of René Pollesch. During 1997-2000 she was editor and head of the news broadcast for children *logo* (ZDF). 1996 editor of *Texte zur Kunst*. Most important publication on Butler and Foucault, the book *Immer Ärger mit dem Subjekt* (1996, edition diskord).

Hubert Machnik, composer and guitarist. Played in various ensembles and orchestras, mainly "Neue Musik". Member of Ensemble Modern 1981–89. Composes piano and chamber music for theatre, dance and film, music for audiovisual installations, computer music, electronic music and "radio pieces". Concerts worldwide. Performances in Tokyo, New York, Montreal, Toronto, São Paulo and in many European cities. Recently: Lecturer at Giessen University (computer music), cooperation with Heiner Goebbels (Geneva), the Berlin Philharmonic Orchestra (Education Dpt., Berlin / New York), Blindman Saxophone Quartet (Brussels), Deufert / Plischke (Vienna / Antwerp) and the William Forsythe Company (Berlin / Frankfurt / Stuttgart / Munich).

Boyan Manchev, philosopher, teaching at the New Bulgarian University, Sofia University and the Academy of Theatre and Film in Sofia. He is also Directorof the programme "Metamorphoses of Community" at the International College of Philosophy in Paris. His work concentrates on the theory of representation, image and body, and on the contemporary conceptualisations of community; it pays particular attention to contemporary visual arts, theatre and dance. He has initiated or collaborated with projects of the Zentrum für Kunst und Medientechnologie (Karlsruhe), Tanzquartier Wien, Institute of Contemporary Art (Sofia), Akademie Schloss Solitude (Stuttgart), Centre national de la dance (Paris), Kunsthaus (Dresden), EHESS (Paris), Netherlands Institute for Advanced Study (Wassenaar), Centre for Advanced Study (Sofia). Author of *The Unimaginable. Essays in Philosophy of Image* (Sofia: NBU, 2003); *The Total Body of Pleasure. Political Representation, Violence and Excess*, in *Zurück aus der Zukunft. Osteuropäische Kulturen im Zeitalter des Postkommunismus* (Eds. Boris Groys, Anne von der Heiden and Peter Weibel, Frankfurt/Main: Suhrkamp Verlag, 2005). Translator of Jean-Luc Nancy, *Corpus*. (Sofia: LIK, 2003). His bibliography includes several edited volumes, essays, articles, reviews and interviews in Bulgarian, French, German, English, Italian and Russian.

Ralo Mayer, has been investigating socio-political issues like migration, new social movements and self-organisation since 2000. Recent artistic works reflect an increased interest in scripting and staging processes in performative research. Since 2003 fellow at the Manoa Free University, projects include the exhibition and conference *W...WirWissen* about collaborative artistic knowledge production. Supported by daegseingcny, an imaginary scholarship for design and agency. Currently setting up the research series *How to do things with worlds* about performative aspects of micro-universes in both Science Fiction and post-Fordist reality. 2x so-called.
http://manoafreeuniversity.org
http://daegseingcny.net

Gil Mendo, choreologist, teaches at Lisbon Polytechnic's Higher School of Dance, where he is Chairman of the Artistic/Scientific Board and co-ordinator of international exchanges. He is currently also Dance Programmer at Culturgest in Lisbon. and for a number of years has been involved in international exchange and networking (IETM, Fonds Roberto Cimetta, DBM, IRIS). From 1996 to 2001 he was Head of the Dance Department at the Institute for the Performing Arts, Portuguese Ministry of Culture.

Louise Neri, editor, curator and writer currently based in Paris. In 1990 she moved to New York to edit the international art journal Parkett. During this time she also co-curated the Whitney and São Paulo Biennials and edited innovative artists' monographs such as *Looking Up: Rachel Whiteread's Water Tower* and *Silence Please! Stories after the works of Juan Munoz*. In 2000 she left Parkett in order to pursue independent activities, moving to Europe in 2002. In 2002–3 she organised a year's programme of monthly exhibitions and events entitled Antipodes at White Cube in London, and wrote and edited an accompanying book by the same name. Most recently, she developed programmes for the Theater am Turm//Bockenheimer

Depot in Frankfurt at the invitation of William Forsythe. *The final season, Why Only Now?* was conceived as a multi-disciplinary programme of dance, performance, music, radio, film and discussion. It included projects initiated and produced by TAT with local and international artists working with the diverse communities of Frankfurt. Neri continues to write on visual and performing artists for journals, catalogues and occasional articles for *The New York Times.*

Christine Peters, studied theatre, English and French literature in Giessen, Dublin and Frankfurt / Main. From 1992–98 she was project director and assistant to the artistic director at Künstlerhaus Mousonturm, Frankfurt / Main, an international and interdisciplinary centre for contemporary arts. There she worked as Artistic Director from 1998–2003, presenting a year round programme dedicated to international and transdisciplinary arts. Her work contained international networking, production, publication and presentation. She initiated, curated, published and produced network projects and symposiums in a European context concerning the dialogue between art theory and practice, such as *Vision Future, plateaux, European Production Centres – Crossing Borders in Theatre, Portrait* and *International Summer Academy.* Since 2004 she has been working as freelance curator, dramaturge and lecturer, e.g. for: Festival Tanz&Theater Hannover, 2004, Festival Theater der Welt, Suttgart 2005, Festival Steirischer Herbst, Graz 2006, The Bakery, Paris 2006, Lecturer at the theatre, media & film department, University Frankfurt 2005 / 2006.

Goran Sergej Pristaš, graduated from the Zagreb Academy of Drama Arts in 1993. Since 1994 teaching at the Academy of Drama Art in Zagreb, now as assistant professor. In 2002, he obtained his MA. From 1990 to 1992, he was artistic director of the ŠKUC theatre. In 1993 a dramaturge and member of the artistic council of &TD theatre. 1994–1999 dramaturge in Montažstroj. He has written a few short scripts for documentary films. As a dramaturge, he participated in numerous dance and theatre productions. In 1999, he produced *Confessions*, his first performance as a director. Active member of the internationally presented and awarded group BADco. Programme coordinator at the Centre for Drama Art since 1995. President of the board of CDU since 2000. From 1996–2005 editor-in-chief of *Frakcija*, a magazine for the performing arts (one of the most highly respected performing magazines in Europe). One of the initiators of the project *Zagreb – Cultural Capital of Europe 3000.*

Jan Ritsema, theatre director. He started dancing when he was fifty. Made a solo. Was invited by Meg Stuart for several *Crash Landings*, worked with Boris Charmatz in his *Entrainements* project in Paris and in a Bocal presentation and made the widely acclaimed *Weak Dance Strong Questions* with Jonathan Burrows. Teaching at P.A.R.T.S, the dance school of Anne Teresa De Keersmaeker since it started in 1995. Currently working on a new dance piece with Sandy Williams.

Gerald Siegmund, studied theatre, English and French literatures at the University in Frankfurt / Main. Completed in 1994, his Ph.D. thesis on *Theatre as Memory* linked the theatrical experience with concepts of memory derived from Freudian psychoanalysis. In 1998, he joined the staff of the Department of Applied Theatre Studies at the University in Giessen, where he is teaching now. Since 1995 he has been working as a free-lance dance and performance critic for *Frankfurter Allgemeine Zeitung, Balletanz* and *Dance Europe*. Since 2005 Professor of Theatre Studies at the University Bern. He has published widely on contemporary dance and theatre performance.

Christine Standfest, studied German literature, paedagogics, cultural and gender studies at FU Berlin and the University of Lancashire. Dramaturgy, political activism, translation and broadcasting work. Since 1997 working and performing with Theatercombinat, since 1999 Theatercombinat Vienna. Last works *firma raumforschung* and *palais donaustadt,* currently engaged in the 2-year project *tragödienproduzenten 1* in Vienna and Geneva. Participant in anatomie sade / wittgestein … (see above). Editing work, lectureships.

Robert Steijn, studied Slavic Languages and Theatre Science / Dramaturgy. Is based in Amsterdam, and nowadays works as dramaturge, performer, director, writer and translator Started a working collaboration with dancer and choreographer Frans Poelstra (*Frans Poelstra, his dramaturge and Bach, In concert),* made installations

for public spaces (*Trilogy of texts),* made a theatre ritual for multi-cultural cities together with Lidy Six (*Tower of Babel*), made two solos about intimacy: *Facing the invisible* and *Fur Stefan,* performed in and co-wrote *Not the real thing* for the theatre company L&O Amsterdam. Did dramaturgical advisor for choreographers as Thomas Lehmen, Paz Rojo, Nicole Beutler, Carolien Hermans, Andrea Bozic, Tale Dolven. Gives workshops on writing, shamanistic strategies for choreography and creativity (PACT Zollverein Essen, ImPulstanz, Tanzquartier Wien, Magpie Amsterdam) and teaches at the SNDO in Amsterdam, and advises at the moment in P.A.R.T.S in Brussells.

Mårten Spångberg, artist living and working in Brussels. He has created a number of works for and with himself which address relations between physicality and language, produced as essays authored for the stage. He was the initiator of Panacea Festivals and has curated a number of events such as *Capitals,* at Gulbenkian Foundation in Lisbon, International Summer Academy Frankfurt, International Festival, a shared initiative together with Tor Lindstand, operates in the field of immaterial performance and temporary architectural structures.

Ritsaert ten Cate, founding artistic director of Mickery Theatre Amsterdam for 25 years, after which he founded DasArts, a postacademic programme for theatre; now he works as a visual artist and will open a shop called Touch Time as a studio and showplace. xs4all.nl / ~rtencate

....

Contributors

Attila Tordai-S., coordinating editor (with Timotei Nădăşan) of Balcon Collection, IDEA Publishing. Attila Tordai-S. has been chief curator of Protokoll Studio in Cluj, Romania, since 2000 and the editor of the magazine *IDEA arts + society* since 2003. From 2001 to 2003, he was editor of the contemporary art magazine *Balkon* (Cluj). He taught art theory and history at Babes-Bolyai University, Cluj, from 1999 to 2003. He regurarly publishes essays on contemporary art and has curated many exhibitions, including *Unstable Narratives*, (hArtware medien kunstverein, Dortmund, 2002) and *The Mistake: stories about mistakes* (Protokoll Studio, Cluj, 2001). He was appointed as co-curator of Periferic 7 contemporary art biennial, Iaşi, Romania, 2006.

Isa Wortelkamp, scientific assistant at the Institute of Theatre Studies, FU Berlin. Her research in the field of theatre and dance studies is centred on: relation of performance and recording, dance literature, dance and architecture. Publications: *Flüchtige Schrift / Bleibende Erinnerung*, in: Gabriele Klein, Christa Zipprich (Hg.), Tanz. Theorie. Text, Münster 2002, *Architektonische Konstellationen*, in: *Tanzdrama 4* (2002); *Sehen mit dem Stift in der Hand. Stille Stellen der Aufzeichnung*, in: Andreas Gelhard, Ulf Schmidt, Tanja Schulz (Hg.), *Stillstellen. Medien, Aufzeichnung, Zeit*, Schliengen 2004.

257

Ana Vujanović, theorist of theatre, performing arts and culture. Ph.D.: Theatre studies, Editor of *TkH*, journal for performing arts theory. Guest lecturer at the University of Arts in Belgrade. Editor of theoretical symposia within Belgrade International Theatre Festival. Publishes regularly in theoretical art journals and books. Many theoretical-artistic works, performance-lectures and exposures at seminars, conferences and art festivals … Publication: Destroying Performance Signifiers, Belgrade: SKC, 2004

Katherina Zakravsky, theorist of culture and performance artist in Vienna; 1999 Ph.D. on Immanuel Kant's concept of the university; 2001 / 02 researcher in theory at the Jan van Eyck Academie, Maastricht; since 1998 solos and collaborations in dance, video and performance; currently working with the choreographer Chris Haring (A, *Fremdkörper*, etc.); various lectures, laboratories and publications on film, culture and politics; since 2002 mainly research on Giorgio Agamben's theory of bare life and the camp. Recent publications: *Re-Membering "Le Sacre"*, in: *Tanz anders*wo: *intra- und interkulturell* (ed. Krassimira Kruschkova, Nele Lipp). Münster, Hamburg, London 2004.

editors

Martina Hochmuth, Ph.D. in French literature. Curator in contemporary dance and performance with a focus on projects together with artists, initiatives and institutions from the East and Southeast of Europe. Curator and artistic coordinatior for T junction Gegenwartstanz, Vienna 1997–2000. Co-director of *Movements on the EDGE*, Bucharest 2001, 2002, Proiect DCM Foundation. Co-curator of OSTWEST *Academy,* Tanzquartier Wien, 2004. Curator of *performing identities*, Vienna Days Bucharest, 2004. Co-curator of *gibanica*, Ljubljana 2005. Since 2004 Dramaturge, Head of Research and Information Centre at Tanzquartier Wien.

Krassimira Kruschkova, studied Theatre and Film Studies in Sofia, was scientific assistant at the Institute for Literature Theory at the University of Sofia, Ph.D. thesis in Vienna in 1994, since 1995 teaching at the University for Applied Arts Vienna, and since 1997 also at the Academy of Visual Arts Vienna. Since 2002 Venia docendi at the Institute for Theatre, Film and Media Studies of the University of Vienna: *Szenische Anagramme. Zum Theater der Dekonstruktion* (Vienna 2002). Since 2003 Head of the Theory Centre at Tanzquartier Wien; curator of the lecture series *Ob?scene* (2003/04), *Gestures* (2004/05), *Potentiality* (2005/06), as well as of the conferences *Dance somewhere else* (2003) *Impossible tears* (2004) and *I say I* (2005). Latest publications: *Tanz anders*wo*: intra- und interkul-turell* (ed. with N. Lipp), Lit 2004; *Ob?scene. Zur Präsenz der Absenz im zeit-genössischen Tanz, Theater und Film* (ed.), Böhlau 2005.

Georg Schöllhammer, editor, author and curator. Lives and works in Vienna. Since 1995 editor-in-chief and co-founder of *springerin – Hefte für Gegenwartskunst*, a quarterly magazine dedicated to the theory and critique of contemporary art and culture. 1988–1994 editor for visual arts at the daily *Der Standard*. 1992–1998 visiting professor for theory of contemporary art at the University of Art and Industrial Design, Linz. Numerous publications, exhibitions and projects on contemporary art and architecture. He directs *tranzit.at*, an initiative to support contemporary art projects in Central Europe. Recently he curated the exhibition *Play Sofia* (Kunsthalle Wien, 2005), and the projects OSTWEST *Academy* (Tanzquartier Wien, 2004) and *Lokale Modernen: Architektur an den Rändern der Sowjetunion* (Local Modernities: Architecture on the Margins of the Soviet Union; Frankfurt/Main and Berlin). As editor-in-chief for documenta 12 he is planning and directing the publication projects.

Contributors

Imprint

It takes place when it doesn't
On dance and performance since 1989

A springerin and frakcija book
Editors: Martina Hochmuth, Krassimira Kruschkova, Georg Schöllhammer
Copy Editing: David Ender, Jill Winder
Design and Cover: Markus Weisbeck, John Russo / Surface Gesellschaft für Gestaltung
Print: RemaPrint, Vienna

ISBN 3-86588-255-2

Published by
Revolver
Archiv für aktuelle Kunst
Fahrgasse 23
D - 60211 Frankfurt am Main
Germany
Tel.: +49 (0)69 44 63 62
Fax: +49 (0)69 94 41 24 51
www.revolver-books.de

We gratefully acknowledge the financial support of Tanzquartier Wien
and THEOREM, an association supported by the Culture 2000
programme of the European Union. Tanzquartier Wien is member of THEOREM.

Printed in the EU